ACTS

Dispensationally Considered

VOLUME TWO

ACTS

Dispensationally Considered

By

Cornelius R. Stam

VOLUME TWO
Acts 15:36 through 28:31

BEREAN BIBLE SOCIETY
N112 W17761 Mequon Road
PO Box 756
Germantown, WI 53022
(Metro Milwaukee)

Copyright 1958
Copyright Renewed 1985

by

BEREAN BIBLE SOCIETY
N112 W17761 Mequon Road
PO Box 756
Germantown, WI 53022

Sixth Printing 2011

ISBN: 0-9644541-9-X

Cover graphic: ©iStockphoto.com/Sascha Burkard

Printed in the United States of America

SHERIDAN BOOKS, INC.
CHELSEA, MICHIGAN

CONTENTS

CONTENTS

CONTENTS

VII

CONTENTS

CONTENTS

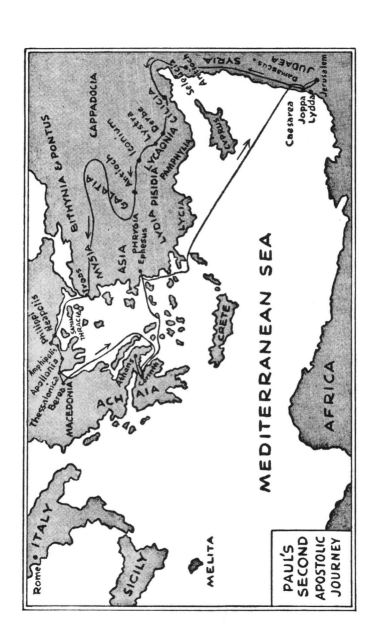

PAUL'S SECOND APOSTOLIC JOURNEY

PAUL BEGINS HIS
SECOND APOSTOLIC JOURNEY

STILL MORE TROUBLE

"And some days after Paul said unto Barnabas, let us go again and visit our brethren in every city where we have preached the word of the Lord, and see how they do.

"And Barnabas determined to take with them John, whose surname was Mark.

"But Paul thought not good to take him with them, who departed from them from Pamphylia, and went not with them to the work.

"And the contention was so sharp between them, that they departed asunder one from the other: and so Barnabas took Mark, and sailed unto Cyprus:

"And Paul chose Silas, and departed, being recommended by the brethren unto the grace of God.

"And he went through Syria and Cilicia, confirming the churches."

—Acts 15:36-41

THE FALLING OUT BETWEEN PAUL
AND BARNABAS

Antioch had already seen enough contention because of the Judaizers, but before leaving the scene we are to witness still another sharp controversy, this time between Paul and Barnabas, those companions in labor who had together accomplished so much for the Lord.

11

The trouble began when Paul proposed that he and Barnabas visit their brethren "in every one of the cities"[1] where they had preached the Word, to see how they were getting on. Here we get a glimpse of the apostle's concern over his children in the faith, so often expressed in his epistles and especially in II Corinthians 11:28, where he speaks of *"the care of all the churches."*

Barnabas evidently concurred with Paul in this, only he "was minded"[2] to take John Mark with them again, while Paul, on the other hand, felt it would be wrong to take with them, as a companion, the one who had "departed"[3] from them so soon after they had embarked on their former journey. In the disagreement neither would yield to the other; Barnabas would not go *without* Mark and Paul would not go *with* him, until the matter developed into an angry dispute. Indeed, so sharp was the contention between these two old friends that they separated from each other, Barnabas taking Mark and sailing to Cyprus, and Paul choosing Silas and (after being commended to God by the Church) traveling through Syria and Cilicia.

WHO WAS WRONG?

It would be folly to water down such a passage as this in order to exempt either party from blame. No justification whatever is offered for this heated quarrel. Unquestionably it was improper and wrong, and by it Paul and Barnabas proved exactly what they had

1. This is the thought in the original. They had already revisited some cities, but this time Paul proposed revisiting them *all*, without exception.

2. "Determined" is too strong for the Gr. *bouluomai*.

3. Gr. *aphistemi*, "fallen away."

12

said to the Lystrians: *"We also are men of like passions with you"* (Acts 14:15). Characteristically, the Scriptures state the facts frankly for our learning and good. We emphasize this because, when we magnify Paul's *office*, as the Scriptures do (Rom. 11:13) there are always some who accuse us of exalting Paul personally.

Some have explained the contention by noting a possible spiritual decline in the change from the words: *"the Holy Spirit said,"* in 13:2, to the words: *"Paul said,"* in 15:36. It should be remembered, however, that in the former passage we have the Spirit's original instruction to *the Church at Antioch* to separate Paul and Barnabas for the work wherein they had now become engaged. Therefore we should not expect another such case, nor are we to suppose that the apostle is acting in the flesh every time we fail to find the words: *"The Holy Spirit said."* Indeed, since the passing of the Pentecostal era believers should be very careful about saying: *"The Spirit said"* or, *"The Spirit told me"* or, *"The Lord said to me,"* unless they are referring to the written Word of God.

There were perfectly natural circumstances leading up to the quarrel between Paul and Barnabas. First, the failure of Mark, Barnabas' cousin,[4] so early in their first journey had had its effects. Then too, Paul had probably begun losing confidence in Barnabas himself since he (Barnabas) had been "carried away" in the "dissimulation" at Antioch (Gal. 2:13).

On the other hand Barnabas may well have been irked at having been involved in Paul's rebuke of

---

4. The Gr. *anepsios* in Colossians 4:10 is better rendered "cousin" than "sister's son."

13

Peter. Indeed, Barnabas may have felt that Paul was personally indebted to him, because he had been the one to bring him to the apostles in Jerusalem and then to the work at Antioch. Also, Barnabas had once ranked first among the prophets at Antioch (See Acts 13:1, where Saul is mentioned *last*) and the two had frequently been spoken of as "Barnabas and Paul." This had been so even as recently as the council at Jerusalem (Acts 15:12,25). Yet, little by little, Paul had been coming to the fore, leaving Barnabas in the background. This, of course, was God's will, but it may have been difficult for Barnabas to recognize it as such.

But while the Scriptures do not offer any vindication of their "sharp contention," it does not follow from this that the principles each contended for were necessarily wrong. Indeed, an examination of the facts indicates they were quite right, and as one places himself in the position of either party in the dispute he "can see his point," only each party failed to place himself sufficiently in the *other's* position or, as Paul himself later put it, to *"look not every man on his own things, but every man also on the things of others"* (Phil. 2:4).

As to *what* the disputants were contending for, it should be observed on Barnabas' side that Mark's desertion must have disappointed him as deeply as it had Paul, and that Mark must have been the subject of his earnest prayers, their being related so closely. What dealings Barnabas had had with Mark by letter, or in Jerusalem, or whether Barnabas had again brought him to Antioch, we do not know. We know he was there, however, and it is evident that Barnabas felt there was sufficient ground for giving him another opportunity; that he had confidence that Mark had learned his lesson and could now be depended upon. It was perfectly natural and right that Barnabas should feel a strong responsibility to his young cousin in this matter. True, Mark had failed, but are faults never to be forgiven, and do not men often learn from their failures?

This is not the *whole* picture, however. Paul had not the same personal reasons nor, probably, the same grounds for renewed confidence in Mark that Barnabas had, and to him it probably seemed an unwarranted *risk* to proceed with *such* a companion on a journey which experience had shown would be fraught with peril. This can be well understood, for above all things "it is required in stewards *that a man be found faithful*" (I Cor. 4:2) and *"confidence in an unfaithful man in time of trouble is like a broken tooth, and a foot out of joint"* (Prov. 25:19). Doubtless too, Paul felt that Barnabas had been influenced by his attachment to a relative; that he was prejudiced in favor of his cousin to the extent that he did not sufficiently consider the arguments against his going.

TWO PARTIES INSTEAD OF ONE

As we proceed with our studies in Acts we shall see how more and more God *overrules providentially* rather than *intervening directly*, as He had at first.

What a change has taken place since the early chapters of Acts! There, for example, *"the multitude of them that believed* [more than 5,000] *were of one heart and of one soul"* (Acts 4:32) and when two impostors sought to join themselves to the number, God intervened and struck them dead.

But now the believers were no longer all of one heart and of one soul—not even those at Jerusalem.

Hence the "dissension and disputation" at Antioch, the "much disputing" at Jerusalem, Paul's rebuke of Peter at Antioch, and the "sharp contention" between Paul and Barnabas.

At Pentecost *"they were all filled with the Holy Spirit"* (Acts 2:4) simply because "the day of Pentecost was fully come" (Ver. 1) and the time had arrived for the pouring out of the Spirit in power. But now, with the raising up of Paul we are coming more and more into the dispensation where the *exhortation* is in order: *"Be filled with the Spirit"* (Eph. 5:18). At Pentecost the Spirit *took possession* of His own and *caused* them to do His will. *Now*, the Spirit's help is *provided* by *grace*, but we must *appropriate* it by *faith*. This, of course, presents a greater *challenge* and permits of greater *victories* and *rewards*, but it also makes defeat possible. Hence the record of so many failures among the believers after the raising up of Paul to usher in the new dispensation.[5]

But while direct divine interventions decrease in later Acts, it is evident that God does overrule providentially. We have seen this in the results of the Jerusalem council, so fraught with disaster. We have seen it too in the whole problem over the Judaizers. Had not the Judaizers come to Antioch, the council at Jerusalem with its important decisions might never have been held. Had not Peter "withdrawn" from the Gentiles at Antioch the argument of Galatians 2 would have lost much of its strength. This does not excuse Peter and the Judaizers, of course, but it does show us that while God no longer intervenes *directly* and *miraculously* in the affairs of men, He nevertheless *remains on the throne,*

---

5. For a fuller discussion of this subject see the author's booklet: *"The Believer's Walk in this Present Evil Age."*

16

"working all things after the counsel *of His own will"* and *"for good to them that love God, to them who are the called according to His purpose"* (Eph. 1:11; Rom. 8:28).

Thus, too, it was in the case of Paul and Barnabas. In the midst of failure we see God overruling, for now there are two parties instead of one going forth to proclaim the gospel, Barnabas taking Mark, and Paul, Silas.[6]

It has been noted that Paul and Silas were commended by the church to the grace of God (Ver. 40) as Paul and Barnabas had been at the first (Acts 13:3; 14:26) but that Barnabas and Mark received no such commendation at this time. This, however, may have been because Barnabas left suddenly or secretly, either from anger or disappointment, or generously, to leave the work there wholly to Paul.

Even at that, it does seem that the main body of the church there probably stood with Paul, though on the other hand again it must be said that the later record indicates that Barnabas' confidence in Mark was justified and that he did well in giving the young man another chance.

At any rate, Barnabas and Mark now sail for Cyprus, while Paul and Silas travel through Syria and Cilicia (we hope not bound for the same destination!). This is the first indication that *churches* had been established in Syria and Cilicia (apparently either after Paul's return to Tarsus or during his ministry in Antioch. See Galatians 1:21 and cf. Acts 9:30; 11:25,26; 15:23).

---

6. One reason for this latter choice was doubtless that Paul needed with him one who could vouch for the decision of the Jerusalem council (See Acts 15:27).

It is heartening to consider that all four of the men we have been discussing really had the same great cause at heart, and that after a time their wounds healed again. In I Corinthians 9:6 Paul speaks highly of Barnabas as a co-worker for Christ. As to Mark, in Colossians 4:10 Paul instructs the Colossian believers to *"receive him,"* in Philemon 24 he calls him a *"fellow-laborer"* and in II Timothy 4:11 he makes the touching request: *"Take Mark, and bring him with thee: for he is profitable to me for the ministry."* Thus Mark came through with colors flying and Paul graciously received him back. Indeed it is touching to note that God used this servant (Acts 13:5) who had failed so dismally, to write the account of the *perfect* Servant, *The Gospel According to Mark*.

This is the last we hear of Barnabas and Mark in the Book of Acts. The dispensational reason for the disappearance of the twelve apostles, and even of Barnabas and Mark, from the record, is that the message and ministry entrusted to Paul might be duly emphasized. It does not indicate that Barnabas became a spiritual "castaway." Alexander Whyte's comments on Barnabas are pertinent here:

"Very soon now, it will be the greatest honor to any house on the face of the earth to entertain the Apostle Paul. But no proud householder of them all can ever steal this honor from Barnabas, that he was the first man of influence and responsibility who opened his heart and his house to Saul of Tarsus, when all Jerusalem was still casting stones at him" (*Bible Characters*, Vol. V, pg. 230).

Paul would undoubtedly miss Barnabas now, not only because they had gone through so many experiences together in their service for Christ, but also because the churches he was now to revisit knew Barnabas and Barnabas' name was linked with his own in the letter from Jerusalem. How would the break now be explained, and might not Barnabas' absence arouse suspicion as to the genuineness of the letter? Surely Silas was *the* man to have with him in such a case, for as one of the "chief men" of the church at Jerusalem, specially sent to "tell [them] the same things by mouth" (Acts 15:27) he could now be of greater help than any.

TIMOTHY CHOSEN TO ACCOMPANY PAUL AND SILAS

"Then came he to Derbe and Lystra: and, behold, a certain disciple was there, named Timotheus, the son of a certain woman, which was a Jewess, and believed; but his father was a Greek:

"Which was well reported of by the brethren that were at Lystra and Iconium.

"Him would Paul have to go forth with him; and took and circumcised him because of the Jews which were in those quarters: for they knew all that his father was a Greek."

—Acts 16:1-3

A PROMISING YOUNG MAN

Those who would serve the Lord acceptably may well learn from Paul's perseverance and courage. The above passage records his *third* visit to Derbe and Lystra, where he had been stoned and left for dead.

It was in this vicinity that the apostle found a young man, remarkably provided by God as another helper and fellow-traveler, and destined to become one of Paul's most faithful and effective co-workers. That the provision was

19

remarkable is indicated by the fact that the account of the incident opens with the exclamation *"Behold!"*

Timothy was the unfortunate offspring of an unwise and unscriptural marriage. His mother was a Jewess, named Eunice, and his father was a Greek. In Judaea such marriages seldom occurred, but here among the Jews of the dispersion they were naturally more prevalent. Perhaps the young Greek lover gave Eunice and her mother, Lois, to understand that when married he would become a true worshipper of the God of Israel, but it is evident that he had not done so, for Timothy had never even been circumcised and the passage we are considering indicates that he, the father, had remained "a Greek." Yet, these untoward circumstances were graciously overruled.

Whatever the temptations that had caused Eunice to accept this unequal yoke and whatever the reasons for which her mother, Lois, had consented to the marriage, it is evident that they both blamed themselves for what had taken place and earnestly sought to undo the wrong, for the apostle refers to their "unfeigned faith" (II Tim. 1:5) and to the fact that "from a child" Timothy had "known the holy Scriptures" (II Tim. 3:15).

With regard to this Dean Howson observes: "It is not a little remarkable that a character which is among the most faultless and charming in the Bible, should be the character of that one person whose domestic relations and early training are thus described" (*Companions of St. Paul*, pg. 269).

Yet, though mother and grandmother had both diligently taught Timothy the Scriptures, which were able to make him "wise unto salvation" (II Tim. 3:15) it was not directly through their instrumentality, but through Paul's, that he had been saved, for Paul calls him *"my own son in the faith"* (I Tim. 1:2 cf. Ver. 18 and II Tim. 1:2; 2:1). Apparently Timothy was saved at, or through, Paul's first visit to Lystra. We know, from II Timothy 3:10,11, that he had an intimate knowledge of Paul's "manner of life" and of his persecutions at Antioch, Iconium and Lystra.

That visit to Lystra had taken place some six years previous and it was probably about twelve years after *this present* visit that Paul could still write to Timothy: *"Let no man despise thy youth"* (I Tim. 4:12) so Timothy must have been but a lad at the time of his conversion. But his thorough instruction in the Scriptures, the "unfeigned faith" of his mother and grandmother, the inspiration of Paul's preaching and his intimate knowledge of the apostle's manner of life and sufferings for Christ, must all have had a great effect upon him,[7] for now *"Behold!"* here is this young man, already a consecrated and promising believer! Indeed, his Christian influence must already have extended beyond the limits of his native city, for we read that he was "well reported of" by the brethren of *two* churches: that at Lystra and that at Iconium (Ver. 2).

From the two epistles to Timothy it is evident that he was cultured and refined, a student from his youth, delicate in health and possessing, as was natural from his upbringing, an almost feminine tenderness, for Paul writes him with regard to his childhood, his mother, his grandmother and his tears, prescribes for his "often infirmities" and urges him not to be ashamed or afraid or weak, but to be strong, as "a good soldier of Jesus Christ."

---

7. His witness of Paul's cruel and unjust treatment at Lystra must have made a profound impression upon his young mind, laying the foundation for a warm and lasting friendship.

Since Timothy was not a robust character, it appears that Paul sometimes feared that, if anything, he might withdraw from the fight. Timothy did not withdraw, however, but proved courageous and faithful to the end. He doubtless came to be Paul's most intimate associate for the greatest length of time.

Besides ministering to Paul and working with him much of the time, Timothy was left with, or sent to, many a church where his help was particularly needed (See Acts 17:14; 19:22; I Cor. 4:17; I Thes. 3:2; I Tim. 1:3) and Paul mentions him as a co-writer of six of his epistles (II Cor. 1:1; Phil. 1:1; Col. 1:1; I Thes. 1:1; II Thes. 1:1; Phile. 1).

The apostle's esteem and affection for Timothy is readily seen in such passages as those in which he describes him as his "brother," a "minister of God," his "fellow-laborer in the gospel of Christ," his "beloved son, and faithful in the Lord," etc.

In one of his last letters, the apostle writes of him:

"But I trust in the Lord Jesus to send Timotheus shortly unto you....

"For I have no man likeminded, who will naturally care for your state.

"For all seek their own, not the things which are Jesus Christ's.

"But ye know the proof of him, that, as a son with the father, he hath served with me in the gospel" (Phil. 2:19-22).

Even in his early ministry for Christ Timothy must have served with Paul in many more places than those of which it is recorded, for Paul, in writing to the Corinthians, explains that Timothy will remind them

22

of his ways: "as I teach *everywhere* in *every* church" (I Cor. 4:17).

Another step in the transition from the old dispensation to the new is seen in the fact that hitherto all of Paul's fellow travelers on his apostolic journeys had been chosen from the Circumcision, while here, for the first time, was one who was only partly Jewish. For reasons which we will consider at length, the apostle, however, had him formally initiated into the Hebrew race by the rite of circumcision.

In addition, a public consecration service was evidently held for the young man, before he embarked on his journey with Paul and Silas. In this service men with the gift of prophecy declared that God had chosen Timothy for this ministry and a special "gift" for the work was imparted to him by the Spirit, as the elders of the Church, together with Paul, and probably Silas, identified themselves with him in the laying on of hands (I Tim. 1:18; 4:14; II Tim. 1:6). While the new dispensation was dawning brighter, the old, with its miraculous gifts, had not yet "vanished away."

Timothy, then, though very young, was by his upbringing, by his personal character, and now by supernatural enduement singularly qualified for the work he was to undertake in accompanying Paul on his journeys and assisting him in his work.

THE CIRCUMCISION OF TIMOTHY

Paul's circumcision of Timothy, so soon after the council at Jerusalem, has puzzled many sincere and diligent students of the Word.

If he had circumcised the young man because it was known that his *mother* was a *Jewess*, the problem might be more easily solved, but the passage under consideration clearly states that he did so because "they knew all that his *father* was a *Greek*" (Ver. 3). Yet, only a short time ago he had insisted, at the council at Jerusalem, that the *Gentiles* should *not* be brought under circumcision and the law. Indeed, he had taken Titus, a Greek, with him as a test case and was later able to say: "And Titus was not compelled to be circumcised either...we gave place by subjection, no, not for an hour" (Gal. 2:3,5).

Why, then, did Paul now circumcise Timothy? Was this consistent? Did he temporize for expediency's sake?

It is often difficult, of course, to draw the line between right and wrong in cases where expediency is involved, yet it seems to us that both a general consideration and a particular examination of the incident will reveal that the apostle did not compromise or violate his principles on this occasion.

First, a compromise in these matters at such a time would have been too obviously inconsistent for, not only had Paul but recently fought for Gentile freedom from circumcision at Jerusalem, but we are distinctly told that both at Antioch and "as they went through the cities" on this very journey, they delivered to the churches the written decision of the council at Jerusalem[8] (15:30; 16:4).

---

8. From Acts 15:28-31; 21:25 and other related passages, it is a fair conclusion that the "decrees" (plural) of 16:4, refer to *copies* of the decree, rather than to a list of decrees. Their *decision* and *decree* was that the Gentiles were not to be placed under the law (21:25) but they hoped that the Gentile brethren would cooperate in refraining from such practices as might alienate them from the Jews at the start (15:21,29).

Second, it must be observed that the case of Timothy differed widely from that of Titus, not only because Timothy was partly Jewish, but because in his case no such principle was involved as there had been in the case of Titus. In the case which involved Titus, *believers* at Jerusalem had sought to establish it as a principle that the Gentiles must be circumcised and keep the law to be saved. In that case Paul "gave place by subjection, no, not for an hour" (Gal. 2:5). The Gentiles, to whom he had been sent with the good news of grace, were *not* to be placed under the law.

In the case of Timothy, however, no such principle was involved. No one here was seeking to impose circumcision upon Timothy. It was for the sake of the *unbelieving* Jews (Ver. 3) that Paul circumcised Timothy, and this was done voluntarily, so as to remove any possible hindrance to their ministry among the people of Israel.

Thirdly, the *time element* is an important factor in the interpretation of the Book of Acts. It must be remembered that Paul himself received the great truths of grace *gradually*, in a series of revelations, and that the circumcision of Timothy took place before he had even written his first epistle. A few years *later* he was to write to the Galatian believers, Jewish and Gentile alike:

"Behold, I Paul say unto you, that if ye be circumcised Christ shall profit you nothing.[9] **For I testify again to every man that is circumcised that he is a debtor to do the whole law" (Gal. 5:2,3).**

These Galatian believers had come to see the law as fulfilled in Christ and had *then*, through the

---

9.   *Logically*, of course, *not actually*.

influence of the Judaizers from Jerusalem, begun to place themselves under the law again.

Thus it would be wrong for *anyone today* to submit to circumcision in compliance with the law, and *even at that time* it would have been out of order for any *Gentile* to do so. But it must be remembered that the council at Jerusalem had not ruled against the circumcision of *Jewish* believers, that Paul's ministry was still "to the Jew first" and that he naturally began his testimony to them by proving that "Jesus is *the Christ*," the Messiah of Israel.

And now Timothy was to accompany him, a young man who had been brought up as a godly Jew and was even half Jewish physically, but had never been circumcised. Had he remained uncircumcised their ministry among the Jews would have been hindered from the very start, for "they knew all that his father was a Greek" and, suspecting that he was not circumcised, would have considered him an "alien from the commonwealth of Israel." Even social intercourse with the Jews would thus have been hindered, for they considered it an abomination to eat with the uncircumcised.

The statement, then, that Paul circumcised Timothy because "they knew all that his father was a Greek," should not lead us to conclude that Paul was making a concession to *Jewish believers* who felt that *Gentile* believers should be circumcised. It was clearly for the sake of the *unbelieving Jews* that Paul circumcised Timothy.

It is true enough that Timothy could have remained uncircumcised and that no one would have had a right to *impose* the rite upon him. Indeed, had *brethren* demanded Timothy's circumcision on the basis of Acts 15:1, Paul would have opposed their attempt to bring him into bondage, but since Timothy was half Jewish, physically, and mostly Jewish in his upbringing, and since circumcision was still the mark of God's covenant people, Paul circumcised him so that henceforth Timothy's ministry to the people of Israel might be as free and unhindered as his own.

In this act, performed at that stage in the transition from Judaism to grace, Paul was simply teaching the lesson that while we have no right to give up our liberty (Gal. 5:1) we do have liberty to give up our rights. This is what he meant, when he exhorted even Gentile believers not to use their liberty for an occasion to the flesh, but by love to serve one another (Gal. 5:13). This is what he meant when he exhorted them in matters of "days" and "meats" to exercise their liberty in love, giving up personal advantage and privilege if necessary, for the spiritual benefit of others (Rom. 14:1-15:2; I Cor. 8:1-10:33). This is what he meant when he wrote:

"For though I be free from all men, yet have I made myself servant unto all, that I might gain the more.

"And unto the Jews I became as a Jew, that I might gain the Jews; to them that are under the law, as under the law, that I might gain them that are under the law" (I Cor. 9:19,20).

But here we must exercise caution. Some good Bible teachers, arguing that a twofold program maintained during the latter part of Acts, have overlooked the significant recurrence of the word "as" in I Corinthians 9:20-22, interpreting the passage to mean that Paul *placed himself under the law* when among the Jews, so as to win them, but lived free from the law while among the Gentiles.

But these brethren must then explain how the Jewish believers at Corinth, for example (to which church he here writes) could possibly have respected Paul if, after giving them to feel that he was a law-abiding Jew so as to win them to Christ, he then sought to win the Gentiles by showing *them* that he was *not* under the law!

It must be recognized that the twofold program of the latter part of Acts was *not* to continue with *equal* force. One was to *displace* the other gradually (though many Judaizers sought to hinder the transition) and it is evident from the record that Paul began to teach the truths of grace to those very Jews he sought to win by sympathetically placing himself in their position. He *was not* guilty of double dealing when, among the Jews, he sought, as far as was consistent, to forbear practices and policies which might violate their standards, so that he could better witness to them of Christ.

Should any be inclined to take Paul's circumcision of Timothy as justification for practicing water baptism today, we have but to remind them that the transition from the former dispensation to the present was completed with Paul's imprisonment in Rome, after which *both* physical circumcision and physical baptism were eliminated from God's program for the Church (See Col. 2:10-12).

FROM LYSTRA TO TROAS

"And as they went through the cities, they delivered them the decrees for to keep, that were ordained of the apostles and elders which were at Jerusalem.

"And so were the churches established in the faith, and increased in number daily.

28

"Now when they had gone throughout Phrygia and the region of Galatia, and were forbidden of the Holy Ghost to preach the Word in Asia,

"After they were come to Mysia, they assayed to go into Bithynia: but the Spirit suffered them not.

"And they passing by Mysia came down to Troas."

—Acts 16:4-8

We now find Paul, Silas and Timothy visiting the cities where Paul and Barnabas had previously ministered, and delivering to the believers, for their observance, the "decrees" (Gr. *dogmata*) that had been "decided upon" (Gr. *krino*, not *"ordained"*) by the apostles and elders at Jerusalem.

The use of the word *dogmata*,[10] translated "decrees" in the *Authorized Version* does not imply that the Gentiles were, after all, partly subjected to the law. As we have pointed out in a footnote, the basic decision of the council at Jerusalem was that circumcision and the law were *not* to be imposed upon the Gentile believers, but the leaders there hoped that for the sake of the Jews in every city the Gentile brethren would co-operate in refraining from such practices as might nullify their ministry among them from the start (See Acts 15:19-21,24-29; Acts 21:25).

Had the intention of the council been to place or keep the Gentile believers *partly* under the law it would have been no great victory for Paul and his message. As it was, however, the communication from Jerusalem brought "joy" and "consolation" to the Gentile brethren (15:30,31) "confirming the churches" (15:41) and establishing them in the faith (16:5).

---

10. From which, our word *dogma*.

29

In a day when so much emphasis is laid upon "getting decisions for Christ" and so little upon doctrine and the study of the Word, it is important to note that the churches *"increased in number daily"* as *believers* were *"established in the faith"* (Ver. 5).

The selective principle in the divine inspiration of the Scriptures is clearly seen in Verses 5 and 7. Paul's whole ministry in Galatia is passed over with a few words, evidently because an account of it would not be in line with the special purpose of the Acts. In his letter to the Galatians we learn that "on account of [Gr. *dia*] infirmity of the flesh" he had preached the gospel to them at the first (Gal. 4:13). The exact nature of the illness that detained him among the Galatians is not stated,[11] though it seems to have been some severe eye trouble (Gal. 4:15; 6:11 margin). However that may be, we know that even in his illness he plainly set forth Christ crucified among them (Gal. 3:1) and that his energy and faithfulness were richly rewarded by the esteem and affection lavished upon him by those whom he had won to Christ (Gal. 4:14,15).

"Asia," a province of Asia Minor, was the natural place for Paul and his companions to go next, but for some reason the Holy Spirit forbade them to preach the Word there at that time. Whether this was done by a vision, or through some who had the gift of prophecy, or by direct revelation, we are not told, but we do know that *later* Paul was permitted to do a great work in this region, "so that all they which dwelt in Asia heard the word of the Lord Jesus, both Jews and Greeks" (Acts 19:10 cf. 19:26; 20:4).

---

11. Nor whether this was the "thorn in the flesh" referred to in II Corinthians 12:7-10.

Next, arriving opposite Mysia, they "assayed," or *attempted* to go into Bithynia, but again "the Spirit[12] suffered them not," so they" passed by" Mysia, not geographically, but as far as laboring there was concerned, and "came down to Troas" (Ver. 8).

Nothing is said in this passage about Paul's having revisited the believers at Pisidian Antioch, but this city was directly in the line of his journey and may be included in the "cities" referred to in Verse 4. The apostle's original purpose to revisit the cities where churches had been established was, however, already being greatly extended.

---

12. Some MSS read: "the Spirit of Jesus." It is still the same Spirit, sent by Jesus (John 16:7; Acts 2:33) who had already sent forth Paul and Barnabas (13:2,4) and had hindered Paul, Silas and Timotheus from preaching in Asia (16:6).

Chapter XXVIII — Acts 16:9-24

THE APOSTLE'S MINISTRY EXTENDED

THE CALL TO MACEDONIA

"And a vision appeared to Paul in the night: There stood a man of Macedonia, and prayed him, saying, Come over into Macedonia, and help us.

"And after he had seen the vision, immediately we endeavored to go into Macedonia, assuredly gathering that the Lord had called us for to preach the gospel unto them.

"Therefore loosing from Troas, we came with a straight course to Samothracia, and the next day to Neapolis;

"And from thence to Philippi, which is the chief city of that part of Macedonia, and a colony: and we were in that city abiding certain days."

—Acts 16:9-12

THE MACEDONIAN VISION

It has been conjectured that since Luke evidently arrived on the scene here at Troas (Note the "we" and "us" in Ver. 10) it may have been he whom Paul saw in his vision. There seems to be no real support for this, however. In the vision Paul saw *"a man of Macedonia,"* and it is doubtful whether Luke was a Macedonian. It is enough to know that Paul's course was again guided by a supernatural manifestation. The apostle was often led in this way during his early ministry, as were others of the Acts period, such as the circumcision apostles (5:19,20) Philip (8:26) Ananias (9:10,11) Cornelius (10:3) Peter (10:10,17,19; 12:7-9) etc.

This experience of Paul's has often been used as an example of what a missionary call should be. In view of the evident character of God's dealings with men in the present dispensation, the application is generally somewhat modified, but still there is the feeling that a "call" to missionary work involves some sort of "supernatural" manifestation: a dream, a feeling that "the Lord spoke to me," a sense of deep assurance or settled peace or urgent necessity or personal responsibility; a burden for the souls of a particular race or nation, the coming upon a particular Scripture passage from a "promise box" or in devotional reading, or the results of "laying out the fleece" or giving God the choice of two alternatives.

But none of these human emotions or experiences should be confused with the definite vision by which Paul was called to go into Macedonia, and those who today look for some supernatural manifestation in seeking God's guidance should reflect that of the many such supernatural "calls" recorded in the Scriptures, this one of Paul at Troas is the last, for with the setting aside of Israel and her kingdom hopes such manifestations vanished away (Acts 2:16-18 cf. I Cor. 13:8).

Today we are to walk entirely *"by faith, not by sight"* (II Cor. 5:7). With hearts burdened for the lost about us, we should ask God for wisdom and providential guidance as to how and where we may best fill the greatest need, and then prepare by His grace to discharge our responsibility to fill that need. It may be that, after earnest prayer and thoughtful consideration, one may conclude that he can best serve God in Africa and may prepare to go, only to be hindered and shown that God really wants him at home or in some other place. But this does not necessarily mean that he was wrong in preparing to go to Africa, as it would if he were called by some supernatural manifestation, or if personal experiences finally settled such things. On the contrary, the Lord may well use the most baffling circumstances for the good of His servant and for His own glory.

In the case before us Paul was called to Macedonia by a supernatural manifestation and, the call obeyed, there could be no question of his arriving there.

OFF TO MACEDONIA

"Immediately" after the vision we find Paul and his companions "endeavoring" to go into Macedonia, evidently enquiring at the harbor for passage on the first ship to sail there.

As we have seen, an addition had been made to the party at Troas in the person of Luke, the author of Acts. This is evident, not only from the grammatical change from *"they"* to *"we"* in Verse 10, but also from the fact that at this point Luke's simple *historical* style gives place to the *autoptical* style of writing, i.e., that of *personal observation*. The arrival of Luke at this time may well be traced to the apostle's illness while among the Galatians. Later Paul called him *"the beloved physician"* (Col. 4:14) referring not merely to the *fact* that he was a physician, but to the affection with which he was regarded *as a physician*—probably most of all by Paul himself—for benefits received. This is another indication of the dispensational change which has taken place since Pentecost (See Acts 5:12-16 and cf. Rom. 8:22,23).

Here Luke accompanies Paul to Macedonia and Philippi, after which he appears to be absent again. But when Paul returns to Macedonia later we detect Luke's presence again by that same change of pronoun from "they" to "we." From here on he appears to have remained with Paul to the close of the Acts record.

Luke's presence was to prove a great help to the apostle in his journeys as the dispensation of miraculous demonstrations passed away. Almost the last word we hear from Paul, in prison at Rome, is *"Only Luke is with me"* (II Tim. 4:11).

Evidently the company was able to secure passage to Macedonia without delay, for the word "immediately" of Verse 10 is followed in Verse 11 by the words: *"Therefore loosing from Troas:"*

The wind, too, was favorable, for Luke says: "We came with a straight course to Samothracia [an island midway between] and the next day to Neapolis [the harbor of Philippi]" (Ver. 11). The thought here is that the wind was directly at their stern, speeding them to their destination so that it was not necessary to "tack," or travel in a zigzag pattern as would have been the case were the wind against them. The voyage must have been remarkably swift, for the whole was completed in two days, whereas it took five days to cover the same distance on a later voyage (Acts 20:6).

It must have proved encouraging to the apostle to have things go more smoothly for a time. In Galatia he had suffered illness, then twice the Spirit had hindered him from ministering in certain areas. The effect must have been depressing to one of Paul's nature. But upon arriving at Troas all was different. The beloved physician had now joined the party, a special vision had called him to new opportunities, a ship was ready to offer transportation and even the wind was favorable.

From the harbor at Neapolis Paul and his party made their way to Philippi, "the chief city of that part of Macedonia, and a colony" (Ver. 12). There has been some criticism of Luke for an "inaccuracy" here. It is contended that Philippi was *not* the chief city of Macedonia. But there is no inaccuracy, except possibly in our translation. The word "chief," here, is at least once rendered "first" in the *Authorized Version* (I Tim. 1:15) and Philippi was the *first* city of Macedonia to which they came after leaving Neapolis harbor. The context, however, seems to agree better with the rendering "chief," only it should be noted that the definite article is not found in the original, and that even if it is correctly supplied, Philippi is still only said to be the chief city of *"that part* of Macedonia."

It was, of course, an important city, named after the Emperor Philip, the father of Alexander the Great. As a Roman colony its citizens enjoyed many of the privileges bestowed upon the citizens of Rome itself. Free from the authority of the governor of the province, they conducted their own local government. They were not liable to examination by scourging and could appeal from Roman lower courts to the Emperor.

Now, after having been hindered from ministering in one place and in another, and having been called by a vision to Macedonia Paul, with his helpers, stood for the first time on European soil, where he was to be used of God in greater measure than ever. We who come from European stock should humbly thank God for this manifestation of His sovereign grace.

The apostle's supernatural call to Europe was but a sequel to God's previous dealings with him. At

Jerusalem, after his conversion, the Lord had appeared to him with the command: *"Depart; for I will send thee FAR hence unto the Gentiles"* (Acts 22:21). Later, while ministering at Antioch, the Spirit had said: *"Separate Me Barnabas and Saul for the work whereunto I have called them"* (Acts 13:2). With that Paul began his apostolic *journeys*. Now, lest he spend too much time in Asia Minor, he is called into Macedonia. Before it is over he will be taken as a prisoner "of the Lord" to Rome, to do the greatest work of all.

PAUL AT PHILIPPI

THE FIRST CONVERTS IN EUROPE

"And on the sabbath we went out of the city by a river side, where prayer was wont to be made; and we sat down, and spake unto the women which resorted thither.

"And a certain woman named Lydia, a seller of purple, of the city of Thyatira, which worshipped God, heard us: whose heart the Lord opened, that she attended unto the things which were spoken of Paul.

"And when she was baptized, and her household, she besought us, saying, If ye have judged me to be faithful to the Lord, come into my house, and abide there. And she constrained us."

—Acts 16:13-15

The vision of the Macedonian calling for help evidently did not indicate an existing attitude toward the gospel, but a *need* and an *opportunity*. Rather than finding thousands eagerly awaiting the message of grace, the apostle and his company (Paul, Silas, Timothy and Luke) spent several days at Philippi (Verse 12) and then had to make their own contacts by going to the riverside outside the city "where prayer was wont to be made"[1] (cf. Acts 21:5).

It would appear that there was no synagogue in Philippi, especially since we read of Thessalonica, the next city he went to, that there *was* a synagogue there (17:1) and that Paul went in *"as his manner was"* (17:2).

In any city like Philippi, where there were not enough Jews to maintain a synagogue, the few who did reside there would choose (or be granted) a place outside the city near a river or stream, to carry on their devotions; outside the city for the sake of retirement, and by flowing water so that they could attend to the baptisms, or washings, which played so prominent a part in their worship.

Surely Israel was not being left without abundant testimony to the person and claims of Christ, for here, where there was not even a synagogue, the apostle and his helpers still made it a point to deal with "the Jew first," seeking out those who might resort to the riverside on the Sabbath day to pray. In this case the company was made up mostly, if not entirely, of women—always apt to be more devoted and faithful than men. And among these women was one named Lydia, a merchant from Thyatira, who dealt in purple goods, the clothing of the rich and of the socially or politically prominent (See Luke 16:19).[2] From her name it would appear that

---

1. R.V. renders this "where we supposed there was a place of prayer," but some scholars believe this change from the *Authorized* is based on a corruption of the early MSS.

2. Ancient writings have much to say about this industry in Thyatira and inscriptions have even been found among its ruins relating to the "Guild of Dyers" there.

she was not a Jewess, but she had evidently come to fear the God of Israel and may have been a proselyte to Judaism.

At any rate we read that here was one "whose heart the Lord opened" to receive the truth (Ver. 14). There is an important doctrinal lesson for us here, for the assertion that *the Lord* opened Lydia's heart implies that it had been, and would by nature have remained closed. This is always man's condition apart from divine grace. The unaided efforts of even the godliest of men to enlighten the unregenerate heart must be vain and ineffectual. God alone can accomplish this (II Cor. 4:6) and having begun the good work, *He will complete it* (Phil. 1:6).

Yet it was not surprising that God, in His foreknowledge of all things, should choose to open this woman's heart for, though far from home and engaged in business, she was found here seeking the fellowship of those whose God had said: *"Remember the Sabbath day, to keep it holy,"* and was seeking that God in prayer. And now, through Paul's preaching, Lydia found God and true sabbath rest *in Christ* (See Heb. 1:3; 4:9,10).

THE BAPTISM OF LYDIA AND HER HOUSEHOLD

Much is often made of the fact that Lydia and her household were now baptized. Does not this prove, we are asked, that water baptism is in order under Paul's administration? No, it does not, for though Paul was already proclaiming "the gospel of the grace of God," Israel had not yet been finally set aside (See John 1:31 and cf. Acts 28:28) hence much of the old program still prevailed. Paul had but recently circumcised Timothy; he had just been called to Macedonia by a vision; having arrived there he was careful to go to "the Jew first"; he was soon to cast a demon out of a damsel, and being imprisoned as a result, the prison doors were to be opened and his bands loosed *by a miracle*. This was the economy under which he had been saved and from which he gradually emerged, but there is no logic by which we can maintain that circumcision and miraculous signs have passed away and still hold on to the practice of water baptism.

But still less does this passage support the doctrine for which appeal is most often made to it: that of *household* baptism. One prominent writer argues that the passage says: 1.) *she believed*, but 2.) does not say *they* believed, 3.) implying that *they* were baptized because *she* believed. Says this writer: "No mention is made of *their* having believed, and the case is one that affords a strong presumptive proof that this was an instance of *household* or infant baptism."

But this is more than "reading between the lines," and such "proof" is too highly presumptive to stand the Berean test, when water baptism is consistently associated with repentance and faith in the Scriptures (Matt. 3:5,6; Mark 1:4; 16:16; Acts 2:38, etc.). The Reformed theologian, Dr. Albertus Pieters made it clear that the doctrine of infant baptism rests on nothing more than *presumptive* "proof," when he wrote in *Why We Baptize Infants*: "If some intelligent being from Mars should come to visit our earth, and we should hand him a Bible....He would not find infant baptism in the Bible, because it is not there, and cannot be gotten out of the Bible," and again: "The Bible is entirely silent about infant baptism, either pro or con. We admit it. We do not profess to get infant baptism from its pages. We *do* profess to *justify* infant baptism from its pages. That is a very different thing."

When an outstanding exponent of Reformed theology admits that infant baptism is not found in the Bible—that it cannot be gotten out of the Bible, then we may be sure that it is our adversary who has caused this teaching to take its place among the cardinal doctrines of some of our greatest denominations. It is he who prompts men to "justify" religious practices not taught in the Scriptures; to "teach for doctrines the commandments of men" (Mark 7:7).

The passage under consideration gives no indication that Lydia was even married, let alone that she had any children. The household referred to may well have been composed of servants or helpers, including perhaps Euodias, Syntiche and others of "those women" referred to in Philippians 4:2,3. Verse 40 speaks of "the brethren," though this may refer to Timothy and Luke, both of whom evidently remained at Philippi when Paul and Silas went on to Thessalonica. Certainly Lydia's household, like Cornelius' household, was composed of individuals whose hearts could be purified *"by faith"* (Acts 15:9).

Those who hold to *immersion* as the Scriptural *mode* of baptism also find "presumptive proof" for their views here, in that Paul found Lydia by the riverside where, presumably, there would be enough water to immerse her. But there is no intimation that Lydia was baptized where Paul first met her. Indeed, the lack of any mention of her household at the riverside and the declaration that her household was baptized, would seem to indicate that some time had elapsed between the two. But even if they were all present at that first meeting and, for some reason were not mentioned at first, that would be no proof that they were baptized, much less *immersed*, in the river.

Let us reject all "presumptive proofs" and stand squarely on *the written Word*. There we shall find undeniable evidence that *water* baptism signifies *cleansing, not burial* (Acts 22:16; Heb. 9:10; etc.).

Having been baptized, Lydia invited Paul and his company to take up their abode in her home, which must have been of ample size to accommodate four additional people. The sincerity of her invitation was evident for, seeking to overcome their natural reluctance, she challenged them: *"If ye have judged me to be faithful* [i.e., *to have acted in good faith*] *to the Lord, come into my house, and abide there. And,"* says Luke, *"she constrained us"* (Ver. 15). No sooner was Lydia saved than she began *helping* the ministers of the gospel, furnishing them a home and headquarters for their work. And she was persistent and faithful in this help (See Ver. 40).

How unostentatiously had the evangelization of Europe begun! There was no advance organization, no campaign to finance the movement, no advertisement of public meetings; there *was not* even a *public* meeting, where an impression might be made on the whole community. Paul and his companions simply spoke to a few women gathered together for prayer; the Lord opened the heart of one of them and a work was begun the magnitude of which can never be measured. We ourselves are some of the fruit of that humble meeting at a riverside nineteen hundred years ago.

SHAMEFUL TREATMENT
AT PHILIPPI

"And it came to pass, as we went to prayer, a certain damsel possessed with a spirit of divination met us, which brought her masters much gain by soothsaying:

"The same followed Paul and us, and cried, saying, These men are the servants of the most high God, which show unto us the way of salvation.

"And this did she many days. But Paul, being grieved, turned and said to the spirit, I command thee in the name of Jesus Christ to come out of her. And he came out the same hour.

"And when her masters saw that the hope of their gains was gone, they caught Paul and Silas, and drew them into the market-place unto the rulers,

"And brought them to the magistrates, saying, These men, being Jews, do exceedingly trouble our city,

"And teach customs, which are not lawful for us to receive, neither to observe, being Romans.

"And the multitude rose up together against them: and the magistrates rent off there clothes, and commanded to beat them.

"And when they had laid many stripes upon them, they cast them into prison, charging the jailor to keep them safely:

"Who, having received such a charge, thrust them into the inner prison, and made their feet fast in the stocks."

—Acts 16:16-24

THE PYTHONESS

Whether the apostle and his company continued to go to the place of prayer where they had begun their ministry at Philippi, or whether Luke now records an incident which had its beginning at that first meeting is, perhaps, difficult to determine. At any rate, it was as the brethren went "to prayer," or rather "to the prayer-place," that they were first met by a poor demon-possessed slave girl.

The phrase, *"a spirit of divination"* would have been more accurately rendered: *"a spirit of Python* [Gr. *Puthonos*]." Python was the name of the god Apollo in his oracular character, and his priestesses were called Pythonesses. His chief seat of worship was, as we know, at Delphi, the most famous oracle in the world and the last to be discredited. That more than mere superstition was involved here is evident from the fact that the Scripture clearly states that this damsel *was* possessed by a spirit of Python and that she brought her masters much gain by "soothsaying," or divining (Ver. 16) not by merely *pretending* to divine.

This particular Pythian priestess was under the control, not only of a demon, but also of a company of men who used her to great financial advantage because she was demon-possessed. Probably she was too valuable a slave for one owner to afford, since great numbers of the heathen would always flock to such, ready to pay a price for advice on politics, business, marriage, or whatever perplexed or troubled them.

This enslaved priestess of Apollo now began crying that Paul and his company were *"servants of the most high God, which show unto us the way of salvation"* (Ver. 17). *"And this she did many days"* (Ver. 18).

What she said was, of course, true, but why she said it is another question. Perhaps it was to gain a reward from them for advertising them thus, or to gain more influence over their hearers by having discerned and declared the truth, or, perhaps the evil spirit prompted her to cry this lest *he* be expelled (cf. Luke 4:33,34). There is still another possible explanation which may well be the correct one: that this was the sad cry of one who was spirit-possessed and knew it and recognized in the One whom Paul proclaimed her only hope of deliverance. Yet, in any case, this *knowledge* came from an evil spirit and her continual crying impeded the work being done for Christ.

Finally the apostle, "being grieved," commanded the spirit, in the name of Jesus Christ, to come out of her. Doubtless there were several factors in the case which distressed the apostle. First, the implications of her declaration were bad. Was he in league with heathen gods? Surely a compliment from such a source was questionable to say the least. This whole system was Satanic and must be discredited. Then, the fact that people were placing their trust in this priestess of Apollo, the base motives of her masters and pity for the damsel herself—all these doubtless combined to cause the apostle to rebuke the demon and command him to depart. Our Lord had similarly refused the testimony of the demon-possessed, for He would have no dealings with Satan (See Mark 1:34).

At this point it should be noted that while we read so much about demon and spirit possession and the casting out of demons in the Gospels and the Acts, we find no mention of these in the epistles of Paul; not even by implication in his later epistles. It would seem that demon possession, at least in the form in which we find it in the Gospels and the Acts, was characteristic of that day, when the kingdom of Satan was being challenged by the kingdom of Christ (See Matt. 12:24-29).

Those who seek to go "back to Pentecost" instead of "on to perfection" with Paul, sometimes make claims of demon expulsion, but true evidence of it is lacking as it is in their other claims of miraculous power.

One of the most popular Bible teachers of the past generation wrote on the very passage we are considering:

"Today we find the same characters. Even in our land, with all its enlightenment, there are literally thousands of people who scarcely make a move without consulting a clairvoyant or spirit medium...."

But when he speaks of present power to *cast out* demons he moves off into pagan lands:

"We have many instances in modern days of missionaries working in pagan lands where they have come in contact with people who seem to be just as truly possessed with demons as this young woman was, and on many occasions these servants of God have cast out those demons, using these same words." And then the writer proceeds to relate one such case of which he *heard*.[3]

But if *other* "servants of God" could do this in *pagan* lands, why could not *this* servant of God do it *"in our land,"* where he says the same condition exists?

Under the "great commission" to the eleven, power was given to "cast out devils," as well as to perform other miracles (Mark 16:17,18) but in harmony with

---

3.   Dr. H. A. Ironside, in *Lectures on the Book of Acts*, pgs. 373-375.

the disappearance of other miraculous powers under Paul's ministry, the casting out of demons also vanished away. Nowhere is the believer today given such power.

Indeed, since the earthly establishment of Christ's kingdom has been deferred, Satan is not presently occupied with opposing it. Today he smarts from what took place at Calvary and occupies himself with perverting the truth as to Christ's accomplishments there.

In Hebrews 2:14 we read that our Lord took part of flesh and blood: *"that through death He might destroy Him that had the power of death, that is, the devil."* In Colossians 2:15 we read, concerning Christ and His death:

"And having spoiled principalities and powers, *He made a show of them openly, triumphing over them in it."*

Thus, in the epistles of Paul we learn that the cross spelled defeat for Satan, purchasing salvation and all spiritual blessings in the heavenlies for all who will believe. This is the blessed truth which Satan now perverts and opposes. He *"hath blinded the minds of them which believe not, lest the light of the glorious gospel of Christ* [Lit. *the good news of the glory of Christ*]...*should shine unto them"* (II Cor. 4:4). He *"now worketh in the children of disobedience"* (Eph. 2:2). But his opposition is subtle. He ostensibly honors Christ, encourages "spirituality" and a high code of morals. *"Transformed into an angel of light,"* his ministers also appear as *"the ministers of righteousness"* (II Cor. 11:14,15). Hence the believer today is instructed to put on the whole armor of God, that he may be enabled to *"stand against the wiles of the devil."*

47

"For we wrestle not against flesh and blood, but against principalities, against powers, against the rulers of the darkness of this world [age] against spiritual wickedness [wicked spirits] in high places [the heavenlies]" (Eph. 6:12).

But while Paul had come to Philippi with the message of grace, God had not yet brought the former program to an end, nor withdrawn his offer to establish the kingdom. Hence the particular manifestation of Satanic opposition and the response to it which we find here.

As we say, these manifestations have since passed away, but he who caused them has not. He it is who blinds the minds of the lost and who wrestles with the saved, to keep them from enjoying their rightful position in the heavenlies in Christ. Let us then not be "ignorant of his devices," failing to recognize his efforts to undo us, but let us be always ready, clad with "the whole armor of God" and strong "in the power of His might."

PAUL AND SILAS BEATEN AND IMPRISONED

The masters of the Pythoness were enraged because "the hope of their gains" had vanished with the demon.[4] This has always been so. The Gadarenes asked our Lord to leave them because demons cast out by Him had destroyed their swine, which they should not have been raising anyway (Mark 5:16,17). Demetrius started a great uprising in Ephesus because the gains from his silver shrines were dwindling (Acts 19:24-41).

---

4. The terms "came out" and "was gone" (Vers. 18,19) are the same in the original.

And still today one of the chief causes of opposition to the truth is "filthy lucre." How many ministers of the gospel, even, would take their stands for the pure Pauline message of grace if it did not cost them financially! Paul had to warn Timothy against the desire to be rich (I Tim. 6:7-11). Peter, by the Spirit, predicts the coming of "false teachers" who "through covetousness" will "make merchandise" of men (II Pet. 2:3).

Had the gospel increased the income of this girl's owners they would doubtless have accepted it, but now, in the light of their loss, it was all wrong, even though their chattel, so basely used, had been restored to sanity and dignity by it. Thus they *"caught Paul and Silas"* (Timothy and Luke evidently escaping) and *"drew* [Lit. *dragged] them into the market-place unto the rulers"* (Ver. 19).

Appearing before the magistrates these men charged Paul and Silas with a very different crime than might be expected, saying: *"These men, being Jews, do exceedingly trouble our city, and teach customs, which are not lawful for us to receive, neither to observe, being Romans"* (Vers. 20,21).

The observation that Paul and Silas were Jews was intended to prejudice the magistrates against them since the Jews, already hated, had been expelled from Rome by Claudius Caesar (18:2). But why this sudden concern about the sanctity of their religion? Had the plain truth been told it would have been to the credit of the apostles, so all of a sudden they affect a zeal for the public religion! How hypocritically conscientious men can become when their crimes are detected and exposed! Though the Romans opposed religious *innovations*, they were tolerant of existing religions and,

49

indeed declared themselves the protectors of the gods of these nations which they had conquered.

But all this meant little now, for a popular tumult was already in the making. As "the multitude rose up together against them" the magistrates, who should have given them a hearing, tore off their clothes and commanded the lictors to "rod" them, i.e., to beat them with rods. After having beaten them with "many stripes" they "cast" them into prison, "charging the jailor to keep them safely," as though they were dangerous criminals. The jailor, "having received such a charge, *thrust* them into the inner prison, and made their feet fast in the stocks" (Vers. 22-24).

This bare account of the incident gives but a glimpse of the shameful treatment Paul and Silas were made to endure. The whole affair was highly improper to begin with. The plaintiffs had made a false charge and the magistrates had disgraced and punished them without a hearing or even an inquiry as to whether they were Roman citizens. Those who had professed such zeal for Roman law were flagrantly disregarding it now.

This was evidently one of the three times when Paul was "beaten with rods" (II Cor. 11:25). Flogging among the Jews was limited to 39 stripes (Deut. 25:3 cf. II Cor. 11:24) but the "many stripes" here inflicted on the naked apostles may well have exceeded that number, for in II Corinthians 11:23 Paul refers to "stripes *above measure.*"

Then, having been "cast" into prison, they were "thrust" into the inner prison. If secular history is correct these inner prisons were horrible dungeons below the ground, damp and reeking with filth. We know this one was below ground level, for we read later that the jailor "sprang in" (Ver. 29). And here they were subjected to still another form of torture—the stocks,[5] in which their feet were made fast. This made it difficult to sit up and practically forced them, backs all bruised and bleeding, to lie on the damp, vile, ground.

Later Paul recalled to the Thessalonians how he and Silas had been thus "shamefully entreated...at Philippi" (I Thes. 2:2). Little wonder he could say: *"Who is weak, and I am not weak? who is offended, and I burn not?"* (II Cor. 11:29).

But Paul and Silas were both Romans (Vers. 37,38). Why did they not let the magistrates know this at the very beginning? The only answer seems to be that by allowing the magistrates to put themselves in the wrong the apostles sought to secure for the Philippian disciples better treatment in the future. As it was, God had graciously overruled. Had the magistrates inquired into their citizenship and given them a formal trial, they might have been condemned to a long imprisonment, their work thus being hindered. *Now* the magistrates had put *themselves* on the defensive!

Doubtless the heroic comrades lay there sick and faint for a considerable period of time, perhaps sobbing in their pain and humiliation, but they who had subdued the spirit of Python were, though cruelly tortured, sustained by the Spirit of Christ and still gloriously triumphant!

---

5.   It is interesting to note that the word for stocks (*timber*) is also used of the cross of Christ (See 5:30; 10:39; Gal. 3:13; I Pet. 2:24).

THE PHILIPPIAN JAILOR CONVERTED

THE PRISON OPENED BY A MIRACLE

"And at midnight Paul and Silas prayed, and sang praises unto God: and the prisoners heard them.

"And suddenly there was a great earthquake, so that the foundations of the prison were shaken: and immediately all the doors were opened, and every one's bands were loosed.

"And the keeper of the prison awaking out of his sleep, and seeing the prison doors open, he drew out his sword, and would have killed himself, supposing that the prisoners had been fled.

"But Paul cried with a loud voice, saying, Do thyself no harm: for we are all here.

"Then he called for a light, and sprang in, and came trembling, and fell down before Paul and Silas,

"And brought them out, and said, Sirs, what must I do to be saved?

"And they said, Believe on the Lord Jesus Christ, and thou shalt be saved, and thy house.

"And they spake unto him the word of the Lord, and to all that were in his house.

"And he took them the same hour of the night, and washed their stripes; and was baptized, he and all his, straightway.

"And when he had brought them into his house, he set meat before them, and rejoiced, believing in God with all his house."

—Acts 16:25-34

What are these sounds at midnight? Praying! Singing!

Strange! Can it be coming from the dungeon where the two latest prisoners were cast? They cannot even kneel; their feet are fast in stocks. And *sing?* Why, only a few hours ago they were brutally beaten with rods and thrown into the dungeon, their backs pitifully bruised and bleeding from "many stripes."

Of course they cannot sleep—yet how can they be praying and singing in their condition, and in such a place? Yet it must be they we hear, for they are the ones who have been going about telling people about salvation through Christ.

How strange and wonderful it sounds! Until now these walls have heard only groans, curses and vile outbursts: Now they are hearing prayers and songs!

What a testimony Paul and Silas bore for Christ that midnight! Though deeply wronged and in physical misery, faith and joy overflowed as they prayed and sang hymns (Gr. *humneo*) to God. They were far from bitter. In their suffering, and not knowing how long they would be confined to this horrible dungeon or what test they might have to face next, they poured out their hearts in prayer to God, calling upon Him for strength and help. And somehow He seemed closer to them now, rather than farther away, so that they burst out in one song of praise after another, coming from

53

hearts overflowing with peace and joy. *"And the prisoners were listening."*[1]

Their consciences were clear and their hearts right with God—and more, like the apostles in Jerusalem in *their* persecutions, they rejoiced "that they were counted worthy to suffer shame for His name" (Acts 5:41). Indeed, in a truer sense than they, Paul was the apostle of the rejected Christ, filling up that which still remained of His afflictions for His Body's sake (Col. 1:24). Thus he later wrote to the saints in this very city:

"For unto you it is given in the behalf of Christ, not only to believe on Him, but also to suffer for His sake;

"Having the same conflict which ye saw in me, and now hear to be in me" (Phil. 1:29,30).

Yes, and the apostle went farther than that, expressing to them his longing to know Christ more intimately in "the *fellowship of His sufferings*" (Phil. 3:10).

This was the joy that filled and overflowed the hearts of Paul and Silas in that dark prison cell.

And suddenly, as they prayed and sang, there was an earthquake, so violent that it shook the foundations of the prison. *"And immediately all the doors were opened, and every one's bands were loosed"* (Ver. 26).

Surely this was a divine intervention. What if history does bear witness that earthquakes were frequent in that vicinity at that time, it would still be a miracle that one should take place just then and do just that—including even the loosing of every one's bands! This last unquestionably bears the stamp of the miraculous.

---

1. "The prisoners *heard* them" is not strong enough. They *listened*, deeply impressed by what they heard.

Those who deny this have argued that an earthquake, besides loosening the doors, might well have broken loose the bolts that fastened the prisoners' chains to the walls. But what of the other ends? It says "every one's bands were loosed," not merely loosed from the walls. Moreover Paul and Silas had had their feet fast in stocks!

And now the jailor awakens to find all the doors of the prison open and naturally supposes that the prisoners have fled. We have already explained how these Roman keepers were made responsible with their lives for the prisoners entrusted to them (See 12:19) hence it is not strange to find the Philippian jailor, in his distress, drawing his sword to take his life. Suicide, he thinks, is better than disgrace and a cruel execution.

But somehow Paul found out or sensed that the jailor was about to take his life and cried aloud from the darkness: *"Do thyself no harm: for we are all here"* (Ver. 28). To the jailor this must have seemed amazingly humane after the rough treatment he had given Paul and Silas, yet it was one of the natural fruits of the gospel they had been proclaiming.

But what power had kept *all* the prisoners in their cells? We are distinctly told that *"all* the doors were opened" and *"every one's* bands were loosed" (Ver. 26). Why did no one flee? We believe it was what they heard as Paul and Silas prayed and sang hymns, for what must have been the reaction in the heathen heart and mind to such conduct! How could they help associating the earthquake with it?

By now the jailor, so narrowly saved from committing suicide, was completely overwhelmed. Calling for lights (plural, probably torches) he *"sprang in"* and *"came trembling"* and *"fell down"* before Paul and Silas. So great was his reverence for them now that he did not even speak until he had "brought them out" of the dungeon. Then he asked the great question which may already have been troubling him, and now had suddenly taken possession of his heart and mind. Addressing them as "Sirs" (Gr. *Kurioi*, Lords) he entreats: *"What must I do to be saved?"* (Ver. 30).

It has been argued by some that the jailor had physical deliverance rather than the salvation of his soul in mind when he asked this question, but the evidence unites to prove that this is not so.

1. Paul and Silas had been pointed out for "many days" in Philippi, as men who proclaimed "the way of salvation" (Vers. 17,18).

2. The earthquake was over. He could hardly be seeking "salvation" from that.

3. None of the prisoners had escaped, so his life need no longer be in danger from that source. Indeed, the jailor seems to have taken no immediate steps to re-secure the prisoners, either because his attendants (Ver. 29) saw to this, or because the salvation of his soul was now his supreme concern. God may also have used the circumstances to cause the prisoners to stay. At any rate, had he feared *Roman* judgment now, his first concern would have been to make certain no prisoner would escape.

4. The earthquake, the open prison doors, the neglect of the prisoners to do that which would have insured his ruin, Paul's solicitude for his life when he was about to commit suicide; all this would tend to make him seek more than physical deliverance.

5. Paul and Silas evidently took the jailor to mean that he sought salvation from sin. They would not have promised physical deliverance in return for faith in Christ.

6. The tender solicitude of the converted jailor toward the men he had so abused, and his joy when he, "with all his house," *did* believe, would seem to indicate that he had been under conviction of sin.

7. The references to the jailor's "house" in connection with both Paul's reply and the jailor's conversion (Vers. 31,32,33,34) harmonize with the cases of Cornelius (11:14) and Lydia (16:15).

How ready the apostles were with just the answer the jailor needed! *"Believe on the Lord Jesus Christ, and thou shalt be saved"* (Ver. 31). This is the core of the message of grace.

When "the people" had asked John the Baptist: *"What shall we do then?"* he had insisted upon the fruits of repentance and of the kingdom (Luke 3:9-11). When a lawyer had asked our Lord: *"What shall I do to inherit eternal life?"* the Lord had asked him: *"What is written in the law?"* and had instructed him: *"This do, and thou shalt live"* (Luke 10:25-28). When Peter's convicted hearers at Pentecost had asked: *"What shall we do?"* Peter had directed them to *"repent and be baptized...for the remission of sins"* (Acts 2:37,38). But now, under Paul, the clear, pointed message is: *"Believe on the Lord Jesus Christ, and thou shalt be saved."* No matter what your sin, no matter what your ignorance, no matter what your fears about "holding on"—*"Believe on the Lord Jesus Christ, and thou shalt be saved."* Whether to the child, with a lifetime of opportunity before him, or to the dying man with only a few moments to live, the message is still: *"Believe on the Lord Jesus Christ, and thou shalt be saved."*

The added words: *"and thy house,"* have sometimes been taken as a promise that the faith of one member of a family secures the salvation of the whole family. If this were so all the world would of course be saved, for we are all related, but the apostles did not mean this, nor is this teaching found anywhere in the Pauline epistles. The meaning is simply: "This goes for your household too. They, as well as you, may believe and be saved."

But while the apostles came right to the point in answer to the jailor's inquiry, they did not stop there, as some evangelists and soul-winners do today. Still sick and sore, they preached "the word of the Lord" to the jailor and to the members of his household, who had by now gathered around (Ver. 32).

Soon enough the jailor showed evidence that he *had* sincerely trusted in Christ as his Savior, for "the same hour of the night" he took them to still another place, where water was available, and there the once brutal jailor tenderly washed their stripes. We are not told what he said when he did this, but we suspect there were many words of regret and apology. And here too, the jailor "and all his" were washed with a baptism that signified cleansing from sin.

It should be observed again that Paul had not required this baptism for the remission of sins according to the "great commission" given to the eleven (Mark 16:16; Acts 2:38). It was added *after*, as in the cases of Cornelius and Lydia, and only because Israel and the kingdom program had not yet been officially set aside. Nor does this mean that Paul *preached* or *taught* baptism. He rightly circumcised Timothy, yet he did not *preach* circumcision (Gal. 5:11). Similarly he says: *"Christ sent me not to baptize, but to preach the gospel"* (I Cor. 1:17) and it would not be long now before the "one baptism" by the Spirit into Christ was all that would remain (Eph. 4:5).

So far from teaching household or infant baptism, the record states that the jailor *"rejoiced, believing* [Lit. *having believed] in God with all his house"* (Ver. 34). Yet able men of God, like Albert Barnes, will say: "The whole narrative would lead us to suppose that *as soon as the jailor believed* he and all his family were baptized.... *The Baptism appears to have been performed on account of the faith of the head of the family"! (Barnes on the New Testament,* at Acts 16:34. Italics ours). Such are the foundations upon which the doctrine of household baptism has been built.

But this passage gives no better support to the immersionists as far as the *mode* of baptism is concerned. There is no indication that there was enough water in the prison to *submerge* people in. Nor is it probable that there would be. Nor is there any indication whatever that they were immersed. They doubtless had water sprinkled or poured upon them in the same place where Paul and Silas had their stripes washed and certainly in "the same hour of the night" (Ver. 33). There had been an earthquake and much excitement and it is doubtful that they took part in a long ceremony. Indeed we read that they were baptized "straightway" (Ver. 33).

And now the jailor takes Paul and Silas into his own home and sets a table[2] before them (Ver. 34). Doubtless they were hungry by now, for it was at the time of

---

2. Not "meat" merely, but a *meal*. With but one other exception the word *trapeza* is consistently rendered "table."

prayer, 9 AM, (Ver. 16 cf. 3:1) that the trouble had begun, and it was now well past midnight. But a deeper hunger had been graciously satisfied for the apostles, for it must have been well worth all their suffering and humiliation to see the jailor *rejoice, having believed in God with all his house.*[3] Here was feasting and fellowship indeed! And the joy of the jailor and his household was typical of the joy that always follows true faith (See 2:46,47; 8:8; Rom. 15:13; I Pet. 1:8).

PAUL ASSERTS HIS ROMAN CITIZENSHIP

"And when it was day, the magistrates sent the sergeants, saying, Let those men go.

"And the keeper of the prison told this saying to Paul, The magistrates have sent to let you go: now therefore depart, and go in peace.

"But Paul said unto them, They have beaten us openly uncondemned, being Romans, and have cast us into prison; and now do they thrust us out privily? nay verily; but let them come themselves and fetch us out.

"And the sergeants told these words unto the magistrates: and they feared, when they heard that they were Romans.

"And they came and besought them, and brought them out, and desired them to depart out of the city.

"And they went out of the prison, and entered into the house of Lydia: and when they had seen the brethren, they comforted them, and departed."

—Acts 16:35-40

---

3. The jailor's case was very different from that of Cornelius, and a greater demonstration of grace. Cornelius had feared God, prayed, given alms, etc. The jailor, on the other hand, had only a few hours before shown how cruel the pagan heart can be. Yet now he was rejoicing in salvation with all his house.

As morning light dawned the sergeants[4] appeared, not with a summons to bring Paul and Silas in for examination, but with a message from the magistrates to "let those men go" (Ver. 35). This could scarcely have been because the magistrates felt that the sufferings endured by Paul and Silas were sufficient to pay for their "crime." The phrase "when it was day," rather indicates that for some reason they were in a hurry to release them.

Probably the magistrates realized, as they thought the matter over, that they had failed to carry out the boasted justice of the Roman Empire in having Paul and Silas beaten and imprisoned as criminals without inquiry or investigation. Perhaps they even suspected that one or both of them were Roman citizens, and the violent earthquake that followed their premature condemnation of the apostles may well have further troubled their consciences. Under such circumstances they would naturally seek to dispose of the case as quickly as possible.

The jailor, evidently pleased at this sudden turn of events, now bears the good news to Paul and Silas and bids them "go in peace," but what is his surprise when they *refuse* to go, Paul replying with a masterpiece of energetic brevity which, in modern English, would be translated about as follows:

"They have beaten us

"publicly,

"uncondemned,

"men that are Romans,

"and have thrown us into prison;

---

4. Lit. *rod-bearers*. Probably the same men who had beaten them the night before.

"and now do they throw us out secretly?

"No indeed;

"Let them come themselves and lead us out" (Ver. 37).

There was irony in the phrase "men that are Romans," for the magistrates had commanded to beat and imprison them on the charge that *"being Jews"* they had troubled Philippi exceedingly. Similarly the apostle points out that they had been *"thrown"* into prison "publicly," and now will the magistrates *"throw"* (Gr. *ballo* in both cases) them out "secretly," as if they had no rights? No, indeed! He will hold them to account for their illegal action. They must come themselves and escort the apostles out as publicly as they have cast them in. A secret pardon will not suffice; the apostle demands formal vindication.

Now the tables are turned. The accused become the accusers and the judges are in danger of being called to trial. The magistrates are now in danger both from Rome, for violating the vaunted sanctity of Roman citizenship, and also from Philippi itself, for its natives, themselves Roman citizens, upon learning that Paul and Silas are also Romans, may well resent the disregard of their rights. The magistrates, knowing this, "feared" (Ver. 38). There was nothing to do but to capitulate.

There are many lessons to be learned from Paul's action here. We may be certain that the apostle did not challenge these Roman rulers merely for the personal satisfaction he might get out of it. It was not from pride, but from a proper sense of the dignity of his office that he took this action. Also, he thought of the Philippian believers. He had always been the first to bear suffering patiently at the hands of his persecutors, but, as Barnes says at this point: "where submission without any effort to obtain justice might be followed by disgrace to the cause...a higher obligation may require one to seek a vindication of his character, and to claim the protection of the laws."

And this was not the only occasion when Paul asserted his rights as a Roman citizen. We find him doing so again in Acts 21:39; 22:25 and 25:10,11. Yet we never find him demanding his rights as a *Hebrew* citizen. Thus God would emphasize the fact that Paul was pre-eminently the apostle of the Gentiles, as he says in his letter to the believers at Rome:

"For I speak to you Gentiles, inasmuch as *I am the apostle of the Gentiles, I magnify mine office*" (Rom. 11:13).

Still we know that he *was* a Hebrew citizen as well; a *born* Hebrew (Phil. 3:5) and a *born* Roman (Acts 22:28) at the same time. In this he represents the Body of Christ, *a joint body of believing Jews and Gentiles* (I Cor. 12:13). Indeed, this is further emphasized by the fact that Paul was a former *enemy* of God and His Christ, now gloriously *reconciled*, for we read, with regard to Jews and Gentiles, that Christ died:

"...that He might reconcile both unto God in one body by the cross, having slain the enmity thereby" (Eph. 1:16).

Thus, as the twelve were sent to Israel, so Paul was sent to the Gentiles, and as the twelve were the appointed representatives of the twelve tribes of redeemed Israel (Matt. 19:28) so Paul was the appointed representative of the "one body" (Col. 1:24,25).

Returning again to the local scene at Philippi, we find the magistrates apologizing to Paul and Silas, yet requesting them to leave the city, evidently fearing that their continued presence there might call attention to the magistrates' blunder and complicate matters further for them.

But the apostles, while graciously complying with the request, did not flee in haste from the city. With a dignity and self-possession which bespoke the justice of their cause, they went first to Lydia's home to comfort "the brethren." Surely *"the wicked flee when no man pursueth; but the righteous are bold as a lion"* (Prov. 28:1).

We may be sure that under God Paul's courage, patience, presence of mind and clarity of judgment through this ordeal, and the faithfulness of Silas as his companion, placed the small church at Philippi in a much more advantageous position and doubtless helped greatly to establish it.

Nevertheless, these believers would not be free from persecution, for the gospel of God's grace having gotten a foothold in Europe, the devil would do all in his power to oppose it. Indeed, the sufferings they were to endure were to give them a deeper appreciation of the one who had himself suffered so much to bring Christ to them, so that again and again they were to seek Paul out in order to "communicate with his affliction" and supply his needs. How could such as Lydia and her household, and the delivered Pythoness, and the jailor and his household ever forget him?

For the present it seems that both Timothy and Luke remained with the infant church, for Luke says of Paul and Silas that "they...departed" (16:40). Indeed, it is possible that Luke remained at Philippi until Paul's next apostolic journey, for the narrative now proceeds in the third person, not returning to the second again until 20:6. Timothy, however, rejoined Paul soon after, being referred to in 17:14.

Thus "the gospel of the grace of God" was first planted in Europe, and still it continues to bring forth fruit, even though the glorious message, ever more fully revealed to the apostle of grace, and ever more fully proclaimed by him, has since been perverted and confused with "the gospel of the kingdom" by the very leaders of the Church.

CHURCHES ESTABLISHED
AT THESSALONICA AND BEREA

PAUL AT THESSALONICA

"Now when they had passed through Amphipolis and Apollonia, they came to Thessalonica, where was a synagogue of the Jews:

"And Paul, as his manner was, went in unto them, and three sabbath days reasoned with them out of the Scriptures,

"Opening and alleging, that Christ must needs have suffered, and risen again from the dead; and that this Jesus, whom I preach unto you, is Christ.

"And some of them believed, and consorted with Paul and Silas; and of the devout Greeks a great multitude, and of the chief women not a few.

"But the Jews which believed not, moved with envy, took unto them certain lewd fellows of the baser sort, and gathered a company, and set all the city on an uproar, and assaulted the house of Jason, and sought to bring them out to the people.

"And when they found them not, they drew Jason and certain brethren unto the rulers of the city, crying, These that have turned the world upside down are come hither also;

"Whom Jason hath received: and these all do contrary to the decrees of Caesar, saying that there is another king, one Jesus.

"And they troubled the people and the rulers of the city, when they heard these things.

"And when they had taken security of Jason, and of the other, they let them go."

—Acts 17:1-9

MANY GREEKS BELIEVE

Departing from Philippi, Paul and Silas made their way along the great Roman road to the west, arriving at Thessalonica, now known as Salonica, situated on the Aegean Sea about one hundred miles distant. They did not stop to evangelize Amphipolis and Apollonia, two cities along the way, doubtless concluding that the former could be reached through Philippi and the latter through Thessalonica, a populous center from which the gospel might be widely proclaimed. Indeed, we are later informed that from Thessalonica "the word of the Lord" did in fact come to be "sounded out" throughout "Macedonia and Achaia" (I Thes. 1:8).

In addition there was a synagogue[1] at Thessalonica and it was still Paul's custom to seek out such places first. This was doubtless partly because the Jews, believing in the true God, and having gathered about them proselytes and interested Gentiles, afforded him a good starting point from which to proclaim Christ. But in the program of God there was another important reason, Israel, as a nation, had rejected Christ and was already being set aside, the establishment of the Messianic kingdom being deferred until a later date. And now, as Paul was sent "far hence unto the Gentiles," he still went to "the Jew first," not with a view to the establishment of the kingdom after all, but that

---

1. Some texts read, "*the* synagogue," which might indicate that the Jews of this whole region were served by this one synagogue.

from Jerusalem to Rome the Jews might be left without excuse for their rejection of Christ and, as he explains: *"If by any means I may provoke to emulation them which are my flesh, and might save some of them"* (Rom. 11:14). The record of these facts is in harmony with the nature and purpose of the Book of Acts which, we must remember, is *not* to relate the story of "the birth and growth" of the Church of this dispensation, but rather to give an account of the fall of Israel and to explain why salvation was sent to the Gentiles apart from her instrumentality.

For three "sabbath days"[2] the apostle "reasoned out of the Scriptures" with the Jews at Thessalonica. That he was permitted to do this for so extended a time indicates what respect they must have had for his character, his ability and his earnest eloquence. Modern evangelists, who give their hearers a minimum of light from the Word and a maximum of entertainment, should take note of this, and should also take note of the amazing results of Paul's short ministry at Thessalonica.

What Paul preached at Thessalonica should also be considered here. Some have felt that Paul, since he reasoned out of the (Old Testament) Scriptures, must have proclaimed the same message as the twelve had been proclaiming: "the gospel of the kingdom" and "the gospel of the circumcision," and they have interpreted Paul's references to the return of Christ in his Thessalonian epistles to conform to this view.

But there is no evidence that Paul proclaimed the gospel of the kingdom, or of the circumcision, here or anywhere at any time. In Galatians 2:7 he states emphatically that "the gospel of the circumcision" had

---

2. Or, *weeks*.

been committed to *Peter*, as "the gospel of the *un*circumcision" had been committed to him. Nor is it said anywhere that "the gospel of the kingdom" had been committed to him or was preached by him.

In "opening" (explaining) and "alleging" (Lit. setting before, facing with, or maintaining a thing to be so) that Messiah, according to Scripture "must needs have suffered and risen again" and that the Jesus whom he preached *was* the Messiah, Paul was simply establishing the identity of Christ so that they might come to trust in Him. This was the natural point of contact, the logical place of beginning.

That Paul did *not* proclaim the same message as the twelve had been proclaiming is evident from the following facts:

1. He did not call upon them to repudiate the nation's part in the death of Christ; an integral part of the message of the twelve (See Acts 2:23,36,38 and cf. Zech. 12:10; 13:6).

2. He did not, here nor anywhere, *offer* the return of Christ and the establishment of His kingdom, as the twelve had done (Acts 3:19-21).

3. God knew that the possibility of Israel's accepting Christ and His kingdom had already passed, hence the raising up of Paul to proclaim *another* message (Acts 8:1; 22:18; etc.).

4. Paul's ministry, both in the Acts and in his early epistles is consistently *distinguished* from that of the twelve (Acts 20:24; Gal. 1:11,12; 2:2,6-9; etc.).

In this part of Acts, however, we have a *transition* from the old program to the new. The old *gradually* disappears as the new takes its place. It is perfectly natural, therefore, to find Paul, here and elsewhere in the Acts record, proving to the Jews by the Scriptures that "Jesus is the Christ," that some may be won to trust in Him and that those who join the nation in refusing to do so may be left wholly without excuse as God continues to set the nation aside. This is where he had to begin, for if the Jesus who had been crucified was *not* the Messiah, He was an impostor and surely could not be the Dispenser of grace to a lost world, nor the Head of the Body.

Paul's ministry at Thessalonica was brief, but as we add to the Acts record, additional information gained from his Thessalonian epistles, written soon after, we get a better idea of how much was accomplished and how so much *could be* accomplished in so short a time.

Luke, by the Spirit, informs us that "some" of the Jews "believed," or rather, were *persuaded*, and cast in their lot with Paul and Silas, along with "a great multitude" of "devout," or *worshipping* Greeks and "not a few" of the leading women of the city, who, evidently, belonged to that category. Again the Gentiles had put the Jews to shame, with "a great multitude" of them turning to the Lord as compared with "some" of the Jews. But, in harmony with the purpose of Acts, Luke does not mention the even greater multitude of pagans won to the Lord during Paul's short stay there.[3] From Paul's epistles to the Thessalonians it is evident that the church there was from the beginning composed mainly of converts from *idolatry*, rather than from Judaism, for he writes to them as those who had "turned to God from idols" (I Thes. 1:9). Certainly the converted Jews

---

3. Unless Verse 4 should read *"devout persons and Greeks"* as a few MSS have it. These MSS, however, are probably the results of the difficulty encountered over Luke's failure to mention the converted pagans of which the church was mainly composed, for this rendering has little MSS support.

in the assembly formed an insignificant proportion, for Paul writes to the Thessalonians almost as if there were no Jews among them (See I Thes. 2:14; etc.).

How was so much accomplished in so short a time? Was it because things just happened to go easily for him during this period? No, indeed; there was much opposition, but the apostle had come to them in the power of the Spirit, exhibiting rare courage and grace.

Writing by inspiration, the apostle recalls: *"Our gospel came not unto you in word only, but also in power, and in the Holy Ghost, and in much assurance...But even after that we had suffered before, and were shamefully entreated, as ye know, at Philippi,*[4] *we were bold in our God to speak unto you the gospel of God with much contention"* (I Thes. 1:5; 2:2). And the Thessalonian believers, too, were introduced to suffering from the very beginning, for the apostle writes that they *"received the Word in much affliction"* and, as usual, *"with joy of the Holy Ghost"* (I Thes. 1:6 cf. 2:14).

But young and suffering believers could have had no greater human support than the Thessalonians received from Paul and Silas during their stay there. Again, by divine inspiration and not from spiritual pride, the apostle recalls: *"Ye know what manner of men we were among you for your sake"* (I Thes. 1:5) reminding the Thessalonians how he and Silas had not dealt with them from motives of "deceit," nor "uncleanness," nor "guile," but as men entrusted with a sacred charge (2:3,4). Nor had they used "flattery" or some other "cloak for greed;" nor had they "sought glory of men," though "as the apostles of Christ" they "might have been burdensome" to the Thessalonians (2:5,6).

---

4. Their backs undoubtedly still sore from the stripes received but a few days previous.

71

Rather, they had been "gentle" among these babes in Christ, "even as a nurse cherisheth her children." "Being affectionately desirous" of them, the apostles "were willing to have imparted unto [them] not the gospel of God only, but also [their] own souls" (2:7,8).

One detail which perhaps surprises us most of all is that in the apostle's short stay here, with so great a work to do, he even took up daily employment, so that he might not need to look to them for support. *"For ye remember,"* he says, *"our labor and travail [toil]; for laboring night and day, because we would not be chargeable unto any of you, we preached unto you the gospel of God"* (2:9).

Finally, the apostle could call on them to bear witness: *"how holily and justly and unblameably we behaved ourselves among you that believe"* and *"how we exhorted and comforted and charged every one of you, as a father doth his children, that ye would walk worthy of God"* (2:10-12).

How could *such* a ministry fail to produce results? And it *did* produce results. It produced results infinitely more extensive and lasting than all the shallow, frivolous "evangelism" of modern times.

Says the apostle: *"Yourselves, brethren, know our entrance in unto you, that it was not in vain....For... when ye received the Word of God which ye heard of us, ye received it not as the word of men, but as it is in truth, the Word of God, which effectually worketh also in you that believe"* (I Thes. 2:1,13). And the Thessalonian believers were, in turn, used to carry the message far and wide, for *"from you,"* says the apostle, *"sounded out the Word of the Lord not only in Macedonia and Achaia, but also in every place your faith to God-ward is spread abroad"* (I Thes. 1:8).

Little wonder the apostle gave *"thanks to God al-ways for [them] all"!* (I Thes. 1:2). Little wonder he ex-claimed: *"What thanks can we render to God...for you!"* (3:9). Little wonder he called them his *"glory and joy!"* (2:20).

THE JEWS INCITE PERSECUTION

In addition to the opposition which they had en-countered from the beginning, a persecution was now to be raised which was to force Paul and Silas to leave Thessalonica under cover of darkness.

The Jews, envious of Paul's success in winning so many to the Christ whom they rejected, resorted again to foul methods to thwart his ministry. Evidently fear-ing, among the Gentiles, to give to their hostility a purely Jewish appearance, they stirred up the pagans against the apostles as the Jews from Antioch and Ico-nium had done at Lystra (Acts 14:19). Here, however, they stooped to even lower levels than had the Jews at Lystra for, taking to themselves certain evil men from among the rabble,[5] they "gathered a company, and set all the city on an uproar," assaulting the house of Jason,[6] where Paul and Silas had evidently been stay-ing, and seeking to bring them out to the people[7] (17:5). Failing to find them, however, they dragged Jason and some of the other brethren to the rulers of the city, cry-ing: *"These that have turned the world upside down are come hither also!"* (Ver. 6). This was a real compliment.

---

5. The word rendered "of the baser sort" is literally *market-loungers* and refers to such idlers as were always ready for mischief. A good rendering would be *rowdies*.

6. If this Jason is the same as the one mentioned in Romans 16:21, he was a relative of Paul's.

7. Either to the mob or before the popular assembly.

73

Would that it could be said of us, for the world is certainly wrong side up!

However, the charge *as they meant it* was not true, nor was it true that Paul and his associates had violated the decrees of Caesar or sought to incite sedition (Ver. 7). But the Jews had put into their mouths that charge which in widely spread Imperial Rome was always most apt to secure the attention of the magistrates—that of treason against the Emperor. This was the same false charge that had been brought against our Lord Himself when brought before Pilate (Luke 23:2).[8]

To what extremes of intolerance and injustice religious bigotry can lead men! *The Jews* had raised the tumult, yet they accused the Christians of doing it. They themselves believed from their Scriptures that Messiah would overthrow the kingdoms of this world to reign over *them*, and they would have been the first to accept a king who would destroy Rome, if only he would leave them in their sins. Yet now they profess allegiance to Caesar! Their malice was much more bitter than that of Paul's pagan persecutors at Philippi. There the blunder was soon corrected, and that openly. But here the hate ran deeper. Indeed, before it was over the Jews from Thessalonica pursued Paul to Berea to persecute him further, just as the Jews from Antioch and Iconium had pursued him to Lystra.

Both the people of Thessalonica and their rulers naturally became troubled at hearing these things, just as "Herod...was troubled...and all Jerusalem with him," upon hearing of another "King of the Jews" (Matt. 2:2,3) for both people and rulers knew what conflict could result from any challenge to the authority of Rome. The

8. Though before the Jewish high priest He was charged with blasphemy (Matt. 26:60,61).

rulers here, however, showed more restraint than the military magistrates at Philippi had done, for taking "security," or bail, from Jason and the others, they let them go.

Under the circumstances it seemed foolhardy for the apostles to remain at Thessalonica, since their very presence there would only tend to stir matters up more. Furthermore a sizeable assembly had already been established there. Therefore the brethren sent them away by night to Berea, a small town about thirty miles further west. But it was not easy for the apostle to leave so great a multitude of believers so recently, yet so thoroughly, converted to Christ. A short time later he wrote to them about *"being taken from [them] for a short time in presence, not in heart"* and about having *"endeavored the more abundantly to see [their] face with great desire"* (I Thes. 2:17). And with regard to the good news of their faith and love, brought to him by Timothy, the apostle wrote:

"Therefore, brethren, we were comforted over you in all our affliction and distress by your faith:

"For now we live, if ye stand fast in the Lord" **(I Thes. 3:7,8).**

And they did!

PAUL'S MINISTRY AT BEREA

"And the brethren immediately sent away Paul and Silas by night unto Berea: who coming thither went into the synagogue of the Jews.

"These were more noble than those in Thessalonica, in that they received the word with all readiness of mind, and searched the Scriptures daily, whether those things were so.

"Therefore many of them believed; also of honorable women which were Greeks, and of men, not a few.

"But when the Jews of Thessalonica had knowledge that the Word of God was preached of Paul at Berea, they came thither also, and stirred up the people.

"And then immediately the brethren sent away Paul to go as it were to the sea: but Silas and Timotheus abode there still.

"And they that conducted Paul brought him unto Athens: and receiving a commandment unto Silas and Timotheus for to come to him with all speed, they departed."

—Acts 17:10-15

THE NOBLE BEREANS

Travelling by night in Paul's day was not as simple a matter as it is now, but the apostle and his companion were urged on, not merely by the necessity to put distance between themselves and their persecutors, but by their desire to go still farther into Gentile territory with the gospel of the grace of God.

Not deterred by their treatment at the hands of the Jews at Thessalonica, the two men, upon arriving at Berea went again into the Jewish synagogue. But here was an assembly of Jews different in character from any they had thus far found or, indeed, were to find. They are called "noble" or "well-born" (cf. I Cor. 1:26) but the word here indicates those *qualities of character* which might be expected of those of high birth: courtesy, generosity, freedom from bigotry, etc. Indeed this passage itself explains that they possessed those

76

qualities of true spiritual greatness which entitled them to be classed among the spiritual aristocracy of their day.

Many who have read this passage again and again still suppose that the Bereans were called "noble" merely because they *"searched the Scriptures daily, whether those things were so."* This last is true, but it is not the *whole* truth. The Scriptures give us a *twofold* reason:

1. "They received the word [which Paul preached] with all readiness of mind."

2. They "searched the Scriptures daily, whether those things were so."

The Bereans were open-minded. This is the *first* lesson we must learn from them. To appreciate this quality in them we must remember that they were *Jews* who met in a *synagogue* each *Sabbath* day. Some of the things Paul preached to them must have seemed strange, if not almost unbelievable and impossible. Yet, if they listened with open mouths, they listened with open minds too. They did not shake their heads in refusal or deem Paul's message unworthy of investigation just because it was so different from that which they had heard all their lives. They were spiritually great enough to give him a sincere and interested hearing.

In this the Jews of Thessalonica compared unfavorably with them. *"These* were *more noble* than those in Thessalonica," where Paul had reasoned out of the Scriptures for three Sabbath days with men who were unwilling to listen, until they stirred up persecution against him and he was driven away.

How sorely this Berean lesson is needed in the professing Church today! So many among God's people, yes, and even among their leaders, lack this quality of true spiritual greatness. Their first thought is to conform to accepted beliefs rather than to conform to the written Word of God. Their desire to stand well with the popular leaders is greater than their desire *to know the truth and to make it known*. They would rather be *orthodox* than *Scriptural*.

We must not suppose that the Berean Jews were gullible, or mistake their broad-mindedness for credulity. If they were broad they were narrow too. They were not willing to accept what Paul said just because he said it. They would listen and consider, but would not concede, without real evidence from the Scriptures, that the *truth* had been preached. Paul's Word must be subjected to God's Word. This was another sign of their true spiritual greatness.

Picture the scene: A husband comes home saying he has heard strange things in the synagogue from the lips of a visiting rabbi. Reaching for the sacred scrolls, he begins an intensive search. The rest of the Sabbath day finds him buried in thought over the writings of the prophets. And not only that day, for he continues the search day after day. Rising early each morning and hurrying home from work each evening, he puts aside the less important things and searches untiringly until he is sure he has the Truth of God. And he is only one of many like him in that Berean synagogue.

How God must have rejoiced over this Bible-loving, Bible-honoring group! They, and not the popular leaders, were the truly great ones in Israel. Oh, for more such congregations today!

In this also the Thessalonian Jews showed up poorly by comparison. They never even got so far as to examine Paul's message in the light of the Scriptures, for they would not give him an interested hearing in the first place.

And here is another strange paradox. Those who reject light and refuse to even search the Scriptures to see whether these things are so, are yet so ready to accept without question what their "orthodox" leaders have taught them. They are so suspicious of other teachers, yet so credulous of their own.

What a rebuke to Rome this passage is with its encouragement to *individual, personal* Bible study! The Bereans were neither slaves to their own religious prejudices nor, on the other hand, would they accept the word of even the greatest man of God, without subjecting it to personal examination in the light of the Scriptures—*and they were commended for it*.

If there is anything this passage teaches it is that every believer is responsible to examine even the best teaching in the light of the Scriptures, that every preacher should *expect* his teachings to be so examined and should *thank God* for those who do this. Indeed, it is a sign of a *lack* of spiritual greatness when men of God resent Scriptural examination of their teachings by their hearers.

The purity of the Church, doctrinally, depends not upon loyalty to the dogmas of the Church, but upon the maintenance of the Berean spirit among the people of God. The Bereans were not satisfied with a bit of devotional reading now and then. They *searched* the Scriptures *daily*, like the "blessed man" of Psalm 1:2. May we not fail to do so! May we not fail to train our children to do so, that we and they may justly deserve a place among the spiritual aristocracy of *our* day!

A word must here be added about the content of Paul's preaching at Berea. The fact that they "searched the Scriptures" for confirmation of it does not indicate, as some suppose, that he did not preach "the gospel of the grace of God" or proclaim Christ "according to the revelation of the mystery" as far as he knew it, for while the Old Testament Scriptures do not, indeed, *teach* these truths, they do *confirm* them. The "gap" in prophecy is surely a confirmation of the mystery revealed later. It proves that God had the "eternal purpose" in mind all the while. Similarly there is not one word in the Old Testament to the affect that the tabernacle and its furniture, the priesthood, the feasts of Jehovah, etc., are typical of Christ and the all-sufficiency of His finished work, but in the light of the revelation to Paul today they are shown to be such. Furthermore, Acts again consistently stresses the *Jewish* side of Paul's ministry at Berea. When the Acts record is compared with Paul's epistles we find that he *did* preach his special message consistently as it was ever more fully revealed to him (cf. Acts 15 with Gal. 2; Acts 16:6 with the whole Galatian epistle; Acts 17:2,3 with I Thes. 1:5; etc.). He was called from the beginning to proclaim "the gospel of the grace of God" (Acts 20:24) but this glorious message, while not *proclaimed* in the Old Testament Scriptures, is amply confirmed by them.

The result of the Scriptural, spiritual attitude of the Berean Jews toward Paul's teaching was that "therefore *many* of them believed," in addition to "not a few" Greek men and leading women. This in comparison with "some" (Gr. *certain, very few*) Jews at Thessalonica (Vers. 4,12). And we may be sure that these Berean believers were the stronger in faith because they had insisted upon an intelligent, Scriptural understanding of the subject. They now possessed not only the "full assurance of faith" (Heb. 10:22) but the "full assurance of understanding" as well (Col. 2:2). Unbelief, on the other hand, is based on ignorance often willful ignorance, of the Word. Thomas Paine's introduction to the *Age of Reason* contains the following words: "I had neither Bible nor Testament to refer to, though I was writing against both, nor could I procure any."

How long did Paul and Silas continue teaching at Berea? The fact that the Bereans *daily* subjected Paul's teachings to Scriptural examination would already seem to indicate that he must have remained more than a few days. From I Thessalonians 2:17,18 it would appear that he lingered in the vicinity of Thessalonica for some time, attempting "once and again," though unsuccessfully, to revisit them. The logical place for him to have remained at this time would doubtless be Berea.

"But when the Jews of Thessalonica had knowledge that the Word of God was preached of Paul at Berea" his ministry there was cut short, for "they came thither also, and stirred up the people" (Ver. 13). How bitter was their hostility in pursuing him, and what malice they displayed as once again they stirred up others against Paul and his message rather than facing him themselves. Thessalonian bigotry had not only kept *them* in spiritual darkness; it had moved them to do all in their power to hinder *others* from receiving it. What a shame! Did they not have Bibles too?

Evidently the danger to Paul's life again became so great that it was necessary for the brethren to send him away immediately. He himself was generally reluctant to flee, even when in the gravest danger, but his safety was of paramount importance for the work's sake, hence from the beginning we find several occasions when "the brethren" sent him away (See Acts 9:25; 9:30; 17:10; 17:14).

The phrase "as it were to the sea" probably does not indicate any stratagem employed to elude the persecutors but rather the want of an immediate plan. The great necessity now was to get Paul *away* from Berea, further plans to be determined by providential circumstances.

At any rate Silas and Timotheus[9] were left at Berea to encourage and establish the believers there, while certain of the brethren accompanied Paul as far as Athens, a journey of nearly three hundred miles. Here for the first time the apostle seems to have been left completely alone. Hence his message to Silas and Timothy to come to him as speedily as possible.

It may be noted that we have no letter from Paul to the Bereans, nor any other mention of a church there. This does not necessarily mean, however, that the church there did not flourish. In the course of Paul's great apostolic journeys many churches must have been founded of which we do not read a single word.

---

9.   Timothy had rejoined the company, perhaps at Thessalonica.

PAUL AT ATHENS

A DIFFICULT ASSIGNMENT

"Now while Paul waited for them at Athens, his spirit was stirred in him, when he saw the city wholly given to idolatry.

"Therefore disputed he in the synagogue with the Jews, and with the devout persons, and in the market daily with them that met with him.

"Then certain philosophers of the Epicureans, and of the Stoics, encountered him. And some said, What will this babbler say? other some, He seemeth to be a setter forth of strange gods: because he preached unto them Jesus, and the resurrection.

"And they took him, and brought him unto Areopagus, saying, May we know what this new doctrine, whereof thou speakest, is?

"For thou bringest certain strange things to our ears: we would know therefore what these things mean.

"(For all the Athenians and strangers which were there spent their time in nothing else, but either to tell, or to hear some new thing)."

—Acts 17:16-21

ATHENS IN PAUL'S DAY

The apostle was now alone in Athens, the most celebrated city of Greece (then called Achaia) and the cultural capital of the world.

Centuries before this Athens had won world renown for her cultivation of the liberal arts. The most celebrated poets and philosophers had either been born or had flourished there. The outstanding models of statuary and architecture were to be found there. And what was more, practically every religion was represented there.

Though the sun of Athens' glory had by now begun to set, she was still distinguished as the intellectual, artistic and religious center of the world.

There was the *Areopagus* (Latin: *Hill of Mars*) so named from the legendary trial of Mars there. Here judges, called Areopagites[1] because they held session there, actually *tried* doctrines and those who taught them! Above this rose the *Acropolis* with the *Parthenon* and its colossal statue of the goddess Athene.

While the city of Athens has continued to this day, her glory, like all earthly glory, has passed away. Only the ruins of her pride remain.

AN IDOL-RIDDEN CITY

While Paul waited for Silas and Timothy,[2] *"his spirit was stirred in him, when he saw the city wholly given to idolatry* [Lit. *crowded with idols*]*"* (Ver. 16).

---

1. One of these appears to have been saved during Paul's visit at Athens (Ver. 34).

2. He remained alone at Athens for some time longer, for though he'd sent word to Silas and Timothy to "come to him with all speed" (Ver. 15) when Timothy did come to Athens bearing news of the sufferings of the Thessalonian believers, Paul couldn't bear to keep him but again "thought it good to be left at Athens alone" and sent him back to establish and encourage them in the faith (I Thes. 3:1-5). Considering the distance between the Macedonian churches and Athens, Paul must have spent a considerable period of time at Athens and mostly alone, except as converts were won. Thus did he sacrifice himself for the good of those he had been forced to leave. Finally Timothy, with Silas, rejoined Paul at Corinth (Acts 18:5) bearing good news from Macedonia (I Thes. 3:6,7).

The apostle was not filled with wonder at the beauty of Athens' art and architecture, at her subtle and refined philosophies, at her union of religions. He saw all this in the light of *truth* and *reality*. He was rather agitated and upset at the spectacle of men bowing down, not merely to that which their own hands had made, but to the spiritual forces of evil that induced them to "worship and serve the creature more than the Creator" (Rom. 1:25 cf. Dan. 10:21; Eph. 2:2; 6:12). And he was appalled at the sin that accompanied these heathen religions (Rom. 1:26-32).

With all their vaunted wisdom, the Athenians could not even settle on a god! One worshipped this "deity" and another that. Most worshipped different gods on different occasions. So great was the confusion that Pliny says that in Nero's time Athens contained over 3,000 public idols in addition to countless idols possessed by individuals. On every hand there were statues to gods and demi-gods. Practically every "deity" was represented including those "unknown." Petronius (Sat. XVII) says humorously that it was easier to find a god than a man in Athens, and our Scripture states that the city was "crowded with idols."

Athenian philosophers had settled nothing. They had but demonstrated the hopeless bankruptcy of human wisdom and the utter depravity of human nature. Athens' myriad superstitions were but a proof that unbelief, though boasting superior intelligence, is always more credulous than faith. Her vile statues were but an evidence of the low moral level to which her religions had let her sink.[3]

---

3. The exaltation of vice by Athens had had much to do with the fall of the Grecian Empire and was even now undermining the strength of Rome.

THE SYNAGOGUE AND THE MARKET

Though the city was "crowded with idols," there *was* still a synagogue there. *God* not quite crowded out! It was not, therefore, into any of the idol temples with which the apostle was surrounded, but into this synagogue that he first made his way. Those who met in this synagogue were primarily to blame for the conditions that existed at Athens, for everywhere the people of Israel had forgotten that, as the seed of Abraham, they were to be the instruments of God's blessing to the world (Gen. 22:17,18). They recognized the true God, but rather than bring God's Word to the nations they merely boasted in it—and that while failing to *obey* it. Thus, said the apostle, *"The name of God is blasphemed among the Gentiles through you"* (Rom. 2:24).

He saw the city crowded with idols. *"Therefore* disputed he in the synagogue with the Jews" (Ver. 17). The Jew still came first in his ministry. God had already begun to give Israel up and had begun to form the Body of Christ as a witness to the nations, but the sentence of doom was not to be pronounced upon the favored nation until the Jews from Jerusalem to Rome had had an opportunity to turn to Christ.

If we may go by Paul's procedure in other synagogues, he doubtless reasoned with them out of the Scriptures, proving that Jesus was the promised Christ and offering them salvation through His finished work—something Peter had not done at Pentecost (Acts 13:38,39 cf. Acts 2:38).

Next he reasoned also with the "devout" or reverent Gentiles, i.e., Gentiles who had come to revere the true God, though not having become Jewish proselytes.

86

Third, he reasoned daily with such as he met at the market place, where the Athenians gathered every day, not only to buy and sell, but to argue their various philosophies. Here the apostle would meet many who were eager enough to discuss man's "chief end" and "highest good."

THE EPICUREANS AND THE STOICS

Among these were the Epicureans and the Stoics, who represented the two leading schools of Greek thought at that time. Secular history indicates that the Epicureans held forth in what was known as *"the Garden,"* while the Stoics met in *"the Porch,"* from whence their name was derived.

The Epicureans were the followers of Epicurus who had flourished at Athens more than three centuries before. They were virtually atheists, in that they taught that whatever god or gods there were, were too far removed from man to be concerned about his sins or sorrows. They believed in neither creation, nor the continued existence of the soul after death, nor resurrection nor judgment. There was nothing to disturb or alarm.

It follows naturally that the Epicureans held that *the enjoyment of pleasure* was man's "chief end" and "highest good" in life. Hence some—evidently most— gave themselves over to lives of gross sensuality and vice. Their philosophy gave them free license to do so. Others, like Epicurus himself, indulged in more refined pleasures, yet all gave themselves to self-gratification. If sensual excesses were to be avoided it was only because they did not ultimately lead to the greatest pleasure.

The Stoics were the disciples of Zeno, a contemporary of Epicurus, whose philosophy was, however, almost exactly the opposite. They were pantheists and fatalists, and taught that *virtue* was man's "chief end" and "highest good." They believed in the suppression of all natural feeling and strove to accept fate with calm composure, indifferent alike to pain and pleasure, that they might become the masters rather than the slaves of circumstances.

With respect to their morals it might appear on the surface that they approximated Christianity, but in fact they were as far from it as were the Epicureans. Their teachings did not rest upon revealed truth. They were but a natural reaction to the excesses of Epicureanism. We must remember that on every hand the most shameless sensuality was glorified in the public works of art. Indeed, the very religions represented at Athens were, for the most part, degraded and licentious. The excesses of immmorality and vice which resulted, naturally had their evil consequences.

The philosophy of the Stoics, with its emphasis on self-repression, was a natural reaction to all this, but it did not stem from grace and faith. It was but man's attempt to make the most of himself. It produced a kind of phariseeism which looked down with scorn upon any who either wept or rejoiced. It knew nothing of the loving sympathy taught in the Scriptural exhortation: *"Rejoice with them that do rejoice, and weep with them that weep"* (Rom. 12:15). What was more, its self-discipline was often affected rather than real and like the Pharisees they were hypocrites, simply unwilling to acknowledge their sin and their need of a Savior. Thus, as *pleasure* characterized the Epicureans, *pride* characterized the Stoics.

It was these representatives of "the Garden" and "the Porch" that "encountered" Paul with their doctrines of self-gratification and self-repression. Some, indeed, asked contemptuously: *"What will* [Lit. *would*] *this babbler say?"* i.e., "What does he mean to say?" The word translated "babbler" in A.V. is literally *seed-picker* and referred to those who, without thoroughly examining any subject would pick up scraps of information here and there as a bird picks up seeds. Others said *"He seemeth to be a setter forth of strange gods,"*[4] because he had been preaching Christ and the resurrection. Yet Paul's arguments must have been presented with great ability and spiritual power for, as Kitto says: "Even the Epicureans and the Stoics, loitering about in learned leisure, did not deem it beneath their dignity to contend with such a disputant" (*Daily Bible Illustrations*, Vol. 8, pg. 366).

Such a stir did the apostle's teachings cause that "they took hold of him," as the original reads, and brought him to the Areopagus. Evidently he was not actually *tried* for his doctrines here, for we read nothing of an accusation or of witnesses or of a trial or sentence. They simply asked: *"May we know what this new doctrine, whereof thou; speakest, is? For thou bringest certain strange things to our ears: we would know therefore what these things mean"* (Vers. 19,20). But it was probably meant to be a preliminary inquiry for what Paul had preached had been "strange" enough to require an explanation before the Areopagites.

---

4. Lit. *demons*. The word occurs 60 times in the New Testament and is always translated *devils* except here. It is significant in this connection that demons *were* behind their idol worship, and that angel spirits are called *gods* in Scripture because, like the rulers of this world, they are supposed to represent God (Psa. 82:1,6; 86:8; 95:3; 96:4,5; 97:7,9; etc.).

"For all the Athenians [Lit. The Athenians, ALL of them] and strangers which were there spent their time in nothing else, but either to tell, or to hear some new [Lit. newer] thing" (Ver. 21).

They had called Paul a "seed-picker" but *they* were the "seed-pickers," always looking about for something newer, and thus betraying their dissatisfaction with what they had. True, they tried any doctrines that seemed to gain prominence, but did not try them by the infallible and changeless Word of God. They subjected them only to the bar of changing human opinion.

Now Paul must take this trait into account as he addresses them. He will give them something new: the one God they are as yet ignorant of, and His Son, Jesus Christ.

THESSALONICA, BEREA AND ATHENS COMPARED

Before considering the apostle's sermon from Mars Hill, let us compare the record with respect to Thessalonica, Berea and Athens, the three latest cities to be visited by Paul. Leaving aside the question whether Jews or Gentiles are referred to, we find a particular characteristic emphasized in connection with those to whom the apostle ministered in each of these cities.

At the synagogue in Thessalonica Paul reasoned out of the Scriptures for three sabbaths (or weeks) with men who were unwilling to listen, with the result that only a few (Gr. "certain") of them believed, while "a great multitude" of the Gentiles believed. What Paul preached was new to them and they refused to consider it, letting the Gentiles put them, God's chosen people, to shame.

The bigotry of the Thessalonian Jews not only kept them in spiritual darkness but moved them to bitter opposition to the truth, so that they not only persecuted Paul and Silas in their own city but followed them to Berea, stirring up the people there against them.

We need to heed this lesson today. Bigotry among God's people today will have the same effect as it had in Paul's day. Let us never close our minds so as to keep error out, for in doing so we will only shut new light out and close old errors in. Moreover, it is but a small step from shutting out new light from God's Word to engaging in bitter opposition to it.

The Athenians went to the other extreme. They lost interest in what was old and clamored only to hear the new. Yet if what they heard did not appeal to them some "mocked" while others said, more politely: "We will hear thee again of this matter," with the result that there too the fruit was meager.

This lesson is equally needed in our day, for all about us the Athenian spirit is rife. The masses are constantly giving up the old and looking for something new. So pronounced is this trend in our day that in nearly every large city "tomorrow's" news is sold on the news stands tonight, and supposing that the latest fashions and the latest advice must be best, men treat their minds like garbage cans, putting almost anything into them.

Significantly, the record of the Bereans comes between those of the Thessalonians and the Athenians. The Bereans possessed the true spiritual greatness to give man's word a respectful hearing, whether old or new, and then to subject it to an examination in the light of God's Word. The result was that "therefore *many* of them believed," in comparison with few of the Thessalonians and the Athenians. What is more, God recognizes them in the Scriptures as the spiritual nobility of their day because *"they received the Word with all readiness of mind, and searched the Scriptures daily, whether those things were so"* (Ver. 11).

How this lesson is needed in the professing Church today among preachers as well as hearers! Modernists cast away precious treasures of the Bible, explaining that they are old and out of date, while Fundamentalists, clinging to old truth (and error) reject new light simply because it is new! Modernists vie with each other to keep up to date, intellectually, while Fundamentalists vie with each other to be orthodox, when both should make it their aim to be *Scriptural*, bowing in faith before the Word of God.

Men of God today do well to remember the words of our Lord after proclaiming the mysteries of the kingdom of heaven. *"Therefore every scribe,"* said He, *"which is instructed unto the kingdom of heaven is like unto a man that is an householder, which bringeth forth out of his treasure THINGS NEW AND OLD"* (Matt. 13:52).

PAUL'S ADDRESS ON MARS HILL

"Then Paul stood in the midst of Mars Hill, and said, Ye men of Athens, I perceive that in all things ye are too superstitious.

"For as I passed by, and beheld your devotions, I found an altar with this inscription, TO THE UNKNOWN GOD. Whom therefore ye ignorantly worship, Him declare I unto you.

"God that made the world and all things therein, seeing that He is Lord of heaven and earth, dwelleth not in temples made with hands;

"Neither is worshipped with men's hands, as though He needed anything, seeing He giveth to all life, and breath, and all things;

"And hath made of one blood all nations of men for to dwell on all the face of the earth, and hath determined the times before appointed, and the bounds of their habitation;

"That they should seek the Lord, if haply they might feel after Him, and find Him, though He be not far from every one of us:

"For in Him we live, and move, and have our being; as certain also of your own poets have said, For we are also His offspring.

"Forasmuch then as we are the offspring of God, we ought not to think that the Godhead is like unto gold, or silver, or stone, graven by art and man's device.

"And the times of this ignorance God winked at; but now commandeth all men everywhere to repent:

"Because He hath appointed a day, in the which He will judge the world in righteousness by that man whom He hath ordained; whereof He hath given assurance unto all men, in that He hath raised Him from the dead.

"And when they heard of the resurrection of the dead, some mocked: and others said, We will hear thee again of this matter.

"So Paul departed from among them.

"Howbeit certain men clave unto him, and believed: among the which was Dionysius the Areopagite, and a woman named Damaris, and others with them."

—Acts 17:22-34

It is more than doubtful whether anything in the choicest oratory of the learned men of Greece could begin to match the dignity, majesty and grandeur of Paul's address before the Areopagites.

The apostle had met paganism; now he faced the philosophical arguments with which it was defended. From beginning to end he showed perfect self-control, while at the same time his discourse was the outpouring of that which had filled his heart, surrounded as he was by idolatry. His intense earnestness stands out in sharp contrast to the flippancy of the Athenians (Vers. 18,21,32) as he makes his reply from "the midst" of the Areopagus.

A TACTFUL OPENING

With utmost respect the apostle addresses his hearers as *"Ye men of Athens,"* acknowledging the fact that they are *"unusually religious"* (Ver. 22).

The *Authorized* "too superstitious" is a most unfortunate rendering. Paul was not so wanting in tact as to offend his hearers by his very opening remarks. The Athenians *were* superstitious but had he accused them of this at the outset he would have closed their minds to his whole discourse. Examine Paul's other speeches and it will be seen that he opens with such observations as will tend to win the interest and the sympathetic attention of his hearers.

The present case is no glaring exception to this rule of Paul's but rather a signal example of it. In a rare combination of compliment and caution the apostle acknowledges the zeal which the Athenians bestowed on their religion,[5] without expressing any opinion as to the religion itself.

Certainly Paul would not have called the Athenians *too* superstitious, when he was convinced that *any* superstition was wrong. Furthermore the same root is employed in Acts 25:19,[6] where very evidently it is used in the sense of *religion*, for surely Festus would not call Judaism *superstition* before Agrippa, who was himself a Jew.

But this opening statement of Paul's is the more remarkable because, while eminently tactful it was also the first blow in his argument against the philosophies of the Athenians.

The Epicureans were, as we have said, virtually atheists. No god or gods—if there were any—had anything to do with man. The Stoics, on the other hand, were pantheists. To them the universe was god. Both parties, had they been logical and consistent, would have scorned idolatry, though they could not have found the true God. Yet it was here that idolatry, in its multiplied forms, held almost undisputed sway. Betraying the weakness of their own positions the Epicureans had admitted gods into their system as phantoms of the popular imagination, while the Stoics had admitted them as minor developments of the great god, the universe. Both had followed the human bent

---

5. Lit. worship of demons or divinities.

6. Where again it is mistranslated "superstition."

toward some sort of worship and were, in practice, idolaters.

THE ALTAR TO THE UNKNOWN GOD

Actually, the original does not say that Paul had beheld, or observed, their *devotions*, but that he had observed the *objects of their devotion* and that among these he had found "an altar with this inscription, TO THE UNKNOWN GOD"[7] (Ver. 23). "This One, whom you worship as unknown,"[8] said the apostle, "I declare to you." There is an evident allusion here to their charge in Verse 18, for the word "declare" in Verse 23 is the same as "set forth" in Verse 18. They said: *"He seemeth to be a setter forth of strange gods* [Lit. *demons* or *divinities*]." He now replies: "I set forth the *true God* [Gr. *Theos, God*] whom you worship as unknown." Thus he pleads "not guilty" to their charge of introducing "strange divinities."

With what delicacy, yet what boldness, the apostle refers to the idolatry with which he is surrounded, even using an inscription on *their* altar as his text![9] This altar—and ancient writers say there were others like it—aptly expressed the sense of uncertainty which must necessarily trouble the minds of the heathen. Instinctively conscious of the limitations of their idol worship (See Rom. 1:19-21) and seeking to avoid the wrath of any god or gods still unknown and unacknowledged, they erected yet *this* altar, that no god might punish

---

7. There is no article in the original, but the Greek does not require one.

8. "Ignorantly" is another unfortunate rendering.

9. He could not have done so if it had not been that the word *Theos*, rather than *daimonion* (demons) was used on this one altar.

them for their neglect to worship him. Recognizing this, and taking advantage of the fact that they had inscribed *this* altar to the unknown *Theos*, Paul declared: "*Him* declare *I* unto you."[10] Continuing this emphasis the apostle proclaims to his hearers *the* God,[11] the one that made the world [the ordered universe] and all things therein. Paul did not spend one moment proving to these philosophers that God exists or that He did create the universe or even that He is Lord of it. He *assumed* all this: *"The God, that made the universe... seeing He is Lord of heaven and earth...."*

He could well take this position. They had *acknowledged* that they did *not* know Him; Paul could say with authority that *he did*. Moreover the apostle well knew that their idolatry was an expression of their rejection of the light which God had given them. They, like the heathen elsewhere, were guilty of "holding," or *suppressing*, "the truth in unrighteousness" (Rom. 1:18).

"Because that which may be known of God is manifest in them; for God hath showed it unto them.

"For the invisible things of Him from the creation of the world are clearly seen, being understood by the things that are made,[12] even His eternal power and Godhead; *so that they are without excuse"* **(Rom. 1:19,20).**

Thus in one short sentence the apostle dealt with the Stoics, who claimed that the universe *was* God,

---

10. *"Him"* as distinguished from other gods; *"I"* as distinguished from their champions. Both words are emphatic in the Greek.

11. The original contains the definite article.

12. "Things that are made" is the Greek *poyeema*, from which our word *poem* is derived, and indicates the *harmony* of creation.

and with the Epicureans, who supposed that any gods who might exist were too far off to concern themselves with this planet. And, tactfully rebuking the idolatry which both inconsistently engaged in, he went on to point out that, seeing God had *made* the universe and was Lord of it, He *"dwelleth not in temples made with hands; neither is worshipped [served] with men's hands, as though He needed anything, seeing He giveth to all life, and breath, and all things"* (Vers. 24,25 cf. Psa. 50:7-15).

Paul here employs some arguments and some of the exact words which Stephen had used before the Sanhedrin in a defense which Paul himself, then Saul, had doubtless heard (Acts 7:48-50). It is remarkable that it had been necessary to tell the leaders of Israel the same things as these pagan philosophers. They had missed the lesson which David had learned (Psa. 51:16,17) looking upon the temple and altars and sacrifices themselves as sacred. Yet the very purpose of the Mosaic dispensation had been to show them that not only the moral law, but the ceremonial law was impotent to save the sinner (Heb. 10:4).

But if divinely-appointed sacrifices to God had no power in themselves to save, how much less those sacrifices which the heathen offered to gods of their own choosing!

Thus the apostle, with a God-given combination of tact and boldness exposed the folly and sin of their idolatry, and his arguments must have been the more impressive because of the location of the Areopagus, for as he spoke from the hill, with the open sky above them, the plain below and the sea in the distance, all must have spoken of the God whom he proclaimed as the Creator and Sustainer of all.

The word "blood," in Verse 26, should probably be omitted, as in the *Revised Version*, for it is not found in some of the best MSS. The meaning doubtless is that from one person God has made "all nations of men" to dwell on "all the face of the earth" and is a refutation of the Athenian notion that different nations were to be represented by different gods.

Here is another of those departures from the kingdom message and program, which we have found in Acts since the raising up of Paul. Our Lord, in His proclamation of the kingdom never went any farther back in human history than David and Abraham.[13] This was because the Gentiles had been cast away and the establishment of the Messianic kingdom was based on promises made to these two patriarchs. Hence the New Testament Scriptures open with the words: *"The book of the generation of Jesus Christ, the Son of David, the Son of Abraham."*

Paul, on the other hand, consistently goes back to *Adam*, "the first man" and points from him to *Christ*, "the second man," "the last Adam" (I Cor. 15:45-47). He shows how *"by one man sin entered into the world"* (Rom. 5:12). Even the children of Abraham must acknowledge that they are the children of Adam too, so that they might be saved through Christ, not as "the King of the Jews" but as the One who died for all.

"For as by *one man's disobedience* many were made sinners, so by *the obedience of one* shall many be made righteous" (Rom. 5:19).

---

13. Once He did *refer* to Adam and Eve without mentioning their names (Matt. 19:4) but this without any reference to the kingdom.

The fact that "all nations of men" come from one is not, however, intended to lend encouragement to the modern "one world" idea, for the apostle goes on to say that God determined, not only "the times before appointed," i.e., the seasons of their rule, but also "the bounds of their habitation" (Ver. 26 and cf. Deut. 32:8). What bloodshed and chaos has resulted from the failure of nations to recognize this fact!

But this, in turn, was in order that "they should seek the Lord." The nations have not been permitted to rule as long as they have wished, nor over as much territory as they have desired. *God* has determined beforehand the duration and the boundaries of their governments, that they might recognize their dependence upon *Him*, "seeking" after Him and "feeling" after Him with a view to "finding" Him. It is true, of course, that *"God looked down from heaven upon the children of men, to see if there were any that did understand, that did seek God,"* and that the verdict was: *"There is none that understandeth, there is none that seeketh after God"* (Psa. 53:2,3; Rom. 3:11) but this does not alter the fact that they *should* do so and are guilty for *not* having done so.

This, of course, was a refutation of the Stoic philosophy that the universe, including man, *was* God. But again the Epicureans come in for their share as the apostle hastens to add: *"though He be not far from every one of us, for in Him we live, and move, and have our being"* (Vers. 27,28). And to substantiate this fact *to them* he draws from the concessions of their own poets, one of which had said: *"For we are also His offspring."*[14] Paul

14. We still have practically the same words in the writings of Aratus of Cilicia (Paul's own province) and Cleauthus of Lystra, either of which Paul may have referred to.

100

does not, of course, support the false doctrine of "the Fatherhood of God and brotherhood of man" here, for he deals, not with regeneration but with creation (Gen. 1:26,27; Luke 3:38) and goes on to conclude:

"Forasmuch then as we are the offspring of God, we ought not to think that the Godhead is like unto gold, or silver, or stone, graven by art and man's device" (Ver. 29).

This was a rebuke to both the Stoics and the Epicureans. His argument was that if we, living, rational, moral beings are His offspring, we ought not to suppose that He Himself is like mere idols made by man from gold or silver or stone. All this must have been tremendously impressive, surrounded as they were by the false and fading glory of their idols and the greater glory of the creation above and about them.

What an evidence it was of the spiritual blindness of the Athenians, and what a rebuke to their vaunted wisdom, that Paul had to teach them the very ABC of theology: that there was one true God, that He was the Creator and Sustainer of all, etc. With all their illustrious philosophers and their renowned schools of learning they were still superstitious idolaters, so far from agreed as to which god to worship that their city was a veritable Babel of religious confusion. They had come no farther, spiritually, than the pagans at Lystra (Acts 14:11-18).

EMPHASIZING THEIR RESPONSIBILITY

But Paul's purpose was not merely to *convince* his hearers. He would *convict* them of their responsibility to the one true God, whom they had "worshipped" as but one among many, and then as "unknown." He

101

would show them that they were to give an account to Him for their idolatry and sin, and would then preach Christ to them.

The statement that *"the times of this ignorance God winked at"* (Ver. 30) does not mean that until this time God had not held the heathen accountable. The apostle's own words in Romans 1:18-32 make it all too plain that he *did* hold them accountable. The Old Testament Scriptures, too, bear abundant testimony that God never regarded idolatry as innocent, or its related sins as of no consequence. What Paul meant was simply that hitherto God had passed over the idolatry of the heathen world *without punishing it*, as though He did not see it.

But now, says the apostle, He *"commandeth all men everywhere to repent; because He hath appointed a day, in the which He will judge the world in righteousness by that Man whom He hath ordained; whereof He hath given assurance unto all men, in that He hath raised Him from the dead"* (Vers. 30,31).

Some have concluded from this passage that Paul, like Peter before Him, was sent primarily to proclaim repentance. This is a mistake.

The word *repent* (Gr. *metanoeo*) is found at least thirty-one times in the Gospels and early Acts. Moreover, we are distinctly told that repentance, in view of the nearness of the kingdom, was the *theme* of the message proclaimed by John the Baptist, Christ and the twelve (Matt. 3:1,2; 4:17; Mark 6:7,12; Luke 24:47). In comparison we find the word used only five times by Paul in Acts and in two of these cases he refers to what John the Baptist *had* preached to Israel (Acts 13:24; 19:4). Then in all of Paul's epistles we find the word

102

used only seven times (including Hebrews, where it is used thrice) and again several of these cases have no connection with the message which Paul preached.

Since the word *metanoeo* means a thorough change of mind, it is evident that any unbeliever who becomes a believer repents in the process. Yet it is also evident from the above that the *emphasis* in the message of John the Baptist, Christ and the twelve, was on repentance, while this was not the case with Paul. An examination both of the latter part of Acts and of his epistles will reveal that the emphasis in his message was upon *grace*, to be appropriated by *faith*.

This is appropriate, for according to "the gospel of the kingdom" Israel was to repent of her backsliding and accept Christ as King and the Gentiles were to repent of their idolatry and accept Him as King. Under the dispensation which Paul ushered in, however, the Jew and the Gentile are both concluded under sin and Christ is offered as the One who died that they might be "justified freely by His grace." Hence the emphasis is upon grace, appropriated by faith.

We repeat, however, that it is a matter of *emphasis*, for any sinner, believing, repents, in the nature of the case and here, where Paul was encountered by the champions of idolatry and had proclaimed to them the one true God, it is surely not strange that he should call for a change of heart and mind. Nor does this at all indicate that he proclaimed the same message as had Peter and the twelve. Indeed, several distinctions should here be noted:

1. *They* had specifically been instructed to preach repentance to *the Jew first* (Luke 24:47) while Paul here shows its relation to *"all men everywhere."* 2. They had

103

been sent to preach repentance *and baptism* for the remission of sins (Mark 16:16; Acts 2:38) while Paul does not mention water baptism here and, indeed, states in I Corinthians 1:17 that he was *not* sent to baptize. 3. Paul clearly brought in repentance and judgment here as a background to the grace he would have proclaimed had he been allowed to proceed. This was another one of the interrupted discourses of the Book of Acts.

To hold, then, that repentance has no place in the Pauline message is to misunderstand the nature of repentance, but on the other hand, to *preach* repentance, rather than grace, is to display ignorance of the message which the risen, ascended Lord committed to Paul and to us.

As we have said, Paul was answering the champions of idolatry. Quite naturally he would, in such a case, call upon them to repent and turn to the true God (cf. I Thes. 1:9). And quite naturally he would confirm what Peter had said with respect to our Lord's resurrection to "judge the world in righteousness."

But this was not all he had wished to say. *Now* he sought to search and awaken their consciences. "*God commandeth* all men everywhere to repent." It was not a matter of human opinion, as the Athenians were wont to suppose, but of *moral responsibility*. And it was in their interest to turn to God without delay because He had appointed a day in which the world would be judged in righteousness by Christ, whom He had raised from the dead as "assurance" of this fact.

PAUL'S DISCOURSE INTERRUPTED

At Paul's mention of the resurrection his address was interrupted. Some began to mock, while others, more politely, said: "We will hear thee again of this matter" (Ver. 32). This implies again that Paul was not defending himself in a formal trial and indicates further that his hearers evidently had concluded that there was not sufficient cause to hold such a trial. Satisfied with their own heathen beliefs they did not even care to hear him further.

"So Paul departed from among them." His efforts had not been wholly in vain, for there were "certain" who did believe; among them a woman (probably of some prominence) named Damaris, and one of the Areopagites themselves, named Dionysius. As a whole, however, the Athenians had proved that they were not the truly great of their day. They gloried, but in their shame. The humble Bereans had risen head and shoulders above them.

How long Paul stayed at Athens after this is not known, but it was probably after this that Timothy arrived with news from Thessalonica and was sent back again to encourage and establish them.

DID PAUL FAIL AT ATHENS?

Certain theologians have criticized Paul for failing to present the way of salvation in his speech at the Areopagus. It must be remembered, however, that he was brought to the Areopagus *because* he had been preaching *"Jesus, and the resurrection"*[15] (Ver. 18) and it is unthinkable that he would not have proclaimed salvation through Christ had he been permitted to finish his address.

---

15. Paul's revelation as to both the death and resurrection of Christ went far beyond that which Peter had preached at Pentecost (See Rom. 4:25).

His discourse before the philosophers at Athens was in fact a masterpiece of God-given wisdom and spiritual power. The dignity and sincerity of his manner, his skillful use of local circumstances, his rare combination of prudence and boldness, the powerful way in which he met human philosophy with divine revelation, the tactful, yet telling manner in which he exposed his hearers as ignorant idolaters, searching their consciences, warning them of judgment and calling upon them to repent and turn to God; the superb manner in which he appealed to the testimony of creation[16] citing such of *their* poets as recognized any of the truths he proclaimed, and even using the inscription on *their* altar as his text, answering atheism, polytheism, pantheism, agnosticism, materialism and fatalism, all in the course of a few moments' time—all this marks his interrupted discourse on Mars Hill "a speech such as became such a place, such a speaker and such an audience."

16. Rather than to that of the Old Testament, as he would among the Jews.

106

PAUL'S MINISTRY AT CORINTH

GETTING SETTLED

"After these things Paul departed from Athens, and came to Corinth;

"And found a certain Jew named Aquila, born in Pontus, lately come from Italy, with his wife Priscilla; (because that Claudius had commanded all Jews to depart from Rome:) and came unto them.

"And because he was of the same craft, he abode with them, and wrought: for by their occupation they were tentmakers."

—Acts 18:1-3

CORINTH IN PAUL'S DAY

At an isthmus only a few miles wide, where the waters of the Mediterranean Sea nearly cut Achaia (now Greece) in two, lay Corinth.

The ancient city had been burned by the Roman armies in 146 B.C., but a new and greater Corinth had risen and grown to be the commercial and political metropolis of Greece as well as one of the great sports centers of the world.

Corinth boasted extraordinary commercial advantages. It was a vital seaport with harbors on both sides of the isthmus, one on the Gulf of Corinth to the west, the other on the Gulf of Saron to the east, only a few miles away. Situated thus it inevitably became a center of commerce, for the sea trade between Asia Minor and Italy would naturally cross this narrow isthmus, and merchants and traders from all parts of Greece would come here to take advantage of its business opportunities.

It was doubtless also because of its advantageous location that Corinth became one of the world's leading centers of athletic entertainment. The world-renowned Isthmian games were similar to our Olympic games[1] and drew additional thousands of visitors to Corinth from many parts of the known world.

Though Corinth was quite different in character from Athens, it also boasted its subtle and accomplished reasoners, skilled in the art of sophistry and given to abstruse and metaphysical argument. There were "the disputers of this world," whose "wisdom," however, was "foolishness with God" (I Cor. 1:20; 3:19).

From what we have thus far observed it will naturally be concluded that Corinth was a wicked city. A city with *two* ports and the amusement center of a heathen population could not be otherwise. Nor would its "higher learning" stem the tide of sin. But the most appalling aspect of Corinthian life was its *religion*.

In Corinth lasciviousness was not merely condoned but encouraged and actually "consecrated" as worship to Aphrodite,[2] the "goddess of love."

There stood her great temple along with smaller ones, where, history tells us, a thousand "sacred" harlots, enriched her coffers with offerings derived from licentious "visits" with men "worshippers."

---

1. The gymnasium, the stadium, the races, the boxing and wrestling matches are all alluded to in Paul's epistles.
2. The counterpart of the Roman *Venus*.

Little wonder Chrysostom called Corinth "the most licentious city of all that are or ever have been." There was no city on earth more profligate. The very name *Corinthian* in Paul's day was synonymous with immorality, so that one who "played the Corinthian" had fallen into immoral wickedness, and a "Corinthian banquet" was a drunken revel. Little wonder Paul had to remind the Corinthian church that *"neither fornicators, nor idolaters, nor adulterers, nor effeminate, nor abusers of themselves with mankind...shall inherit the kingdom of God"* (I Cor. 6:9,10).

This was Corinth; celebrated for its wealth, luxury and dissipation: "the Paris of antiquity." In its crowded streets the apostle found himself surrounded by all sorts of people: Roman freedmen, slaves, businessmen on the look-out for gain, travelers out to see the world, sailors from two seas, sports enthusiasts, gamblers, pleasure seekers—and a large proportion of them away from home.

Those who wonder how Paul could call the failing Corinthian believers "saints" should bear in mind their background and surroundings. Actually the church at Corinth, with all its faults, was one of the wonders of church history and one of the triumphs of God's grace. Indeed, Paul, by the Spirit, calls them the "seal" of his apostleship (I Cor. 9:2).

But let us not get ahead of ourselves. Doubtless Paul made his way to Corinth, hoping to establish headquarters for the gospel in Achaia, as Thessalonica had been for Macedonia. Doubtless too, he trusted that from this center of travel the good news would spread the faster.

Today Corinth is easily reached from Athens by railway, but Paul had no such convenience at his disposal.

Probably he went by ship across the Gulf of Saron rather than taking the tedious and roundabout land route. The trip by sea would take him no more than a day or two, while that by land would take five or six.

AQUILA AND PRISCILLA

Still alone upon his arrival at Corinth the apostle would need lodging and remunerative employment. He had no board or finance committee to which he might apply for funds. The church at Antioch had not underwritten his expenses. The believers left behind at Philippi had sent gifts "once and again" to relieve his "necessity," but as he kept travelling they "lacked opportunity," finding it more and more difficult to locate him (Phil. 4:10,15,16).

The Jews held that a parent who did not teach his son a craft taught him to be a thief, and evidence is plentiful that of all men Paul was most conscientious about financial matters. Thus we find him on several occasions working with his hands to supply his needs and sometimes even the needs of those who were with him (Acts 18:3; 20:34; I Cor. 4:11,12; I Thes. 2:9; II Thes. 3:8).

In the provision made for the apostle at this time we find a beautiful illustration of God's *providence* in using the seemingly natural order of events to fulfill His purposes. Even before Paul had *"departed from Athens"* to come to Corinth, "Claudius had commanded all Jews to *depart from Rome*," and so it was that Aquila and Priscilla, refugees from Italy, were already on the scene, waiting, as it were, for Paul to call on them, and were able to supply him with *both* lodging and employment.

110

Regarding Claudius' decree, the Roman historian Suetonius says that Claudius expelled the Jews from Rome because "they were constantly exciting tumults under their leader Chrestus." We know that *Christ* was now in heaven, so that this *Chrestus* may have been some other person, yet we know also that Christ *did* cause tumults wherever He was preached, so that either Claudius or Suetonius, later, may have mistaken such a tumult to have been aroused *under His leadership*.

Of course the record says merely that Aquila and Priscilla had "come from *Italy*" so that it might be gratuitous to conclude that they had necessarily lived in *Rome*. While Claudius' drastic decree extended only to Rome it doubtless affected Jews in all parts of Italy adversely.

Yet the latter part of Verse 2 of our passage seems to particularize upon the former, and we know that not long after this Aquila and Priscilla were found at Rome (Rom. 16:3) so it seems probable that this was their residence.

The question naturally arises in our minds whether Aquila and Priscilla were believers in Christ at the time Paul met them or whether they were won to Christ later through Paul. We cannot, probably, determine this with certainty, for while, on the one hand, the record states that Aquila was a *Jew* and that Paul joined the couple *"because he was of the same craft,"* it must be observed on the other, that it is unlikely that Luke would have failed to mention their conversion if this had taken place under Paul's ministry. Furthermore Aquila had resided in Pontus and probably in Rome, and Christ had been preached in both places (Acts 2:9 cf. I Pet. 1:1; Rom. 1:8). Indeed, as we have pointed out, there is the

111

distinct possibility that they were banished from Rome because of a tumult raised about Christ.

It is a singular fact that Aquila is never mentioned apart from his wife, and also that in three out of five times her name precedes his. Perhaps Priscilla was of higher birth or somewhat more capable or energetic than her husband, yet we never find her acting independently of him. Evidently *both* were mature in character to be able, for example, to later show such a popular and gifted preacher as Apollos "the way of God more perfectly" and to help Paul in his labors as they did, conducting church services in at least two of their homes (Rom. 16:3-5; I Cor. 16:19).

Ever since his arrival at Athens Paul's path had been a difficult one. Athens had been too frivolous to consider his message seriously and Corinth was profligate. Would he fare any better here? He had no human companion to help and sustain him (Acts 17:15; I Thes. 3:1). Loneliness and depression were telling on him.

What a comfort then, must the newfound friendship and work with Aquila and Priscilla have been! What earnest conversations they must have engaged in as Paul led them into precious truths which they had never known before! What a sacred spot their home must have become to him!

In Acts 19:21 we find Paul announcing his decision to visit Rome. Was this the result of his contact with Aquila and Priscilla and of their reports concerning the need and opportunities there?

One thing is certain: Aquila and Priscilla came to understand the glorious truths committed to Paul[3]

---

3. And so were used to show Apollos "the way of God more perfectly" (Acts 18:26).

and became faithful co-workers with him. Soon they were to accompany him to Ephesus (Acts 18:18,19) and later, at Rome, they were to receive his greetings as *"my helpers in Christ Jesus; who have for my life laid down their own necks"* (Rom. 16:3,4).

FROM JEW TO GENTILE AGAIN

"And he reasoned in the synagogue every sabbath, and persuaded the Jews and the Greeks.

"And when Silas and Timotheus were come from Macedonia, Paul was pressed in the spirit, and testified to the Jews that Jesus was Christ.

"And when they opposed themselves, and blasphemed, he shook his raiment, and said unto them, Your blood be upon your own heads; I am clean: from henceforth I will go unto the Gentiles.

"And he departed thence, and entered into a certain man's house, named Justus, one that worshipped God, whose house joined hard to the synagogue.

"And Crispus, the chief ruler of the synagogue, believed on the Lord with all his house; and many of the Corinthians hearing believed, and were baptized.

"Then spake the Lord to Paul in the night by a vision, Be not afraid, but speak, and hold not thy peace:

"For I am with thee, and no man shall set on thee to hurt thee: for I have much people in this city.

"And he continued there a year and six months, teaching the Word of God among them."

—Acts 18:4-11

113

REASONING AT THE SYNAGOGUE

As Paul labored week days at the shop of Aquila and Priscilla he used the sabbath days to take advantage of the synagogue services, where he "reasoned... and persuaded the Jews and Greeks."

Perhaps it was during these early days at Corinth that, observing the character of the city, he "determined not to know anything among [them] save Jesus Christ, and Him crucified" (I Cor. 2:2). Not that this was not part of his special message, for, as we have seen, Paul's *"preaching of the cross"* was vastly different from that which Peter had preached at Pentecost when he *accused* his hearers of the crucifixion of Christ and called upon them to *"repent, and be baptized...for the remission of sins"* (Acts 2:38). "The preaching of the cross" was the very *heart* of the great "mystery" revealed to Paul, only he could not, on account of their condition, *explain* the mystery to them or show them its transcendent glories (I Cor. 2:1,6,7). Here he must preach only "Jesus Christ, and Him crucified," as God's power to save and the appeal to holy living.

THE ARRIVAL OF SILAS AND TIMOTHY

As the apostle toiled to provide for his needs and ministered on sabbath days at the synagogue, there were anxious thoughts which troubled him day and night. What about the small band of believers at Thessalonica, where the persecution had been so bitter? What afflictions were they bearing now? Were they standing true? And what about the other groups he had left behind? (II Cor. 11:28).

At Athens Paul had been sought out by Timothy,[4] but the apostle, hearing of the plight of the Thessalonian

---

4. Who with Silas had been left behind at Berea (Acts 17:14).

believers, had sent him back to establish and encourage them, even though it meant that he himself had to be "left at Athens alone" (I Thes. 3:1-3). Since then he had received no first hand news from them, though reports of their conversion had travelled far (I Thes. 1:8).

Picture the joyful scene, then, as the burdened apostle looked up one day, perhaps from his work in Aquila's shop, to see his beloved Silas and Timothy approaching! And see his face, radiant with both smiles and tears of joy, as his brethren bring him so much good news!

Timothy had come with most heartening reports from Thessalonica. They were standing—firmly! True, some were confused about what Paul had said with regard to the rapture of believers to be with Christ, and were mourning for their deceased brethren, whom they feared would now be excluded from that glorious event, but their faith and love were strong and they remembered him affectionately, longing to see him again (I Thes. 3:6).

And he longed to see them too, to complete that which was lacking in their faith (I Thes. 3:10) but this glad news made his heart overflow with gratitude and joy (I Thes. 3:7-9) and he would write them without delay to establish them further especially with regard to the coming of the Lord to catch His own away (I Thes. 4:13-18).

But there was more to gladden the apostle's heart. Silas doubtless brought good news from Berea, where Paul had last left him (Act 17:14) and there was also a special surprise: *a gift from his beloved Philippians!* (II Cor. 11:9). How it spoke to him of their steadfastness and their love for him! And how well he could use it now! Aquila and Priscilla had but "lately come from

115

Italy" (Ver. 2) and it is doubtful that their business was prospering as yet and, as he later wrote the Corinthians, it was his "rule" to reach out with the gospel only as the needs were supplied, lest he "stretch" or reach, beyond that which God had provided (II Cor. 10:13-16).

Little wonder that with the coming of Silas and Timothy we find Paul preaching Christ with new fervor. Heavy burdens had been lifted from his heart. Financial needs had been supplied. Trusted co-workers would now be at his side.

Once more we find him wholly occupied with his message.[5] He *must* get his kinsmen at the synagogue to see and confess that Jesus is the Christ.

It must not be supposed, from Verse 5, that the apostle had not already presented Christ to these Jews. Verse 4 tells us that "he reasoned in the synagogue every sabbath, and *persuaded* the Jews and the Greeks." Certainly he would not trouble to *persuade* them with regard to minor matters. Yet Verse 5, in our version, seems to give the impression that he only *began* testifying that Jesus was the Christ after the arrival of Silas and Timothy. The explanation is that the word rendered "testified" here is a strong word, even stronger than "persuade," in Verse 4, meaning *"to testify or protest solemnly."* Thus Paul had been trying to persuade the Jews, sabbath after sabbath, evidently with little success, but now with the coming of Silas and Timothy he did this with greater zeal, solemnly protesting to them that Jesus *was* the Christ.

Lest any of our readers wonder how the preaching of Jesus as the Christ could harmonize with Paul's

---

5.   Most texts read that he was "engrossed in" or "constrained by *the Word*."

special message, we repeat that from both Acts and the early epistles it is abundantly evident that he preached *much more* than this wherever he went, but he had to *begin* here with these *Jews*, for if they, like their brethren in Judaea, *denied* that Jesus was the Messiah, how could they believe that He was the Lord of grace? Furthermore, it must be remembered that the Book of Acts is primarily the record of Israel's rejection of her *Messiah* and the explanation of her expulsion from divine favor. Hence Paul's special message of grace is given secondary notice here.

THE MESSAGE OPPOSED
AND BLASPHEMED

Paul's testimony to the Jews at Corinth was not merely rejected; it was *opposed* and *blasphemed*, and that in a most definite and final manner. It is a military term Luke uses in Verse 6. The phrase *"they opposed themselves"* means that they set themselves in opposition as in battle array. And their blasphemy indicates that their rejection of Christ was as bitter as it was stubborn.

Once more the favored people were putting the Word of God from them[6] and *judging themselves* unworthy of everlasting life (cf. Acts 13:46). Thus it is that we read:

"And when they opposed themselves and blasphemed, he shook his raiment, and said unto them, Your blood be upon your own heads; I am clean: from henceforth I will go unto the Gentiles" (Ver. 6).

---

6. The recurrence of Jewish blasphemy here recalls our Lord's words in Matthew 12:31,32. That generation in Israel was committing the unpardonable sin.

117

Paul's act in shaking his raiment out against them had deep symbolic significance. It was the indignant protest of one who had found appeals to the Scriptures, to reason and to conscience fruitless. He would cease trying to persuade them.

Moreover, he again (as in 13:46) fixes the blame on *them*, as he exclaims: *"Your blood be upon your own heads; I am clean."* This is an evident allusion to Ezekiel 3:18,19. If they perished in their sin they could never complain that *he* had not warned them.

It should be further observed that the apostle's statement about going to the Gentiles is considerably stronger than that recorded in Acts 13:46. There it was purely a local matter (though a symbolic one); here it is the announcement of a policy. There, with Gentiles clamoring to hear the Word of God and the Jews refusing to hear it, Paul had said: "seeing ye put it from you, and judge yourselves unworthy of everlasting life, *lo, we turn to the Gentiles*." Here he declares: *"From henceforth I will go unto the Gentiles."* From this point on he will be in a fuller sense *"the apostle of the Gentiles."*

It is deeply significant that Paul's first recorded epistle, First Thessalonians, was evidently written in connection with the arrival of Silas and Timothy and the opposition of the Corinthian Jews (see I Thes. 1:1; 2:14-16; 3:6,7; etc.) and that his epistles thus begin with his declaration: *"From henceforth I will go unto the Gentiles."*

THE CHURCH IN THE HOME

It is remarkable how often the work of God has been furthered by meetings held in *homes*. A nucleus of believers, perhaps, has become interested in the study of the Word, when some godly couple has come forward to offer the hospitality of their home for regular services. Many a great work has been done for God in this way, and many a church founded.

Here at Corinth, rejected in the synagogue, the apostle is invited by a man named Justus, to conduct his ministry in his home, and it was evidently while using this home as a base of operations that so great a work was done for God in Corinth.

Similarly Aquila and Priscilla,[7] later opened their homes for regular services both while residing at Ephesus and while residing at Rome, and in connection with each Paul speaks of them with particular affection. This is so also of Philemon, who entertained the church, or *a* church, at Colosse (Phile. 1,2). And Nymphas, of Laodicea, might never have been heard of, had he not been host to the church there (Col. 4:15).

THE CHURCH NEXT DOOR

The apostle was now taking a bold and aggressive step, moving into a home which the Jews would have shrunk from entering:[8] the house of a Gentile "worshipper" named *Justus* who, moreover, lived *right next door to the synagogue*.

Some have questioned his ethics in now conducting services in a home which "joined hard to the synagogue." Imagine the strained feelings as members of the two congregations met outside! Imagine how it must have infuriated the Jews at the synagogue to have Paul start meetings right next door!

---

7. Who had already opened their home to *Paul* while at Corinth.
8. Clearly, to *teach* there. He probably continued to *live* with Aquila and Priscilla unless the coming of Silas and Timothy changed this.

119

To be sure it *is* a breach of ethics and worse, when the pastor or some member of a Bible-believing congregation allows personal considerations to induce him to foster or approve a division in the church in order to draw away some of its members and start a new assembly nearby. This is a negation of the Spirit's assertion that "there is *one body*," a disgrace before the world and an offense against God.

But this was far from the case at the Corinthian synagogue. Paul did not take this action out of spite or for personal reasons. These Jews were rejecting the Word of God and their own Messiah, and Paul, for the sake of any who might not be as adamant as the rest, began holding meetings next door as an open protest and a testimony against the unbelieving majority. He *wished* the members of the two congregations to meet, in order to keep the issue alive. It was entirely a doctrinal matter. His choice of the home of a Gentile[9] for a meeting place would moreover be apt to draw more Gentiles, and the new congregation would stand as a visible symbol of God's purpose to send salvation to the Gentiles despite, yea, *through*, Israel's unbelief. Thus it is written:

"...Through their fall salvation is come unto the Gentiles, for to provoke them to jealousy" (Rom. 11:11).

Surely Israel had no cause to complain. First, Messiah had come to His own, only to be rejected and

---

9. In some MSS the name is Titus Justus; in others simply Justus. This has given rise to the question whether he was the Titus of Galatians 2:3 or whether he was surnamed Justus to *distinguish* him from that Titus. In either case he was doubtless an uncircumcised Gentile, for otherwise there would be no point in stating that he "worshipped God." This term, in the original, is used elsewhere of God-fearing Gentiles (Acts 13:50; 16:14; 17:4; etc.).

crucified. But God had raised Him from the dead and, in infinite mercy, had offered "repentance to Israel, and forgiveness of sins" (Acts 5:31). Even as she stood stubbornly by her evil deed God still dealt with her, provoking her to jealousy by the believing remnant, the "little flock," the "foolish nation" (Luke 12:32; Rom. 10:19). And God did even more than this, for *now* He was provoking Israel to jealousy by the conversion of the Gentiles. Surely Isaiah's prophecy had been *more* than fulfilled.

"Esaias is very bold, and saith, I was found of them that sought Me not; I was made manifest to them that asked not after me."[10]

"...*All day long have I stretched forth my hands unto a disobedient and gainsaying people*" (Rom. 10:20,21).

THE RULER OF THE SYNAGOGUE IS SAVED

The conversion of the "chief ruler" of the synagogue and his household must have made a profound impression upon the community and have given great impetus to the cause of Christ in Corinth. Indeed, it is in this connection that we read that *"many of the Corinthians hearing believed, and were baptized"* (Ver. 8). Thus God already placed His stamp of approval on the bold step Paul had taken.

---

10. This refers, not to the Gentiles, but to Israel, with whom God kept dealing though they wished He would leave them alone. Note: Isaiah is *"bold,"* not *kind*, and the passage in Isaiah 65:1 continues with the words: *"I said, Behold Me, Behold Me, unto a nation that was not called by My name."* That this can refer only to Israel is clear from the whole context, as well as from Paul's conclusion in the next verse

It is important that we observe here that while *many* of the Corinthians were baptized, *Paul* baptized only a *few* of them. One of these was *Crispus*, doubtless baptized by Paul himself because he was so outstanding a convert. Another was *Gaius*, who later made his home a meeting place and was Paul's host on his second visit to Corinth (Rom. 16:23). Then he also baptized *"the household of Stephanas,"* perhaps because they were "the firstfruits of Achaia" (I Cor. 16:15).[11] Looking back, some years later, he could not recall having baptized any beside these.

This was not, as some have supposed, because Paul let others do the baptizing for him to save him time and energy. There was a deeper reason. Water baptism is clearly associated with the manifestation of Christ to Israel in John 1:31 and since He was still being made manifest to Israel water baptism was not out of order. Yet this rite had not been included in Paul's special commission; it *could not* be. He was not sent to baptize,[12] but to preach the gospel, and that simply, *"lest the cross of Christ should be made of none effect, for,"* said he, *"the preaching of the cross*[13]*...is the power of God"* (I Cor. 1:17,18). Thus it was, too, that Paul never baptized anyone *"for the remission of sins,"* as John the Baptist and the twelve had done before him (Mark 1:4; Acts 2:38).

This explains the seeming lack of divine inspiration in the preceding passage (I Cor. 1:14-16). First the apostle states categorically that he thanks God that he

---

11. See Romans 16:5. Either Epaenetus belonged to this household or he was another of the "firstfruits."

12. As both John the Baptist and the twelve had been (John 1:33; Matt. 28:19).

13. See the author's booklet: *The Preaching of the Cross*.

baptized *"none"* of them, but Crispus and Gaius; *only* those two. *Then* he recalls that he *also* baptized the household of Stephanus. And then, becoming more cautious, he states that he does not *recall* having baptized any others!

This does not represent any failure in divine inspiration. Rather it *is* divine inspiration, demonstrating the fact that water baptism was becoming less and less important in the ministry of Paul and that it was *not* included in his special commission.

ENCOURAGEMENT TO A WEARY SOLDIER

But the strain of battle was telling on the apostle. He found himself haunted by fear and depression. Later he wrote of it:

"I was with you in weakness, and in fear, and in much trembling" (I Cor. 2:3).

It must not be supposed that fearlessness was characteristic of a nature so sensitive as Paul's. On the contrary, he was often afraid. His, by the grace of God, was rather the courage that went on braving dangers *in spite of his fears*.

The strain of meeting, week after week, right next door to the synagogue, with all the embarrassing situations inevitably involved, may well have caused some of his followers, and possibly himself, to question the wisdom or propriety of the step he had taken, adding to his mental depression. But the Lord was to endorse the act again in an unmistakable way.

It would appear from several passages in the Second Epistle to the Thessalonians (especially 3:1,2) that this letter was written while Paul was becoming apprehensive about the work at Corinth, and that it was after this that the Lord appeared to him in a vision[14] to encourage him.

Let the reader try to place himself in Paul's position while reading Verses 9 and 10 so as to appreciate its force more fully:

"Then spake the Lord to Paul...:

"Be not afraid,

"but speak,

"and hold not thy peace:

"for I am with thee,

"and no man shall set on thee to hurt thee:

"for I have much people in this city."

How this gracious intervention must have encouraged the heart of the faithful warrior! How it must have stimulated his zeal for his beloved Lord, to hear His voice, encouraging him to speak out boldly and assuring him not only of the fellowship of His presence, but also of physical protection and—*many souls!* Tomorrow he could begin the work anew, assured in advance of the outcome.

Whether he "continued"[15] in Corinth a year and six months *longer* or *all together*, is perhaps impossible to ascertain, but we know that his ministry there was exceedingly fruitful. At Athens and Corinth respectively it had been demonstrated that *"the world by wisdom knew not God"* and that *"God hath chosen the foolish things of the world to confound the wise...that no flesh should glory* [boast] *in His presence."*

---

14. *Horama*, an *objective* vision; not the same as Acts 2:17. This was one of the many occasions on which the Lord appeared to Paul.

15. Lit. *"sat,"* as a teacher.

PROFITABLE PERSECUTION

"And when Gallio was the deputy of Achaia, the Jews made insurrection with one accord against Paul, and brought him to the judgment seat.

"Saying, This fellow persuadeth men to worship God contrary to the law.

"And when Paul was now about to open his mouth, Gallio said unto the Jews, If it were a matter of wrong or wicked lewdness, O ye Jews, reason would that I should bear with you:

"But if it be a question of words and names, and of your law, look ye to it; for I will be no judge of such matters.

"And he drave them from the judgment seat.

"Then all the Greeks took Sosthenes, the chief ruler of the synagogue, and beat him before the judgment seat. And Gallio cared for none of those things."

—Acts 18:12-17

THE APOSTLE BROUGHT BEFORE GALLIO

As God had used Paul to place the Philippian church in an advantageous position with the civil government, before his departure from Philippi, so He now used Gallio, a Roman proconsul, to do the same for the Corinthian church.

Though the Lord had appeared to Paul to encourage and reassure him as to his ministry at Corinth, this did not mean that he was to experience no further opposition. It did mean, however, that any such opposition would turn out to the advancement of the work there. A signal example of this is given to us in the account of Paul's appearance before Gallio.

When Gallio was made proconsul of Achaia,[16] the Jews were quick to take advantage of the change in administration to stir up a tumult and bring Paul before the "judgment seat."

Gallio was the brother of Seneca, the famous statesman, philosopher and counsellor of Nero during his early days. Seneca wrote of Gallio with great affection and described him as an amiable and gracious character, easy to get along with. Doubtless the Jews knew of his reputation and hoped he would accede to their demand that Paul be punished.

Their complaint was that Paul sought to persuade men to worship God "contrary to the law." They *could*, of course, have referred to *their* law (cf. Ver. 15) for the Hebrew religion was then protected by the Roman government. It seems more probable, however, that they meant that Paul was setting up an *unlicensed* religion— one not included among those which were permitted under Roman law. When we consider the wicked and degrading religions which Roman law *did* permit, right here in Corinth, this charge against Paul was a shabby one indeed.

From what follows it appears that Gallio must have questioned the plaintiffs further about their charge, noting that it was wholly a dispute *between Jews*. Thus, when Paul was about to speak in his own defense Gallio interrupted to explain that the case was entirely out of his jurisdiction. Were it a matter of open wrong or "wicked villainy" (R.V.) he explained, he would have conducted a trial, but "if it be a question of words and

---

16. Greece, in a general way, was sometimes called Macedonia and sometimes Achaia, but properly speaking, Macedonia was the northern province of Greece and Achaia the southern, each governed by a proconsul.

names, and of your law, look ye to it; for I will be no judge of such matters."

While the Roman government permitted and protected almost all religions, its magistrates were instructed to keep out of religious controversies if possible. In addition, the Jews had already stirred up much trouble and consequently had only lately been expelled from Rome. Gallio acted shrewdly, then, in not permitting Paul to speak and in declining to even hear the case. What did *he* know about their law or the words and names they were quibbling about.[17]

Mark well, Gallio did *not* give Paul into their hands as Pilate had done with Christ (Luke 23:23,24) for, unlike Pilate, he refused to even *hear* the case, much less to pass sentence. Nor did his "look ye to it" imply permission to *them* to try Paul civilly, or Paul would have appealed to Caesar as he did later, when Festus suggested a trial at Jerusalem (Acts 25:9-12,20,21).

Gallio *dismissed* the complaint—with emphasis, for he *"drave them from the judgment seat,"* doubtless ordering the lictors to clear the court.

To the Greeks standing by, who already hated the Jews, this was an opening to second the work of the lictors and give Sosthenes, the chief ruler of the synagogue[18] (and doubtless Paul's chief accuser) a sound beating.[19]

---

17. At least so it seemed to him, though the issue between Paul and these Jews was actually whether Jesus was the Christ.

18. Evidently the successor to Crispus (Ver. 8). That Sosthenes also was eventually saved seems probable from the fact that Paul later mentions a Sosthenes as a co-worker with him in a letter to the *Corinthian* church (I Cor. 1:1). This would make *two* former persecutors now preaching Christ!

19. In the continuous tense the word *tupto* means a *series* of blows.

"And Gallio cared for none of these things." His behavior harmonized with Seneca's description of his easy-going nature. He was careful not to hear Paul's case and failed to stop an outbreak of violence before the very judgment seat. Yet this may have been partly intentional. Some have supposed that a trial and verdict by Gallio *in favor* of Paul would have helped him more. Actually, however, Gallio's behavior must have proved a greater rebuff to Paul's accusers, and given him and the Corinthian church a better standing in the community than they otherwise would have had.

At Philippi Paul's sagacity had helped gain the young church there recognition by involving his opponents in blame and putting *them* on the defensive. Here Gallio's response to Paul's accusers had done the same. The Lord was fulfilling His promise to His faithful apostle. *"And Paul after this tarried there yet a good while"*—the full year and six months.

"Not many" prominent Corinthians were reached during Paul's stay at Corinth (I Cor. 1:26) but a large number of the common people did turn to Christ, and there *were* such outstanding conversions as those of Crispus, the chief ruler of the synagogue, and probably Sosthenes, his successor; also Gaius and the household of Stephanus. These more prominent ones were later to be joined by Erastus, the city treasurer (Rom. 16:23). Thus those higher up in the scale of life may thank God that I Corinthians 1:26 reads "not *many*" rather than "not *any*."

It was some time before Paul's departure from Corinth that he wrote another epistle to the Thessalonians. Their problems regarding the Lord's return had not yet been solved. Some dishonest persons had taken advantage of Paul's absence, evidently forging a letter, or letters, in his name (II Thes. 2:2) further disturbing and confusing them, so that Paul had to impress upon them that it was his custom to sign his letters personally (II Thes. 3:17).

Some now seemed sure that the prophesied *"day of the Lord,"*[20] with its terrible judgments, was at hand. Indeed some, evidently confusing their persecutions with the coming "great tribulation," were giving up their daily employment and becoming "busybodies," thus dishonoring their Lord. "The prince of the powers of the air" was attacking again. Paul must write without delay to combat his influence and strengthen the little band of believers.

PAUL RETURNS TO JERUSALEM AGAIN

"And Paul after this tarried there yet a good while, and then took his leave of the brethren, and sailed thence into Syria, and with him Priscilla and Aquila; having shorn his head in Cenchrea: for he had a vow.

"And he came to Ephesus, and left them there: but he himself entered into the synagogue, and reasoned with the Jews.

"When they desired him to tarry longer time with them, he consented not;

"But bade them farewell, saying, I must by all means keep this feast that cometh in Jerusalem; but I will return again unto you, if God will. And he sailed from Ephesus.

"And when he had landed at Caesarea, and gone up, and saluted the church, he went down to Antioch."

—Acts 18:18-22

---

20. This is the correct rendering in 2:2.

PAUL'S VOW

After Paul had completed a full year and six months at Corinth he "*took his leave* of the brethren," that is, he bade them farewell, and "sailed" (Lit. "*sailed away*") to Syria. With him on part of this journey were Priscilla and Aquila. Whatever their reasons for leaving Corinth and accompanying Paul as far as Ephesus, God was in it, for they were subsequently used to impart spiritual light to no less a man of God than the great Apollos (Ver. 26).

What Paul did at Cenchrea,[21] before leaving for Syria, presents a complex problem.

There were various vows which one might make to God under the Mosaic law (Deut. 23:21,22) but the one which involved letting the hair grow during the term of the vow and shaving it off again at its expiration was the *Nazarite* vow, in which the subject consecrated himself to the Lord in a special way for a week, a month, a year or any designated period of time (Num. 6:1-21). This appears to be the vow which Paul had taken and which expired at Cenchrea.

This vow, however, was supposed to be consummated at "the door of the tabernacle" at Jerusalem, where blood sacrifices were to be offered and the hair, which had not been cut during the period of consecration, was to be shaven off and also offered in sacrifice.

In the Acts record we are told that Paul had "shorn his head in Cenchrea; for he had a vow," and also that he hastened to "keep this feast[22] that cometh in Jerusalem" (Vers. 18,21).

---

21. The eastern seaport of Corinth, where a church may well have been already established.

22. It has been debated whether this was Passover or Pentecost.

John Kitto is therefore probably correct in explaining that "as these [sacrifices] could not be offered out of Jerusalem, those who took this vow in foreign parts, made their offerings at their next visit to the holy city" (*The Apostles and The Early Church*, pg. 382).

The important question whether Paul was in the directive will of God in taking a vow involving blood sacrifices, or in observing a Jewish feast at Jerusalem, or indeed, in going to Jerusalem at all, will be discussed at length in a later chapter, but here we may say that while it is true, as some have pointed out, that the taking of a Nazarite vow was a wholly voluntary matter and not one commanded by law, the blood sacrifices involved in that vow *were* definitely and minutely controlled by the law (Num. 6:1-21).

Some have pointed out that the language, in the original, might be interpreted to mean that it was Aquila who took the vow[23] but this seems too evidently to be an attempt at escaping from a difficulty.

From Verse 19 it would seem that upon their arrival at Ephesus the company separated and Paul alone entered the synagogue. No reason is given for this, but it is possible that pressing business matters detained Aquila and Priscilla during these first days at Ephesus.

What is more singular is the fact that the apostle did not continue to minister to the Jews in this synagogue *even though they urged him to stay*, for it was seldom indeed that he found doors so wide open. But then, he was hurrying to get to Jerusalem, so declining their invitation he "bade them farewell, saying,

---

23. The *Latin Vulgate* adopts this rendering but the *Syriac* and the great majority of texts and translations reject it.

I must by all means keep this feast that cometh in Jerusalem; but I will return again unto you, if God will" (Vers. 20,21).

Strangely, however, a veil is cast over his visit to Jerusalem and the inference is given that his stay there was extremely brief. The record merely states that *"when he had landed at Caesarea, and gone up,*[24] *and saluted the church, he went down to Antioch"* (Ver. 22). We are not even told whether he reached Jerusalem in time for the feast; indeed, the language may well imply the contrary.

It is strange, too, that nothing is said about any welcome or rehearsal of his activities at Antioch, from whence, about three years previous, he had started out with Silas to "visit the brethren."

---

24. I.e., to Jerusalem.

132

PAUL BEGINS HIS
THIRD APOSTOLIC JOURNEY

HIS THIRD DEPARTURE FROM ANTIOCH

"And after he had spent some time there, he departed, and went over all the country of Galatia and Phrygia in order, strengthening all the disciples."

—Acts 18:23

As we have observed, the kingdom Church of early Acts had its headquarters at Jerusalem, where Messiah was to reign (Isa. 24:23) with His twelve apostles (Matt. 19:28) and from whence the law was to go forth to His whole domain (Isa. 2:2,3).

The Church of Rome, however, teaching that the Church of today (she herself) is Messiah's kingdom, has arbitrarily changed its capital from Jerusalem to *Rome*, from whence her hierarchy dictates the policies and practices of her subjects all over the world. This, while scores of plain passages from the Word of God insist that the Church which is Christ's *kingdom*, was—and is—to have its headquarters at *Jerusalem*,[1] while "the Church which is His *Body*" has *no headquarters on earth*. Its headquarters are *in heaven* where its Head is (Eph. 1:22,23; Phil. 3:20, R.V.).

Sad to say, much of Protestantism still follows Rome in teaching that the Church of this dispensation is Christ's *kingdom*; that it began at Pentecost or before, when the kingdom message was proclaimed by the

---

1. While Rome is not once mentioned in this connection.

PAUL'S THIRD APOSTOLIC JOURNEY

twelve apostles. Little wonder the various denominations have set up their own hierarchies to "govern" the affairs of their members near and far. Little wonder that the free recovery of truth has been hindered by Protestant political machinery almost as much as by Roman religious dictatorship.

We stress this here because some have called Syrian Antioch the *headquarters* of the early Gentile Church. This is a mistake, for there is no indication that any Christian hierarchy ruled from Antioch. Indeed Paul's most prominent associates (except Barnabas) are found almost everywhere *but* in Antioch.

Yet, as if to emphasize the fact that Paul was *not* associated with the twelve in their kingdom ministry, the Spirit has indicated that all three of Paul's apostolic journeys began from *Antioch*, the city to which Barnabas had first brought him to minister among the Gentiles.

Thus it was that, after spending "some time" at Antioch, the apostle "departed, and went over all the country of Galatia and Phrygia in order,[1] strengthening all the disciples" (Ver. 23).

Dean Howson feels certain that on a journey from Syrian Antioch to Ephesus Paul would have revisited most, if not all of the churches he had founded and ministered to, and not only those in Galatia and Phrygia. It may be, however, that the churches in these two regions needed special attention and that he was eager to return to Ephesus in fulfillment of his promise. Also, the churches of Syria, Cilicia, Lycaonia, Pamphylia and Pisidia had already been visited twice. In any case there must have been many a touching scene as the apostle reappeared among friends he had won to Christ and now established them in the faith.

---

1. These words imply the carrying out of a systematic plan.

APOLLOS AT EPHESUS AND CORINTH

"And a certain Jew named Apollos, born at Alexandria, an eloquent man, and mighty in the Scriptures, came to Ephesus.

"This man was instructed in the way of the Lord; and being fervent in the spirit, he spake and taught diligently the things of the Lord, knowing only the baptism of John.

"And he began to speak boldly in the synagogue: whom when Aquila and Priscilla had heard, they took him unto them, and expounded unto him the way of God more perfectly.

"And when he was disposed to pass into Achaia, the brethren wrote, exhorting the disciples to receive him: who, when he was come, helped them much which had believed through grace:

"For he mightily convinced the Jews, and that publicly, showing by the Scriptures that Jesus was Christ."

—Acts 18:24-28

During Paul's absence from Ephesus there appeared on the scene a man with outstanding qualities of spiritual leadership, and one who was to play an important part in the life and ministry of the apostle.

The Scriptures tell us first that he was a Jew from Alexandria. This background already gave him a spiritual advantage over others. The Jews at Alexandria placed more emphasis on the Scriptures than on "the traditions of the fathers," as witnessed by their world-famed library and school of Biblical interpretation, and especially by the fact that the first Greek translation of the Old Testament Scriptures, the *Septuagint*, was produced there.

136

We read, moreover, that Apollos was *"an eloquent*[2] *man,"* and *"mighty in the Scriptures"* (Ver. 24). In addition to this he was thoroughly *"instructed* [Lit. *catechized*] *in the way of the Lord"* (Ver. 25).

"The way of the Lord," we take it, refers to the way He taught His disciples to live in view of the establishment of His kingdom, and the way they *did* live after the coming of the Holy Spirit (Acts 2:42-47; 4:32-37). Paul himself had once gone to the high priest for letters of authority to the Damascene synagogues that if he found any of *"this way"* he might bring them bound to Jerusalem (Acts 9:2) and later he testified that he had "persecuted *this way* unto the death" (Acts 22:4).

Apollos' eloquence, then, came from a background of profound knowledge of the Old Testament Scriptures and a thorough understanding of "the way of the Lord." Perhaps the greatest testimony to the fact that he was painstakingly *thorough* in his studies is the statement in Verse 25, that "being fervent in the spirit, he spoke and taught *diligently* [Lit. *accurately*] the things of the Lord."

What a combination! "Fervent in the spirit" and "eloquent"—and with so much to back it up: a thorough knowledge of the Old Testament and of "the way of the Lord" and the gift for painstaking *exactness* both in study and in teaching. Doubtless Apollos was one of the most powerful and popular preachers of the day; one who could command large audiences almost anywhere.

Yet we are informed that he knew *"only the baptism of John"* (Ver. 25) i.e., he did not know that the Spirit had come (See Acts 1:5) and of course did not know the greater

---

2. The word *logios* may also mean *learned*, but the context and Paul's letters to the Corinthians seem to favor *eloquent*.

truths revealed through Paul. He was like Luther and Calvin, mighty in the truth, *as far as he knew it*.

Here is an important lesson for every man of God to learn. In the writer's library are the works of men like Luther, Calvin, Ellicott, Moule, Howson and Kitto; men who did not understand the great truth of the mystery, yet were thorough in their study of the Scriptures and signally used of God. What was the secret of their power? It was their passion to know the truth and to make it known. These men, from Luther on, were emerging from the dark ages—as we still are today—and could not see many of the great truths which have since become so plain and precious to many of us. But with an earnest passion for the *truth* they studied the Word of God and imparted to others the light they received, often at great cost.

Any man of God who follows their example today will also be mightily used despite his limitations. It is when unbelief enters and light is refused or when, for fear or favor, men do not stand true to the light they have received, that spiritual power is lost. This is why in these days when the great truth of "the mystery" is being recovered, so many who reject it are losing the power that once attended their ministry for Christ. May God help them to pay the price to find it again!

How Apollos had come to know "the baptism of John" and "the way of the Lord," we do not know. Probably either he had visited Palestine some time previous, or disciples from Palestine had reached him in Egypt. At any rate he was so filled with what he had learned that he freely "spake and taught" about it and now "began to speak boldly in the synagogue" (Vers. 25,26). Thus the place which Paul had declined to fill was now occupied by one who knew only "the baptism of John."

But the greatest qualities of this great man, and also of Aquila and Priscilla, are yet to appear.

As the couple first heard Apollos preach they, of course, recognized him as a truly great teacher of the Word, but as he continued teaching they noticed that he got no further than the baptism of John and the teachings of Christ on earth.

In this matter, which must have proved a disappointment to them, they showed their fine Christian character. They did not take him to task for his limitations or criticize him to others. Instead *"they took him unto them,"* perhaps inviting him to dine or visit with them, and *then* they "expounded unto him the way of God more perfectly" (Ver. 26).

The Greek word here rendered *"more perfectly"* is the comparative of that rendered *"diligently"* above. Here Apollos had found a couple who could lead him further into the truth with the same painstaking exactness which he had himself exhibited, and therefore could appreciate.

It should be noted that whereas he had been instructed in *"the way of the Lord,"* Aquila and Priscilla now led him further into "the way of *God* [Gr. *Theos*]" (Ver. 26). They could now tell Apollos the great basic truths of the mystery as they had learned them from Paul in his "gospel of the grace of God." They could show him the crucifixion, resurrection and ascension (of which he *may* have heard) *in the light of that grace*— all of it harmonizing perfectly with the Old Testament Scriptures, though not taught there.

It is noteworthy that Apollos received his advanced theological training, not at a seminary or from any of the great leaders of the day, but from two humble tentmakers and one of them a woman. Nor is this the last we hear of the service of this godly couple for Christ, for later Paul writes of them as having opened their home to regular church services here in Ephesus (I Cor. 16:8,19) and still later he writes of them as *"my helpers in Christ Jesus, who for my life have laid down their own necks,"* and indicates that again in Rome the church services were held in their home (Rom. 16:3-5). For their heroism and faithfulness, says the apostle, *"not only I give thanks, but also all the churches of the Gentiles"* (Ver. 4). Perhaps few of us have thought of the debt of gratitude we owe to such as Aquila and Priscilla.

But Apollos also showed his greatest qualities at this time. It is inspiring to think of the powerful and popular preacher so sincerely willing to be taught that he sits with unaffected humility at the feet of two members of his audience—a tentmaker and his wife. And this is not all.

Apollos could now, of course, have returned to the synagogue, explaining that he had preached to them without full knowledge of the truth, and claiming that he now knew the way of the Lord more perfectly, but this would doubtless have served only to arouse the suspicion of his hearers, destroying his usefulness among them. Evidently feeling, therefore, that Aquila and Priscilla could better carry on the testimony at Ephesus and wishing to minister where Paul had already established the truths he had so recently learned, Apollos thought to go to Achaia, whereupon "the brethren" wrote the "letters of commendation," evidently referred to in II Corinthians 3:1. The result was that upon his arrival at Corinth he *"helped them much which had believed through grace"* (Ver. 27). Not that he *immediately* led them further into the truths

140

of grace, for he himself had but recently begun to see them, but he encouraged the believers as *"he mightily convinced the Jews,*[3] *and that publicly, showing by the Scriptures that Jesus was Christ"* (Ver. 28).

And thus the chain of circumstances ran: Paul had helped Aquila and Priscilla at Corinth, *they* help Apollos at Ephesus and *he*, in turn, helps the brethren at Corinth, watering what Paul had planted (I Cor. 3:6).

As might have been expected, however, some at Corinth began to prefer Apollos to Paul. Unlike Paul, they contended, Apollos had come with "letters of commendation" (II Cor. 3:1).[4] Furthermore, Apollos was an orator while Paul was not, for *"his letters,"* said they, *"are weighty and strong, but his bodily presence is weak, and his speech of no account"* (II Cor. 10:10, R.V.). Thus Apollos unintentionally became involved in division and rivalry in the church at Corinth. One party boasted of him and another of Paul. There were others, but Apollos was chiefly involved, for after mentioning four such divisions (I Cor. 1:12) Paul deals mainly with his own and Apollos' connection with the case (I Cor. 1:13; 3:4-6).

But neither Paul nor Apollos condoned, much less fostered this party spirit among the Corinthians. Indeed, it is touching to witness the humility of these two great men and their mutual consideration for one another.

In writing to the Corinthians about it later Paul does not ask: "Was *Apollos* crucified for you? or were ye baptized in the name of *Apollos?*" He rather makes

---

3. Lit. *overwhelmed with argument.*
4. Quite forgetting that *they themselves* were Paul's "letter of commendation" (Vers. 2,3).

141

little of *himself*, and asks: "Was *Paul* crucified for you? or were ye baptized in the name of *Paul*?" (I Cor. 1:13). Indeed, such confidence did Paul have in Apollos that he strongly urged him to return to Corinth just when the party rivalry was so great, and such consideration did Apollos have for Paul that in spite of Paul's urging he would not go. In Paul's words: *"As touching our brother Apollos, I greatly desired him to come unto you...but his will was not at all to come at this time..."* (I Cor. 16:12).

Evidently the experience brought these two great men of God closer together, for in Titus 3:13 the apostle writes most solicitously of Apollos with regard to a forthcoming journey, to make certain that he will be well cared for and will want nothing.

THE THREE YEARS AT EPHESUS

THE DISCIPLES OF JOHN

"And it came to pass, that, while Apollos was at Corinth, Paul having passed through the upper coasts came to Ephesus: and finding certain disciples,

"He said unto them, Have ye received the Holy Ghost since ye believed? And they said unto him, We have not so much as heard whether there be any Holy Ghost.

"And he said unto them, Unto what then were ye baptized? And they said, Unto John's baptism.

Then said Paul, John verily baptized with the baptism of repentance, saying unto the people, that they should believe on Him which should come after him, that is, on Christ Jesus.

"When they heard this, they were baptized in the name of the Lord Jesus.

"And when Paul had laid his hands upon them, the Holy Ghost came on them; and they spake with tongues and prophesied.

"And all the men were about twelve."

—Acts 19:1-7

Fulfilling his promise, Paul returned to Ephesus and doubtless had a happy reunion with his beloved Aquila and Priscilla and the other "brethren" referred to in 18:27.

Before entering the synagogue he found "certain disciples" who were no farther advanced dispensationally,

143

than Apollos had been before his contact with Aquila and Priscilla. They, like Apollos, knew only "the baptism of John."

It is doubtful that they became disciples of John through Apollos' ministry at Ephesus for Aquila and Priscilla dealt with Apollos as he "began" to minister in the synagogue (18:26) and there is no indication whatever that Apollos baptized any of his hearers with John's baptism.

However, the fact that Paul "found" these disciples before entering the synagogue, and his direct question about the Holy Spirit may well indicate the possibility, if not the probability, that they were *associates* of Apollos, whom he (and perhaps Aquila and Priscilla) had been unable to lead into further truth, so that Aquila and Priscilla now mentioned their case to Paul, hoping that he might succeed in doing so before commencing his ministry in the synagogue.

The *Authorized* renderings of both Paul's question and their answer are misleading. The word *"since"* in the question is as incorrect as the *"after"* in Ephesians 1:13, for Paul's question was whether they had received the Holy Spirit *"upon believing."* Nor did their answer indicate that they questioned the *existence* of the Holy Spirit. They could not have questioned this, for the Old Testament Scriptures contain many references to the Holy Spirit, and John's baptism itself was a preparation for the baptism with the Spirit (Matt. 3:11).

Furthermore Paul's question must be understood in the light of its background. It concerned their receiving the "pouring out" of the Holy Spirit in *miraculous*

144

power (Acts 2:17,18). Our Lord had distinctly stated, with regard to the promise of the Spirit:

"And, behold, I send *the promise of my Father upon you:* but tarry ye in the city of Jerusalem, until ye be endued with *power from on high"* (Luke 24:49).

"But *ye shall receive power, after that the Holy Ghost is come upon you"* (Acts 1:8).

This too was the promise of Old Testament prophecy, so that these disciples actually replied: "We have not even heard whether the Holy Ghost has *come"* (Ver. 2). This word *"come"* should have been supplied by the translators as they supplied the word "given" in John 7:39.

This must not be confused with the Spirit's operation in *regeneration*, much less with His present work in *sealing* believers (Eph. 1:13) *baptizing* them into Christ and His Body (Rom. 6:3; I Cor. 12:13) and *indwelling* them as His temple (Eph. 2:22).[1] Indeed, at Pentecost it was Christ who baptized men in the Spirit while today it is the Spirit who baptizes men into Christ (Matt. 3:11 cf. Rom. 6:3; I Cor. 12:13).

Finding that these disciples had *not* received the Spirit (in miraculous power) the apostle asked: *"Unto what then were ye baptized?"* to which they replied: *"Unto John's baptism"* (Ver. 3).

This, of course, explained why they had not received the Spirit, for had they been baptized with Peter's baptism at Pentecost they would have received "the gift of the Holy Ghost" (Acts 2:38).

---

1. While all this had in fact taken place in these believers, nothing is said of it here since the theme of Acts is the fall of Israel, not the formation of the Body. This is an instance of the selective principle in divine inspiration.

WERE THESE DISCIPLES REBAPTIZED?

Now Verses 4 and 5 have been used by those who speak of "Christian baptism"—especially our Baptist friends—to show the great importance of water baptism and of being baptized *in the right way*.

This, they argue, is the last mention of water baptism in the Acts and in it these disciples actually had to be baptized over again because they had not been baptized with "Christian baptism"—the baptism of the "great commission" and/or Pentecost.

No argument for "Christian baptism" could be weaker, and we here propose to prove that these disciples were not rebaptized at all.

It is regrettable that Verses 4 and 5 have for so long been read through Baptist spectacles that it is almost impossible for some to read them correctly.[2] Even the general run of commentaries have been affected by the continuous repetition of the Baptist view of this passage even though it presents insurmountable difficulties.

The misinterpretation of this passage springs from the mistaken notion that Verse 5 records the *rebaptism* of these disciples, while in reality it is the continuation of Paul's explanation in Verse 4. In Verse 5 Paul recalls the *response* of John's hearers to his message.

Among the many arguments which support this view are the following:

1. There was no basic difference between John's baptism and that of Peter at Pentecost. Both were baptisms of *"repentance"* and both were *"for the remission*

---

2. Though some translations render Verse 5 so that it cannot be misunderstood, notably the Dutch, which reads: *"Those who heard him...."*

of sins" (Mark 1:4; Acts 2:38). There was a difference in the *result*, however, for at Pentecost those baptized received *"the gift of the Holy Ghost"* in addition to the remission of sins. This explained why these disciples had not received the gift, and why, with the laying on of Paul's hands, they now "spake with tongues and prophesied."

2. Paul's main question did not concern water baptism but the gift of the Holy Spirit. These disciples had not received this gift because they had been baptized *before the coming of the Spirit*. Therefore Paul laid his hands on them, imparting the Spirit to them.

3. Why should these few disciples alone be rebaptized? Why not the twelve apostles, Apollos and *all* who had been baptized before Pentecost?

4. How could the rebaptism of only these few prove the importance of "Christian baptism" over John's baptism? Would not the lack of evidence that all the others were rebaptized rather prove the opposite?

5. Why should Luke's record be interrupted to record the rebaptism of these twelve men without explaining why *only these* had to be rebaptized?

6. The record does not *say* that these men were baptized *again*.

7. If the popular interpretation of Verse 5 were correct it would more probably read: "When they heard this, *Paul* baptized them..." or "they were baptized *again*...." As it is, Verse 5 records the response of John's hearers to his message (Ver. 4) and then Paul enters in Verse 6 ("And when Paul..." etc.) laying his hands upon them that they might receive the Holy Spirit.

8. In Acts 8:12-17 there were believers who *had* been baptized with so-called "Christian baptism" yet,

147

for another reason, had not received the gift of the Holy Spirit. These, like the disciples here under discussion, received the Spirit by *the laying on of hands.*

9. If this "last record" of water baptism in Acts proves the importance of "Christian baptism," does it not also prove that tongues and prophecy go with Christian baptism? When these disciples were "rebaptized," the Holy Spirit came upon them and *"they spake with tongues and prophesied"* (Ver. 6).

It is passing strange that so few of those who use this passage to prove the importance of Christian baptism, seem to notice these obvious objections to their view. We know of only one who holds the rebaptism theory who freely admits the near impossibility of holding this view. He is Dr. W. M. Ramsay of Aberdeen, Scotland. In his book, *"St. Paul the Traveller and Roman Citizen,"* he says: "This episode I must confess not to understand.... If there were any authority in MSS or ancient Versions to omit the episode, one would be inclined to take that course" (pg. 270).

Some stress has been laid on the so-called "formula" in Verse 5 as proof that this could not refer to John's baptism.

As we have written again and again there is no Scriptural warrant whatever for the notion that the phrases, "the name of the Father, and of the Son, and of the Holy Ghost" (Matt. 28:19) and "the name of the Lord Jesus" (Acts 19:5) were *formulae* to be used at baptism. This unfounded notion caused the late Dr. Haldeman to refuse church membership to one who had been baptized by Dr. Pettingill, because he had not been baptized in the name of the Trinity (according to Matt. 28:19) but in the name of the Lord Jesus

148

(according to Acts 2:38 and 8:16). This same unscriptural notion has led some to the conclusion that the twelve apostles did not work under the commission recorded in Matthew 28.

When our ambassadors to other lands represent us at diplomatic conferences they speak, to be sure, *in the name of the United States of America,* but they do not keep repeating these words as a formula. And who can deny that John, the forerunner of Christ, went forth and baptized in His name and by His authority, as well as did the apostles?

The record closes by pointing out that the disciples at Ephesus numbered "about twelve." If any significance may be attached to this it would appear to link their experience with *Israel* and the divine *government,* and this would be consistent with the purpose of Acts.

FROM THE SYNAGOGUE TO THE SCHOOL OF TYRANNUS

"And he went into the synagogue, and spake boldly for the space of three months, disputing and persuading the things concerning the kingdom of God.

"But when divers were hardened, and believed not, but spake evil of that way before the multitude, he departed from them, and separated the disciples, disputing daily in the school of one Tyrannus.

"And this continued by the space of two years; so that all they which dwelt in Asia heard the word of the Lord Jesus, both Jews and Greeks."

—Acts 19:8-10

Paul's previous visit to Ephesus, along with the testimonies of Apollos and, doubtless, Aquila and Priscilla,

149

had evidently served, at the very least, to stir up keen interest at the Ephesian synagogue, so that upon his return Paul was permitted to minister there for three months. Nor, should we conclude that he managed to retain his position among them for this length of time by maintaining a "discreet silence" on the most vital subjects of all, as some "diplomatic" preachers do today, for we are distinctly told that he *"spake boldly,"* without reserve, all this time.

More than this; all this time he *"disputed,"* or *debated* with these Jews and sought to "persuade" them of the truths concerning "the kingdom of God"[3] (Ver. 8).

It is a sad commentary on the state of the Church today that *controversy* over the Word of God is frowned upon. Christian leaders often consider it a personal affront when their teachings are questioned. Debates about great Bible doctrines are considered "unspiritual" and why, they ask, should we try to *persuade* others "to believe as we do"? Why not just leave it to the Holy Spirit to show them? So little does *the Word of God* mean to them; so utterly has the spirit of the noble Bereans died in their hearts.

Let all such take careful note of the conduct of the Apostle Paul in this matter, for he is constantly found the center of contention and controversy.[4] No one could ever say that *he* did not care what men believed. And let them hear the words of one who wrote at a time when great numbers of our choicest Bible commentaries and works of theology were written:[5]

---

3. This term must not be confused with the "kingdom of heaven." It will be discussed at length when we reach Acts 28:31.

4. Though by no means *contentious* by nature.

5. Great Britain's Dean John S. Howson.

"We live in a time of much religious debate....and debate has a tendency to bring out truth more clearly into view" (*Companions of St. Paul*, pg. 14). "I say it is a happy circumstance that these subjects are eagerly debated. For debate leads to improvement, and diversity of opinion is far better than indifference" (*Ibid*, pg. 51).

But once again "divers were *hardened*"[6] and *"believed not,"* lit. *"were unbelieving,"* i.e., they *would not* believe, and their stubborn unbelief caused them to oppose Paul publicly by "speaking evil" of his teachings, as the Jews had done at Paphos, Pisidian Antioch, Iconium, Lystra, Thessalonica, Berea and Corinth.

Convinced that his ministry in these surroundings had now been brought to an end, and desiring to transfer those who had believed to a more edifying environment, the apostle "departed" from the synagogue and "separated the disciples" from the unbelieving Jews, taking up a daily ministry in *"the school of one Tyrannus"* (Ver. 9). The school of Tyrannus became to the Ephesian synagogue what the house of Justus had been to the Corinthian synagogue: a public condemnation of Israel's rejection of Christ.

Whether this new place of ministry was one of the divinity schools so often connected with synagogues, or a secular institution of learning; whether Tyrannus offered free use of the school because he had been converted to Christ or had become interested, or whether Paul and his associates *rented* it from him; indeed, whether Tyrannus was then the lecturer at this school or whether it was merely named after a Tyrannus, we do not know. We do not even know the hours at which

---

6. "Stiffnecked," in Acts 7:51 is derived from this word.

Paul held forth there. We only know that we find him, earnest and zealous as ever,

"disputing daily in the school of one Tyrannus.

"And this continued by the space of two years; so that all they which dwelt in Asia[7] **heard the word of the Lord Jesus, both Jews and Greeks" (Vers. 9,10).**

Thus the church at Ephesus became a distinct body and Ephesus became the center of Paul's apostolic labors and the chief seat of Christianity in the province of Asia.

A few years previous he had been "forbidden of the Holy Ghost to preach the Word in Asia" (Acts 16:6) but now he was used of God to evangelize the whole province thoroughly. It is possible that the province was evangelized spontaneously as the gospel of the grace of God was carried from one to another, for even in our shallow day the continued presence of a prominent evangelist often has an effect on a large area surrounding the city in which he ministers. More probably, however, the province was evangelized by an organized campaign, as the apostle sent his helpers forth with the message. It is doubtful that Paul himself left Ephesus to take part in this, however, for not only is there no record of it, but our text states quite specifically that "this" daily ministry in the school of Tyrannus "continued by the space of two years" and that *as a result* "all they which dwelt in Asia heard the word of the Lord Jesus." Furthermore Paul, in an epistle written later, distinctly states that the believers in Colosse and Laodicea, two of Asia's principal cities, had *not* seen his face (Col. 2:1).

7.　The *province* of Asia, in Asia Minor.

From the record it appears probable that the work outgrew the school of Tyrannus and that in addition to the three months in the synagogue and the two years at the school of Tyrannus he spent approximately nine more months at Ephesus (See Acts 20:31). It may be that the rest of Chapter 19 records events that transpired during this time. Certainly there is the "season" of Verse 22.

PAUL'S UNCEASING TOIL

Before considering the two examples of the power of Paul's ministry given to us in Chapter 19, we should take note of some of the additional information about his stay at Ephesus which is given to us outside that chapter.

First it should be noted that during *most* of his stay at Ephesus he worked with his hands—probably again with Aquila and Priscilla—to support not only himself but also his associates in the work. In Acts 20:34 he reminds the Ephesian elders: *"Yea, ye yourselves know, that these hands have ministered unto my necessities and to them that were with me."* And writing to the Corinthians toward the close of his stay at Ephesus (as we shall later see) he says: *"Even unto this present hour we...labor, working with our own hands"* (I Cor. 4:11,12).

And besides this he debated daily in the school of Tyrannus for two of these years and *also* made time for much personal visitation, teaching *"publicly, and from house to house"* (Acts 20:20). Pastors who put a minimum of energy into their ministry for the Lord and then wonder why it does not prosper would do well to consider these facts prayerfully and act accordingly.

HIS PERSECUTIONS AND SUFFERINGS

The apostle bore many heavy burdens while at Ephesus.

Writing to the Corinthians about the matter, he says there were *"many adversaries"* (I Cor. 16:9). It is doubtful that the *"beasts"* with which he *"fought...at Ephesus"* (I Cor. 15:32) were actual wild beasts, but his phraseology in this passage gives us some idea of the ferocity of the opposition he encountered.

At Ephesus there was a great arena or amphitheatre where foot races and boxing and wrestling matches were staged. At the close of such entertainments they often sent men into the arena to fight with wild beasts. These were called *"last victims."* Sometimes they were trained, armed men, but more often condemned criminals, completely unarmed. These closing "shows" were considered the climax of the day's entertainment for the blood-thirsty throngs that had gathered.

Almost certainly alluding to this, the apostle wrote to the Corinthians:

"For I think that God hath set forth us the apostles last, as it were appointed to death: for we are made a spectacle unto the world, [both] to angels and to men" (I Cor. 4:9).

One aspect of his sufferings not mentioned in Acts 19, yet one which we might have suspected, is also referred to in his farewell to the Ephesian elders: the vicious and relentless opposition of the unbelieving Jews. As he bids his friends good-bye, he recalls the *many tears and trials* "which befell me by the lying in wait of the Jews" (Acts 20:19). Those from whom he had been forced to separate himself at the synagogue,

154

and perhaps others from other cities where he had ministered, would not leave him alone but, again and again, sought opportunity to slay him. Constantly his life was in jeopardy. As he went to call on interested hearers he was always conscious that danger and death might lurk nearby. It was dangerous to ever be alone. This constant pressure told on him and often caused him to burst forth in tears.

Then, too, there was *"the care of all the churches"* (II Cor. 11:28). Beside the new assemblies in Asia (I Cor. 16:19) which required more and more attention, there were the other churches, farther off, which he had founded, and from which he received news.

It appears that it was before or during his stay at Ephesus that he heard such disturbing news about the Galatian churches that he wrote them immediately with his own hand, warning them of the dangers of the course they were taking. There was news from other churches, too, that caused concern, and there can be no doubt that as he labored at his tent-making these companies of believers were continually on his mind.

Since Corinth was situated just across the Aegean Sea from Ephesus and there was constant intercourse between the two cities, Paul doubtless kept better informed about the Corinthian church than about any other outside Asia. Indeed so disturbing were the reports from Corinth that the apostle was constrained to pay them a short visit during this time. How soon reports about their party divisions, legal battles, disorderly gatherings, etc., began to arrive we do not know, but it is evident that already he began to learn about the gross immorality practiced among them—immorality which would have been considered a disgrace even among the heathen.[8]

This second visit to Corinth is not actually recorded but there is clear internal evidence that it took place. For one thing, the second *recorded* visit to Corinth (Acts 20:1-3) is twice called his *"third"* visit (II Cor. 12:14; 13:1) so that there must have been a visit between the two which are recorded. The apostle describes this visit as one in which he had come to them *"in heaviness"* (II Cor. 2:1) and one which had caused him great *personal humiliation* (II Cor. 12:21). Hence he writes in II Corinthians 13:2 *"If I come again I will not spare."*

Besides Paul's unrecorded visit to Corinth there is also another letter which though not included in Sacred Scripture, he evidently wrote to them at about this time. This is "the[9] epistle" alluded to in I Corinthians 5:9. Evidently after his brief visit to them he had received further disturbing reports about their moral conduct so that it had become necessary to send them an epistle in which, by apostolic authority, he forbade them to keep any company with fornicators. Evidently this injunction was misunderstood (perhaps even purposely by some) so that they then wrote him an epistle to which First Corinthians (actually his *second* letter to them) was in part the reply (See I Cor. 7:1). In this letter he further explains that his previous letter had referred to keeping company with *professing believers* who practiced fornication (I Cor. 5:9-11).

All this anxiety and sorrow of heart did the apostle have to bear while toiling physically to support himself

---

8. The number involved must have been large and a considerable number of them must have *persisted* in their sin, for in II Corinthians 12:21 the *unrepentant* ones are still called "many."

9. The original contains the definite article.

and his co-workers, and carrying on an extensive public and private ministry at the same time. Yes, this and more, for while still at Ephesus he wrote to these carnal believers:

"We are fools for Christ's sake, but ye are wise in Christ; we are weak, but ye are strong; ye are honorable, but we are despised.[10]

"Even unto this present hour we both hunger, and thirst, and are naked,[11] **and are buffeted, and have no certain dwelling place;**

"And labor, working with our own hands: being reviled, we bless; being persecuted, we suffer it:

"Being defamed, we entreat: we are made as the filth of the world, and are the offscouring of all things unto this day" (I Cor. 4:10-13).

GOD'S BLESSING ON HIS MINISTRY

It must not be supposed from all this that Paul was crushed in spirit and continued his strenuous ministry only out of a sense of stern duty. Far from it! In reliance upon God and doubtless with the inspiration and encouragement of faithful helpers in the work,[12] he maintained a remarkable spiritual balance. As he wrote to the Corinthians not long after:

"We are troubled on every side, yet not distressed [crushed]; we are perplexed, but not in despair;

---

10. This is a sample of the biting sarcasm so typical of this epistle.
11. This does not mean to be *without* clothing, but without *sufficient* clothing.
12. Including Onesiphorus, who helped him in many ways (II Tim. 1:16-18).

"Persecuted, but not forsaken; cast down, but not destroyed" (II Cor. 4:8,9).

Thus his ministry at Ephesus was blessed beyond measure. In Verse 10 of Acts 19 we learn that through his ministry there all in Asia heard "the word of the Lord Jesus"; in the remainder of the chapter, which we have yet to consider, we find a large portion of the Ephesian populace voluntarily burning their heathen books at a public bonfire; *"so mightily grew the Word of God and prevailed"* (Ver. 20). And these spiritual victories are attested to by Demetrius the silversmith, who complained that *"not alone at Ephesus, but almost throughout all Asia, this Paul hath persuaded and turned away much people, saying that they be no gods, which are made with hands"* (Ver. 26). Little wonder that Paul wrote to the Corinthians: *"For a great door and effectual is opened unto me"* (I Cor. 16:9). In all his persecutions and sufferings God was working.

Before we close this examination of Paul's ministry at Ephesus we have yet to consider two specific cases of God's blessing upon it: one relating to Israel and the other to the Gentiles.

JUDGMENT UPON ISRAEL
BLESSING TO THE GENTILES

"And God wrought special miracles by the hands of Paul:

"So that from his body were brought unto the sick handkerchiefs or aprons, and the diseases departed from them, and the evil spirits went out of them.

"Then certain of the vagabond Jews, exorcists, took upon them to call over them which had evil spirits

the name of the Lord Jesus, saying, We adjure you by Jesus whom Paul preacheth.

"And there were seven sons of one Sceva, a Jew, and chief of the priests, which did so.

"And the evil spirit answered and said, Jesus I know, and Paul I know; but who are ye?

"And the man in whom the evil spirit was leaped on them, and overcame them, and prevailed against them, so that they fled out of that house naked and wounded.

"And this was known to all the Jews and Greeks also dwelling at Ephesus; and fear fell on them all, and the name of the Lord Jesus was magnified.

"And many that believed came, and confessed, and showed their deeds.

"Many of them also which used curious arts brought their books together, and burned them before all men: and they counted the price of them, and found it fifty thousand pieces of silver."

—Acts 19:11-20

In the passage before us we have another of those significant narratives of Acts which set forth, symbolically, the blessing of the Gentiles through Israel's fall.

It begins with the "special" miracles which God wrought through Paul. Actually the word "special" should have been rendered in the negative as it is in the Greek: *"not common"* or *"not ordinary."* The idea is that though Ephesus, being more oriental in character than Athens or Corinth, had many magicians and wonder-workers about her streets, God used Paul to

159

work miracles which they could not duplicate, just as Moses and Aaron, more than fifteen centuries earlier, had wrought miracles which Pharaoh's magicians found it impossible to imitate.

Among these were the curing of diseases and casting out of demons by handkerchiefs and aprons which had touched Paul's person. The era of demonstrative miracles had not yet passed.

But among those who witnessed these miracles there was a company of Jews who were a symbol of what their nation was fast becoming and has since become.

They were "*vagabond* Jews," wanderers, far from their land, certainly *not* typical of redeemed Israel of the future who "*shall* dwell in their own land" (Jer. 23:8) but rather of the present apostate Israel, wandering homeless in other lands.

Moreover these Jews were "exorcists," men who expelled, or presumed to expel, evil spirits, not, of course, by the power of God, but by magical rites, incantations and other means, the implication being that they went from place to place offering to cast out demons for a price.

Now some of these, observing the power that Paul exercised in the name of the Lord Jesus Christ, presumed to use Christ's name in their sorceries, saying: *"We adjure you by Jesus whom Paul preacheth."*

How low these vagabond Jews had fallen, spiritually, is evidenced by the fact that, for personal gain, they would use the name of the Lord Jesus Christ, their Messiah, whom they rejected, in a traffic with evil spirits which was strictly forbidden by Scripture and

160

punishable with death (See Ex. 22:18; Lev. 20:27; Deut. 18:10,11; I Sam. 28:3,9).

In this too they were symbolic of their nation, for rather than representing *God* before the nations now, Israel has become a *false prophet* by rejecting Messiah. Yet, while rejecting Christ as an imposter, no one has been more ready to make financial gain of Him than the Jew, on "Good Friday" at Easter time, Christmas time and all through the year.

Among these wandering exorcists were seven sons of a leading priest, named Sceva who used the name of Christ on one occasion with disastrous consequences, for the evil spirit replied contemptuously: *"Jesus I recognize and Paul I know,*[13] *but who are ye?"* whereupon the demon-possessed man, with the strength of the Maniac of Gadara, leaped upon them, overcoming all seven of them "so that they fled out of that house naked and wounded" (Ver. 16). Such was the consequence of the unauthorized use of that holy name.

In this these seven vagabond Jews were again symbolic of the nation as a whole, for in their ill use of Christ, Satan has prevailed against them and left them, spiritually, naked and wounded.

But there is even more in this narrative that is symbolic, for as a result of this incident "the name of the Lord Jesus was magnified" and there were "many," evidently including some Jews, who now "believed... confessed, and showed their deeds" (Vers. 17,18).

Once more, then, we have salvation going to the Gentiles *through Israel's fall* (See Rom. 11:11-15) and

---

13. Lit. *"recognize,"* as an authority; *"know,"* have familiar knowledge of.

more: through their fall there is grace to *all*, both individual Jews and individual Gentiles, as it is written:

"For there is no difference between the Jew and the Greek; for the same Lord over all is rich unto all that call upon Him.

"For whosoever shall call upon the name of the Lord shall be saved" (Rom. 10:12,13).

"For God hath concluded them all in unbelief, that He might have mercy upon all.

"O the depth of the riches both of the wisdom and knowledge of God! How unsearchable are His judgments, and His ways past finding out!" (Rom. 11:32,33).

As a result of the judgment upon these exorcists the believers who had used "curious"[14] arts brought their books of instructions, secret formulae, incantations, etc., and staged a large public bonfire, burning books totaling about fifty thousand pieces of silver, or nearly ten thousand dollars in cost. *"So mightily grew the Word of God and prevailed"* (Ver. 20).

Thus the "special" miracles which God wrought through Paul were by no means an encouragement to idolatrous practices or superstitions, but were rather a supernatural testimony, especially to Israel,[15] that Paul's ministry was the work of God.

PLANS TO VISIT JERUSALEM AND ROME

"After these things were ended, Paul purposed in the spirit, when he had passed through Macedonia

---

14. Lit. going beyond that which is legitimate.
15. See I Corinthians 1:22.

and Achaia, to go to Jerusalem, saying, After I have been there, I must also see Rome.

"So he sent into Macedonia two of them that ministered unto him, Timotheus and Erastus, but he himself stayed in Asia for a season."

—Acts 19:21,22

We are not to presume that Paul had received any revelation instructing him to go to Jerusalem and Rome, for it is distinctly stated that he "*purposed*" this "in the spirit" i.e., *his* spirit. The *Companion Bible* explains: "The meaning is that he was firmly resolved."

The apostle's heart constantly yearned for Jerusalem and his kinsmen (Rom. 9:1-3; 10:1) and he had long had a desire to go to Rome (Rom. 1:13; 15:23) but little did he imagine that soon he would be *taken* from the one to the other as "the prisoner of Jesus Christ for [the] Gentiles" (Eph. 3:1).

Planning to pass through Macedonia and Achaia before traveling to Jerusalem, he sent Timothy and Erastus ahead, evidently especially to prepare the Corinthians for his coming, so that he might not again embarrass both them and himself by his coming (I Cor. 4:17).

It was doubtless at this time that *First Corinthians* (actually his *second* letter to them) was written.

We know that this letter was written while he was at Ephesus (I Cor. 16:8). We know also that it was written while his ministry there was prospering (I Cor. 16:9) which would probably place it at or after Acts 19:20. We are informed, furthermore, that it was written when he planned to visit them after remaining briefly at Ephesus (I Cor. 16:8). This again would set the date at Acts 19:22b. Finally, it was certainly written before the great tumult over the goddess Diana (Acts 19:23-41) for immediately after this he departed for Macedonia and Greece (Acts 20:1,2).

The epistle which we know as *First Corinthians*, then, was almost certainly written between the public bonfire of Acts 19:19 and the uproar over Diana, or during the "season" referred to in Verse 22. Evidently the church at Ephesus, or a segment of it, met in the home of Aquila and Priscilla at this time (I Cor. 16:19).

The plan to visit Macedonia and Achaia again was doubtless largely due to continued disturbing reports from the church at Corinth. Members of "the house of Chloe" had reported that a factious spirit prevailed among the believers there. The constant intercourse between Ephesus and Corinth must have brought many believers from one city to the other, for the apostle had also learned of their going to court one against another, their disorderly conduct at their services and many other serious failings. Indeed, the most serious defection of all was *"commonly reported"*: immorality so wanton that even the heathen considered it too disgraceful to speak of (I Cor. 5:1).

Then too there was the letter which he had received from *them* regarding marriage. This too must be dealt with. Thus it is that we have "First Corinthians" in our possession today.

In this great epistle we learn that the apostle had preached much which the Book of Acts, because of its nature and purpose, does not mention. There he shows that "the preaching of the cross" had been his theme (I Cor. 1:17-25). There he also rebukes the Corinthians because, due to their carnality, he could not explain to them the "deep things of God" and the great truths of "the mystery," which he *had* taught to more mature believers (I Cor. 2:1,2,6,7; 3:1-4). To those who boasted of their party connections or went to law against each other, he declared that "by one Spirit" they had all been *"baptized into one body,"* that with all their failings they were "the Body of *Christ*"; members of *Him* and therefore of each other (I Cor. 12:13,14,27). To those who boasted of their miraculous powers, especially speaking in tongues, he showed the transcendent glory of love (I Cor. 13:8-13). To those who lived as though they were responsible to no one, he declared that Christ was indeed alive and revealed the additional "secret" that at any "moment" He might come to call them to Himself (I Cor. 15:12,20,51-53).

THE MIRACLES AT CORINTH

Those who suppose that the miraculous powers of the apostolic era were a sign of spirituality, and who contend that if we were but more spiritual we too would possess these powers, should stop and consider the case of the Corinthian believers.

From Paul's letters to the Corinthians it is evident that they were of all the churches the most *un*spiritual, yet he acknowledges: *"...ye come behind in no gift"* (I Cor. 1:7). That "gifts of healing...working of miracles...prophecy...divers kinds of tongues," etc., were included with these "gifts" is evident from I Corinthians 12:9,10.

From the fact that the *Corinthian* church stood ahead of others in the possession of miraculous gifts, then, we must conclude that the possession of such gifts was *not* an indication of spirituality.

165

What, then, *did* they indicate? Simply that *God was working*. They were *signs* to the unbelieving, and especially to the unbelieving *Jews* (I Cor. 1:22).

Thus it becomes particularly significant that it was just this *un*spiritual church that possessed most of the sign gifts. Whether or not the believers at Corinth still met in the home that "joined hard unto the synagogue" at this time, they were certainly under constant observation by the Jews of the synagogue there. These Jews would certainly not be impressed by the *lives* these carnal believers led, but, looking at the signs, would have to acknowledge the new movement to be *the work of God* (See John 3:2).

THE UPROAR AT EPHESUS

SATAN ENRAGED

"And the same time there arose no small stir about that way.

"For a certain man named Demetrius, a silversmith, which made silver shrines for Diana, brought no small gain unto the craftsmen;

"Whom he called together with the workmen of like occupation, and said, Sirs, ye know that by this craft we have our wealth.

"Moreover ye see and hear, that not alone at Ephesus, but almost throughout all Asia, this Paul hath persuaded and turned away much people, saying that they be no gods, which are made with hands:

"So that not only this our craft is in danger to be set at nought; but also that the temple of the great goddess Diana should be despised, and her magnificence should be destroyed, whom all Asia and the world worshippeth.

"And when they heard these sayings, they were full of wrath, and cried out, saying, Great is Diana of the Ephesians.

"And the whole city was filled with confusion: and having caught Gaius and Aristarchus, men of Macedonia, Paul's companions in travel, they rushed with one accord into the theatre.

"And when Paul would have entered in unto the people, the disciples suffered him not.

167

"And certain of the chief of Asia, which were his friends, sent unto him, desiring him that he would not adventure himself into the theatre.

"Some therefore cried one thing, and some another: for the assembly was confused; and the more part knew not wherefore they were come together.

"And they drew Alexander out of the multitude, the Jews putting him forward. And Alexander beckoned with the hand, and would have made his defence unto the people.

"But when they knew that he was a Jew, all with one voice about the space of two hours cried out, Great is Diana of the Ephesians.

"And when the townclerk had appeased the people, he said, Ye men of Ephesus, what man is there that knoweth not how that the city of the Ephesians is a worshipper of the great goddess Diana, and of the image which fell down from Jupiter?

"Seeing then that these things cannot be spoken against, ye ought to be quiet, and to do nothing rashly.

"For ye have brought hither these men, which are neither robbers of churches, nor yet blasphemers of your goddess.

"Wherefore if Demetrius, and the craftsmen which are with him, have a matter against any man, the law is open, and there are deputies: let them implead one another.

"But if ye enquire any thing concerning other matters, it shall be determined in a lawful assembly.

"For we are in danger to be called in question for this day's uproar, there being no cause whereby we may give an account of this concourse.

"And when he had thus spoken, he dismissed the assembly."

—Acts 19:23-41

The nineteenth chapter of the Acts is a record of tremendous victories for Christ. It tells of the *extraordinary* miracles wrought through Paul and of the discomfiture of deceivers who sought to use the name of Christ to their own advantage. It tells also of the deep inroads being made into the heart of heathenism as large numbers of those who had practiced the black arts came and burned their books, valued at fifty thousand pieces of silver, in a public bonfire. Thrice in the chapter the mighty effects of Paul's ministry are particularly noted (Vers. 10,20,26).

It is not strange, then, to read of a great popular uprising against Paul and his teachings, incited, not first of all by men, but by the "wicked spirits in the heavenlies" against whom believers, especially *faithful* believers, still "wrestle" today (See Eph. 6:12).

DIANA

It was actually Diana who incited "no small stir" about the "way" which Paul proclaimed, for the real "Diana," back of that carved statue, was a fallen angel or group of fallen angels. It is they, the demons, who were behind all idolatry. The philosophers at Athens were evidently aware of this, for when Paul appeared among their idols to preach Christ, they said: "He seemeth to be a setter forth of strange *demons* [Gr. *daimonion*]" (Acts 17:18).

Whether the advocates of the unspeakable lewdness practiced in the "groves" and temples of Ashtoreth and Venus, or the protectors of young men and maidens and the champions of chastity, like the earlier Artemis, all idols represented attempts by Satan to pervert truth and divert worship away from God.

169

Thus it is that God commanded the children of Israel:

"Thou shalt have no other gods before me....for I the Lord thy God am a jealous God..." (Ex. 20:3,5).

And thus it is that Psalm 82 presents God "judging among the gods," and saying:

"I have said, Ye are gods; and all of you are children of the most High.

"But ye shall die like men, and fall like one of the princes" (Vers. 6,7).

Idolatry, on the human side was, of course, not based upon truth, but upon the changing superstitions of unregenerate men. Hence the Diana of Ephesus (the later Artemis) was, unlike her various predecessors, the many-breasted personification of fruitfulness and bounty in nature, and as a woman, she called forth a fanatical loyalty from her devotees.[1]

The image of Diana was supposed to have fallen from heaven, sent down to earth by Jupiter, but it is easily possible, especially considering its unshapely form, that it was nothing more than a meteor made into a crude statue.

But if the *image* of Diana was crude, her *temple* was world-renowned for its beauty. Situated at some distance from the city, it was magnificent to behold, with its one hundred twenty massive marble pillars,[2] each

---

1. A similar devotion is rendered to Mary in Roman Catholicism, so that those who readily take the name of Christ in vain and so carelessly exclaim "My God!" are offended if Mary's name is as lightly used. Take the name of God in vain, but not that of Mary!

2. Each pillar is said to have been sixty feet high, weighing one hundred fifty tons. Pliny says that the temple took two hundred twenty years to complete (Lib. 36, C. 14).

the gift of a prince, and was considered one of the seven wonders of the world. So great was the national pride in this sanctuary that it is said that when Alexander the Great offered the spoils of his eastern campaign on condition that he be permitted to inscribe his name on the building, the honor was declined.

Ironically, however, Diana, whom "all Asia and the world" was once said to have worshipped, is not worshipped by a single man today, and her magnificent temple lay buried in the dust for centuries until fragments of it were uncovered by Mr. J. T. Wood for the British Museum in the late eighteen hundreds.

DEMETRIUS

Demetrius, the silversmith, was, of course, the human instrument whom Satan used to touch off the uprising at Ephesus. He appears to have been at the head of a guild of silversmiths and others of "like occupation" and had been instrumental in bringing them "no small gain" through the sale of silver shrines "for"[3] Diana. The devotees of Diana would buy these miniature shrines to carry on their persons, display in their homes or leave at the temple itself as an act of worship, much as Romanists today present their rosaries and images at Lourdes and Ste. Anne de Beaupre. Moreover, Ephesus, being one of the largest seaports on the Aegean Sea, travelers from far and near would also purchase these silver shrines to take home as mementos of the world-renowned Diana and her temple.

Concerned because of the sharp decline in business since Paul's appearance at Ephesus, Demetrius called the guild members together to discuss the situation.

3. Evidently the facade of the temple, with the figure of Diana in the center.

With almost naive simplicity he stated the purpose of the gathering and the real reason for his concern over Diana and her temple: *"By this craft we have our wealth"* (Ver. 25). Paul, by contending that *"they be no gods, which are made with hands,"* was *hurting business*. This was the *human* cause behind the uproar. Little matter whether Paul was right or wrong in his contention; he was causing them personal loss.

This passage teaches further that those who stood to gain by idolatry, actually wanted the gullible masses to attach supernatural significance to this merchandise "made with hands," otherwise why object to Paul's contention that these objects were *not* gods?

As we have pointed out, Satan, "the god of this age" (II Cor. 4:4) was the moving power behind all this, diverting men's worship away from *God*, and his efforts in this direction have continued to this day.

Even the Church of Rome, while contending about representation and symbolism before Protestants, actually leads her devotees to attach supernatural significance to things "made with hands."

The writer has before him a letter received from the Franciscan Friars of the Atonement, at Graymoor, New York. It contains, as an "Easter gift," a medal[4] of St. Pius X, supposed to have touched his body and to have been blessed by Pope Pius XII. The Graymoor Friars send the medal, of course, to promote devotion to St. Pius X, but also—of course—with the prayer and the *suggestion* that St. Pius X will inspire the recipient to make some sacrifice to help educate young men for the priesthood!

"Let St. Joseph Solve Your Problem," says a paid newspaper ad and, incidentally, a chaplet of St. Joseph

---

4. Worth almost nothing in actual value.

will be mailed to anyone sending a contribution of one dollar or more to the Catholic institution placing the ad. In another periodical small advertisements keep appearing urging its readers to "Burn a Votive Light" in honor of *"Our Lady of the Miraculous Medal,"* or *"St. Christopher,"* for a "safe journey," or *"St. Anthony*, finder of lost things," or *"The Infant of Prague"* for "finances," or *"St. Anne,"* for a "happy marriage," or *"St. Joseph,"* for "employment and good death." How to get these "votive lights"? That is explained on page 32, where the prices are given.

These are only a few of the evidences seen on every hand that *Rome promotes superstition and idolatry for financial gain.* Well do we remember our amazement at the almost unbelievable prices charged for the cheapest religious trinkets at Ste. Anne de Beaupre in Quebec.

Thus the spirit that prompted Demetrius to call a meeting of his guild still prevails today. Even among Protestants, yes, and Fundamentalists, *vested interests* play a prominent role in the stubborn resistance to spiritual advances and reforms.

How transparent is Demetrius' complete argument! "Paul's teaching is endangering our business—and, of course, the glory of our goddess, Diana"! Why did he have to cover his greed with a cloak of religion? It was the danger to their "gain," their "wealth," their "craft" that had roused Demetrius and his fellow guild members, otherwise they would have cared little about the glory of Diana and whether or not the masses of common folk worshipped her. At any rate "our wealth" came first with the leaders; then the glory of Diana, but the glory of Diana would come first with the masses, and would be used to restore the wealth of the leaders.

THE UPROAR

Money and religion! Where could two more inflamatory elements be found with which to start a mad uprising!

As the guildsmen, "full of wrath," went about crying aloud to Diana, "the whole city was filled with confusion" (Vers. 28,29).

It would appear that at this point the guildsmen sought to capture Paul, whom Demetrius had mentioned by name, but, failing to find him had caught Gaius and Aristarchus (two of Paul's traveling companions) and were now taking them to the theatre to subject them to their own form of "justice." If the home of Aquila and Priscilla was Paul's lodging place at Ephesus, this may well have been the occasion on which they "laid down their own necks," for him (Rom. 16:4); at least we know of no other specific occasion to which this tribute by Paul could more appropriately refer.

Seeing Gaius and Aristarchus taken by force, and concluding that in the theatre, if anywhere, they might learn what the commotion was all about, the populace "rushed with one accord into the theatre" (Ver. 29).[5]

Where the apostle had been in the meantime, we do not know, but learning of the tumult, he now would have entered in among the people, had not the disciples prevented him from doing so. It is a testimony to the character of Paul that at this point "certain of the chief of Asia [Lit. *Asiarchs*[6]] *which were his friends*" sent a message to him, entreating him not to venture into the theatre (Ver. 31). Evidently Paul had gained the

---

5. The ruins of this ancient amphitheatre still stand. It probably seated upwards of twenty-five thousand persons.

6. The *Asiarchs* were men of wealth and position chosen to preside over public festivals and games.

respect and admiration, and even the affection, of these prominent men, so that now, though not themselves believers, they proved to be his true friends.

Meantime bedlam reigned at the theatre. *"Some cried one thing, and some another; for the assembly*[7] *was confused; and the more part knew not wherefore they were come together"* (Ver. 32).

In the excitement, a man named Alexander was being singled out from the multitude, "the Jews putting him forward" (Ver. 33). Some have supposed that this was the Christian Alexander of I Timothy 1:20, before his defection, and that the Jews put him forward to deliver him to the vengeance of the mob. But there are insurmountable objections to this view, especially since the Jews themselves were opposed to the worship of Diana and would hardly place themselves in so compromising a position.

It is far more likely that this Alexander is the "coppersmith" referred to in II Timothy 4:14, who did Paul "much evil," probably at this very time. It is evident that this man, put forward by the Jews, was about to make "a defence" (not *"his* defence") to the people. Probably the Jews, themselves opposed to idol worship, feared that *they* might suffer the wrath of the silversmiths and thus chose from among themselves a man of "like occupation," a coppersmith, to explain that *they*

---

7. Gr. *ekklesia*, rendered *church* well over a hundred times in A.V., but *assembly* here and in Verses 39,41. The occurrence of this word here is further confirmation of the fact that its use in Acts 2 is no proof that the Body of Christ began at Pentecost. God has had His *ekklesia* all down through the ages. See Acts 7:38 and LXX (the Greek translation of the Old Testament) where the word occurs more than sixty times. The *ekklesia* of Acts 19:32 was not, of course, the Church of *Christ* at all, though what is said about it may well describe the confusion prevailing in the professing Church.

had not caused the defection from Diana—this, when they as worshippers of the one true God, should have supported Paul in this conflict .

Alexander was not even given a hearing, however. The multitude well knew that the Jew was the hereditary foe of idolatry and when they saw that Alexander was one of that race, their confusion was immediately dispelled and as one man they cried out *"Great Diana*[8] *of the Ephesians"* (Ver. 34) continuing this for two hours.

We have here an example of how wrong the majority can be, and how little sight and feelings are to be trusted. Here was a mass demonstration of deep emotional feeling but it was wholly unsound, and its effect utterly unpredictable. Such a demonstration was fraught with great peril, for a fanatical mob like this, with emotions aroused to so high a pitch, might do almost anything.

After two hours, however, the "townclerk" (the chief officer of the city) succeeded in appeasing the people. Showing himself to be both tactful and persuasive, as a man of the world, he first soothed the feelings of the multitude with regard to Diana.

"What man is there," he asked, *"that knoweth not how that the city of the Ephesians is a worshipper* [*temple-sweeper*[9]] *of the great goddess Diana and of the*

---

8. The insertion of the word "is" in A.V. and R.V. is probably incorrect. *"Great Diana"* was a common formula of *devotion* and *prayer*, as attested by several ancient inscriptions. "Great *is* Diana" could be a calm expression of recognition of her greatness. *"Great Diana"* gives a more natural and far more effective tone to the scene. Four times in this chapter Diana is called "great" by the devotees.

9. This is the literal meaning of the word here rendered *"worshipper."* Thus is Ephesus personified as Diana's devotee.

image which fell down from Jupiter?   Seeing then that these things cannot be spoken against, ye ought to be quiet, and to do nothing rashly" (Vers. 35,36).

This, we say, was well calculated to calm the storm of emotions, but the townclerk's conclusion was as weak as his premise. *"What man knoweth not?"   "Seeing then that these things cannot be spoken against"!* The masses, of course, readily accept as truth that which they are told *"everybody knows."* Indeed, there is perhaps nothing that holds even the great majority of believers back spiritually like the thought that they must not repudiate that which is *commonly* believed, nor accept that which is *not* commonly accepted, and thus they actually set human opinion above divine revelation.   Let us thank God that *truth* rests upon a firmer foundation than the confused and changing opinions of fallen men! The townclerk spoke so confidently of Diana and her glory, but already Diana and her temple are memories of the past, and their glory withered and gone.

Next the townclerk had a word to say in defense of Paul and his associates. They had not been "robbers of temples"[10] nor "blasphemers" of Diana (Ver. 37). Their care not to deride this heathen goddess shows what restraint Paul's fellow-workers had practiced under his leadership and by his example. In the record of his ministry among both Jews and Gentiles, we find him often *reasoning, debating* and *persuading*, but never *insulting* or *ridiculing*. Now this was all to his advantage.

In the light of all this, argued the townclerk, Demetrius and the craftsmen should present any complaint against Paul and his associates in the manner

---

10. Since many of Diana's worshippers brought their gifts to her at the temple, robberies there were quite common.

prescribed by law. And this he capped with a serious reminder that the Roman government looked with stern displeasure upon any outbreak of lawlessness.

Having thus calmed the passions of the multitude and restored order, the townclerk declared the assembly dismissed.

THE POSITION OF THE BELIEVERS AGAIN ENHANCED

Once more God had overruled the opposition of Satan to enhance the position of a young and struggling church. At Philippi He had used Paul's Roman citizenship, at Corinth the sagacity of a heathen judge, and here the appeal of the townclerk. The church at Ephesus would now be in a much more favorable position in this period when her growth and establishment were so important. Thus does our God take the wise in their own craftiness and cause even the wrath of man—yea, and of the devil—to praise Him.

Finally, it should be noted that Israel falls more and more in the background in this episode, as both the persecution and protection involved originate with the Gentiles.

THE RETURN TO
MACEDONIA AND GREECE

PAUL'S ACTIVITIES THERE

"And after the uproar was ceased, Paul called unto him the disciples, and embraced them, and departed for to go into Macedonia.

"And when he had gone over those parts, and had given them much exhortation, he came into Greece,

"And there abode three months. And when the Jews laid wait for him, as he was about to sail into Syria, he purposed to return through Macedonia.

"And there accompanied him into Asia Sopater of Berea; and of the Thessalonians, Aristarchus and Secundus; and Gaius of Derbe, and Timotheus; and of Asia, Tychicus and Trophimus.

"These going before tarried for us at Troas."

—Acts 20:1-5

Very little is told us here of a ministry which must have consumed many months. Paul departed for Macedonia, went over those parts, exhorting the believers "much" and then arrived at Greece, where he stayed three months; that is all the information we have from Luke's record.

As we meditate upon what *is* told us, however, and examine Paul's early epistles as to his activities at this time, a much more complete picture unfolds.

Whether the uproar at Ephesus cut short the apostle's stay there, we are not clearly told. In any case, though, it would be wiser for him to leave now. A tremendous work had been done there, and since he, personally, had become the chief target of the enemy's fury, it would be better for the work to entrust it now to the care of those with whom he had labored for three years.

Thus, taking affectionate leave of the disciples, he left for Macedonia, doubtless revisiting the believers at Thessalonica, Berea and, of course, Philippi. What happy reunions, after at least six years' absence, there must have been with old friends and co-workers such as Lydia and her household, the Philippian jailor and his, Jason, and scores of others! The apostle must have experienced much joy, some apprehension and also some sorrow at their reports of spiritual victories and defeats, and he gave them "much exhortation" (Ver. 2).

On the way to Macedonia he would doubtless stop (perhaps to change ship) at Troas, and it is probably regarding this occasion that he wrote to the Corinthians some time later:

"Furthermore, when I came to Troas to preach Christ's gospel, and a door was opened unto me of the Lord,[1]

"I had no rest in my spirit, because I found not Titus my brother: but taking my leave of them, I went from thence into Macedonia" (II Cor. 2:12,13).

The apostle had, as we shall see, sent Titus to Corinth to deal with some of their problems and to learn, and report to him, the effects of his recent letters to them. Evidently he had hoped to meet Titus at Troas, but had been disappointed, with the result that he became so anxious that he failed to enter the open door of opportunity set before him, proceeding to Macedonia instead.

---

1. Perhaps through his evangelization of Asia (See Acts 19:10).

And this state of spiritual depression continued even after he had reached Macedonia. We have already mentioned the happy reunions that must have taken place, especially at Philippi, yet even here he could not shake off the apprehensions he felt with regard to the Corinthian church.

It was here in Macedonia, however, that Titus finally reached the apostle with news that was generally good. Thus he wrote:

"For, when we were come into Macedonia, our flesh had no rest, but we were troubled on every side; without were fightings, within were fears.

"Nevertheless God, that comforteth those that are cast down, comforted us by the coming of Titus" (II Cor. 7:5,6).

TITUS

It is remarkable that Titus, who occupied so large a place in Paul's ministry, is not even mentioned in the Book of Acts. Conversely, the notice he is given in just *one* of Paul's epistles (II Corinthians) is altogether unique in Paul's writings. In that epistle alone he is mentioned nine times, and always with affection and esteem.

Ramsay believes that had he not been a Gentile he would have been recognized sooner, and reads in II Corinthians a possible wish on Paul's part to compensate for the neglect that had for many years sacrificed him to the thankless policy of conciliating the Jews (See *St. Paul the Traveller and Roman Citizen*, pgs. 285,286).

Titus had probably been converted to Christ through Paul's ministry while at Syrian Antioch. From there Paul and Barnabas had taken him up to Jerusalem as a test case in the controversy over Gentile freedom from the law of Moses (Acts 15:2; Gal. 2:3). As we have already pointed out, he *may* have been the Titus Justus of Acts 18:7 (See R.V.) whose house adjoined the Corinthian synagogue. If so, his inviting the believers to meet in his home would correspond well with his nature as it is described for us in the Scriptures. After performing many difficult and valuable services for Paul, Titus was left in charge of the churches on the island of Crete (Titus 1:5) a difficult assignment indeed (See Titus 1:12,13) and finally we find him at Dalmatia (II Tim. 4:10) again among a rough class of people.

Titus and Timothy were probably closer to Paul than any of his co-workers, and in this fact we learn how wonderfully God provided the moral and spiritual support the apostle so often needed in his strenuous ministry, for these two young pastors differed greatly in nature and character, yet both were so valuable to Paul.

As we have already pointed out, it is evident from Paul's letters to Timothy that he was cultured and refined, a student from his youth, delicate in health and possessing, as was natural from his upbringing, an almost feminine tenderness. The apostle writes to him about his childhood, his mother, his grandmother and his tears; prescribes for his "often infirmities" and begs him not to be ashamed or afraid or weak, but to be strong, as *"a good soldier of Jesus Christ."* This sincere and refined young man, a teacher by nature, proved a great help to Paul and served with him as *"a son with the father"* (Phil. 2:19,22).

Titus was a very different character. This is quite evident from Paul's letter to him, in which he addresses him as an army general might address his lieutenant; directing him to *set in order the things that are wanting*, to *exhort and convince the gainsayers*, to *stop the mouths of unruly and vain talkers*, to *rebuke sharply* those who lived careless lives, to *show himself a pattern of good works* and to *reject wilful heretics*.

An interesting comparison between Timothy and Titus is to be found in what Paul has to say with respect to visits they made to Corinth.

Timothy was head and shoulders above the Corinthian believers, both morally and spiritually, yet when Paul sent him there, he had to write a letter ahead, exhorting them: "Now if Timotheus come, *see that he may be with you without fear*; for he worketh the work of the Lord, as also I do. *Let no man therefore despise him...*" (I Cor. 16:10,11). But later, when Titus had been to Corinth and had returned, Paul wrote them: "And his inward affection is more abundant toward you, whilst he remembereth the *obedience* of you all, how with fear and trembling *ye* received *him*"! (II Cor. 7:15).

Titus, then, was the more robust character of the two, yet far from *coarse* or *crude*. Indeed, he was by nature a remarkable combination of enthusiasm and discretion and, certainly, integrity (See II Cor. 12:18).

REPORT FROM CORINTH

Paul needed a friend like Titus. We have discussed the apostle's anxiety and mental depression both at Troas and in Macedonia, and while this state of mind was partly due to his apprehensions regarding the church at Corinth, it was also partly due to his disappointment at failing to find Titus, whose bouyant faith had so often encouraged and refreshed him.

He left Troas, he says, *not* first of all, because he had failed to hear from Corinth, but *"because I found not Titus, my brother"* (II Cor. 2:13) and regarding his "troubled" condition in Macedonia, he says that "God, that comforteth those that are cast down," comforted him, first of all, *"by the coming of Titus,"* and *then* by the news he brought from Corinth (See II Cor. 7:5-7).

It was a relief to Paul to learn from his friend that conditions at the Corinthian church had improved measurably; that the majority had sincerely mourned over their conduct, had shown an earnest desire to live pleasing to God and were still devoted to him (II Cor. 7:7); also that they were still glad to do their part with regard to the offering being gathered for the poor saints in Judaea (II Cor. 9:1,2).

There was, however, an obstinate minority whom Paul's letters, and perhaps the visits of his associates, had only embittered. From Paul's replies to them we gather that they attributed his interest in the collection for the Judaean saints to personal monetary motives (II Cor. 12:17,18) yet asserted that he could be no true apostle, since he accepted no financial support! (II Cor. 11:7); that they compared, to his disparagement, the credentials Apollos had presented (Acts 18:27) with Paul's lack of them (II Cor. 3:1,2); that they sneered at his bodily infirmities (II Cor. 10:10) and charged that his declared intentions to come and visit them were all a bluff; that he was actually *afraid* to appear among them (II Cor. 1:15-18; 13:1-3).

Thus it was that Paul sent Titus[2] back to Corinth[3] with another letter, that which we know as the *second*

---

2.   Along with two other trusted brethren (II Cor. 8:18,22).

3.   That II Corinthians was written from Macedonia (possibly Philippi) at this time, and sent by the hand of Titus, is concluded from the following facts: Paul had come from Asia, via Troas to Macedonia (II Cor. 1:8; 2:12,13) was now in Macedonia (II Cor. 9:2,4) had met Titus there and had received the news from Corinth (II Cor. 7:5,6) had sent Titus back with this letter (II Cor. 8:6,16-18) and was soon himself to follow (II Cor. 9:4; 13:1).

epistle to the Corinthians. This letter had a twofold character containing expressions of love and joy to the obedient, and of rebuke and warning to the disobedient. Paul sent this letter to prepare the way for his third visit to them, to defend himself against the charges of his enemies and to warn them that their enmity would not deter him from exerting his apostolic authority and power if they persisted in their rebellion (See II Cor. 10:2-6; 13:1-3). And there was still another reason:

THE COLLECTION FOR THE JUDAEAN SAINTS

As we have already intimated, the apostle had for some time been gathering an offering for the poor saints in Judaea. He had several reasons for engaging in this project. First, he felt it was the *duty* of the Gentiles, who were now being made partakers of Israel's spiritual things, to minister to *them* in material things (Rom. 15:25-27). Second, he had *promised* to remember Israel's poor (Gal. 2:10). Third, he hoped that a generous gift from the Gentile believers would serve to *improve relations* between the church at Jerusalem and the Gentile churches (Rom. 15:31; II Cor. 9:12,13).

Evidently the churches of at least four provinces had joined in this undertaking. In the Corinthian letters three of these provinces are mentioned in this connection: *Galatia* (I Cor. 16:1) *Macedonia* (II Cor. 8:1-4) and *Achaia* (II Cor. 9:2). Then, if Acts 20:4 is a list of the delegates thus far entrusted with the delivery of the gift (as it appears to be) *Asia* must also be included.

This was not the first time, of course, that the Gentile churches had helped the Judaean churches

185

financially. Regarding the request of the leaders at Jerusalem that the Gentile churches remember their poor, Paul had commented to the Galatians: *"Which very thing I was also zealous to do"* (Gal. 2:10, R.V.).

And indeed the apostle had been used to deliver Gentile bounty to Jerusalem years before this, when the believers at Syrian Antioch had "sent relief unto the brethren which dwelt in Judaea" (Acts 11:29,30).

This alone is evidence enough that the Pentecostal program, with its "all things common," had broken down. *Then* the Church at Jerusalem had enjoyed great prosperity, *"neither was there any among them that lacked"* (Acts 4:32-35); but since then the Gentile church at Antioch, and now those in the provinces of Galatia, Asia, Macedonia and Achaia, had all had to come to the support of *"the poor saints...at Jerusalem."* Thus the picture, unlike that presented in prophecy, is one of needy Jews receiving "alms" from the Gentiles (Acts 24:17).

PAUL THE PROMOTER

Probably the great majority of believers have looked upon Paul as one who devoted himself almost entirely to prayer, Bible study and preaching, and had as little as possible to do with organization and finances.

How wrong they are! It is doubtful, in fact, whether there ever was a greater *promoter* than Paul. Wherever he went he *organized* churches and great evangelistic endeavors, and during the period of Acts which we are now considering he was actively engaged in an organized campaign to raise funds—large funds—for the needy saints in Judaea.

HIS INTEGRITY

One reason why he could do this so well was because, unlike some modern money raisers in the Church, he had a fine sense of honor with respect to pecuniary transactions, and his conduct in financial matters was beyond reproach.

He could sincerely say to Felix:

"And herein do I exercise myself, to have always a conscience void of offence toward God, and toward men" (Acts 24:16).

Evidently Felix considered this a mere platitude at first, but finally he learned that he had "hoped" in vain for a bribe from the apostle (Acts 24:26).

When Paul besought Philemon to forgive his runaway slave and to accept him now as "a brother beloved" (Phile. 15,16) he was careful to offer to assume personally any indebtedness Onesimus may have incurred—and *this* was no empty gesture, for he declared: *"I Paul have written it with mine own hand; I will repay it"* (Vers. 18,19).

He could challenge those who knew him well: *"We have defrauded no man"* (II Cor. 7:2) *"Did I make a gain of you?...Did Titus make a gain of you? Walked we not in the same spirit...in the same steps?"* (II Cor. 12:17,18). *"I have coveted no man's silver, or gold, or apparel"* (Acts 20:33) and, as proof, he could add: *"Yea, ye yourselves know, that these hands have ministered unto my necessities, and to them that were with me"* (Ver. 34).

And thus, too, he managed the campaign to raise funds for the circumcision saints in Judaea.

The men listed in Acts 20:4 were doubtless trustees,[4] chosen by the churches themselves to transport their gifts to Jerusalem. To the Corinthians he had sent explicit instructions that whoever *they* should approve, *in writing*, would be delegated to bring *their* liberality to Jerusalem and that, *if it seemed proper*, he would head the delegation (I Cor. 16:3,4). And now he introduces to them *"the messengers of the churches"* of Macedonia (II Cor. 8:23) two men of God, *"chosen of the churches to travel with us with this grace"* (Ver. 19).

All these precautions were taken, as he explains:

"...that no man should blame us in this abundance which is administered by us:

"Providing for honest things, not only in the sight of the Lord, but also in the sight of men" (II Cor. 8:20,21).

Leaders in Christian work would do well to learn these lessons from the great apostle of grace, lest they bring reproach upon Christ and His cause by careless or illicit handling of funds committed to their trust.

HIS FUND-RAISING METHODS

It is an interesting fact that many who would commend the preacher for exhorting believers as to their testimony and conduct, would soon condemn him for exhorting them as to *giving*.

Indeed, some men of God have actually boasted that they tell no one but the Lord[5] about the needs of His work. This is a distinct departure, not only from Scripture, but from the *Pauline* Scriptures on this

---

4. Possibly excepting Timothy.
5. Though, inconsistently, they generally keep telling *others* how they tell *only the Lord!*

subject, for *giving* is as much a part of the Christian life as are testimony and conduct, and the man of God who forbears to exhort his hearers as to giving, on the ground that "the Lord knows all about it," may as well also forbear to exhort them as to their witness and walk on that basis.

This is not to deny, as we have said, that *some* fundraising in the professing Church does indicate a lack of faith, spirituality and even honesty, and those who are responsible, under God, for the financing of His work should search their consciences and ask God for the sincerity, integrity and spirituality of Paul in this matter.

The letter which Paul wrote to the Corinthians at this time contains more instruction as to giving and fund-raising than any other.

In soliciting funds for the poor saints at Jerusalem, the apostle did not engage in dramatic emotional appeals or in schemes by which the donors would be giving more than they realized. On the contrary, he frankly tells them the need, and reminds them of their privilege and responsibility in the matter. Nor is there any indication of the hysteria that has often characterized frantic appeals for funds to carry on the Lord's work. He is *sane* and *reasonable* in the matter.

Indeed, he carefully *avoided* making dramatic and frantic appeals, for he had written them some time previously, urging them to *save systematically* toward this contribution (I Cor. 16:1,2). And rather than using high-pressure methods, he made it very clear to them that each should give only *"as he purposeth in his heart...not grudgingly, or of necessity"* (II Cor. 9:7).

He exhibited a spirit of *fairness*, too, in his appeal for funds. "Upon the first day of the week," he had said,

"Let every one of you lay by him in store, *as God hath prospered him*" (I Cor. 16:2) and in the letter before us he emphasizes this:

"For if there be first a willing mind, it is accepted according to that a man hath, and not according to that he hath not.

"For I mean not that other men be eased and ye burdened" (II Cor. 8:12,13).

It must be remembered, however, that the carnal Corinthians had been far from liberal in their support of the Lord's work or of Paul, His servant. Doubtless the largest of the assemblies, they could easily have supplied Paul's meagre needs, yet, while toiling so earnestly among them he had had to work with his hands for his own support, and that while other churches, especially the Philippians, had sought him out to help him (Phil. 4:15,16 cf. II Cor. 11:7-9).

Regarding the contribution to the Judaean saints the Corinthians had exhibited the same trait. They had shown great zeal in the matter a year previous and had evidently begun the weekly collection, but this was now being neglected (II Cor. 8:10) and Titus' latest visit, having resulted only in more promises, the apostle sent him back with further instructions and exhortations about it.

With God-given tact the apostle tells them that it is, in a sense, "superfluous" to write to them about this ministry to the saints, for he knows the forwardness of their *minds* and has boasted to those of Macedonia "that Achaia was ready[6] a year ago" (II Cor. 9:1,2). He

---

6. Not with the complete offering, but ready to put their plans into operation.

190

informs them, too, that their *zeal* (not their performance) has "provoked very many" (II Cor. 9:2).

But their intentions must be carried out without further delay. Thus the apostle apprises them of the large contribution already made by the churches of Macedonia, and this not out of an abundance, but out of their *"deep poverty"* (8:1-3). Indeed, he bore the Macedonians record that they had earnestly besought him to accept a larger contribution than they could reasonably afford (II Cor. 8:3,4). And, he is careful to point out, this was all the result of *a healthy spiritual condition* (II Cor. 8:2,5).

To this challenge the apostle adds several others. They abound in *other* graces, why not in *this*? (II Cor. 8:7); should they not *prove* the *sincerity* of their professed love to Christ and His people? (II Cor. 8:8); they were ready and eager a year ago; now they should *"perform the doing of it"* (II Cor. 8:11); they now have an "abundance" with which to supply the "want" of others; some day the tables may be turned, so that *they* will need the help (II Cor. 8:14). And, of course, he advances what must always be the strongest argument of all:

"For ye know the grace of our Lord Jesus Christ, that, though He was rich, yet for your sakes He became poor, that ye through His poverty might be rich" **(II Cor. 8:9).**

Paul had praised the Corinthians before others, but now found it necessary to send "the brethren" lest this "boasting...should be in vain" and lest, perchance the delegates from Macedonia, coming with him, should find them unprepared, and both he and they should be made ashamed (II Cor. 9:3,4). The chief of these "brethren" was, of course, Titus, sent to "finish" what he had "begun" some considerable time previous (II Cor. 8:6).

Together, these brethren were to "make up beforehand" the offering of which the Corinthians had now had ample "notice," that it might be *ready* as a *surplus*, gladly bestowed, rather than an incomplete offering turned over as a matter of necessity before it was ready (II Cor. 9:5). Thus the apostle challenges them:

"Wherefore show ye to them, and before the churches, the proof of your love, and of our boasting on your behalf" (II Cor. 8:24).

"He which soweth sparingly shall reap also sparingly; and he which soweth bountifully shall reap also bountifully.

"Every man according as he purposeth in his heart, so let him give; not grudgingly, or of necessity; for God loveth a cheerful giver.

"And God is able to make all grace abound toward you; that ye, always having all sufficiency in all things, may abound to every good work" **(II Cor. 9:6-8).**

How many of God's children need these exhortations today! Even those in ordinary circumstances here in America have much of this world's goods—so much that too often they only want more for themselves and forget their responsibility toward God and others. The rich, generally begin by wanting "security." When they have *that*, they tell themselves, they will do their part in the Lord's work. As though there could be a place of greater security than the center of God's will! The result is almost always the same. They are never sure that they have *enough* security and their funds are always "tied up" in business so that they fail to meet the challenge and enjoy the privilege of having a substantial part in the Lord's work. Thank God for the exceptions, for they are few. Any leader in the cause of Christ

192

witnesses the contrast between the Macedonians and the Corinthians over and over again as some who have so little bear so large a part of the financial load, while others, who have so much, share so little.

Before leaving the subject of this letter to the Corinthians, it should be observed that it contains much additional information about Paul's sufferings not found in the Book of Acts.

Here he tells about the "trouble" that had overwhelmed him in Asia, how he had been "pressed out of measure, above strength, insomuch that [he had] despaired even of life" (1:8). Here he tells of his physical frailty and the pain that he endured everywhere he went (II Cor. 4:7-5:10; 12:7-9). Here he tells about his mental anxiety at Troas (2:12,13) his struggles, fears and discouragement in Macedonia (7:5) and gives a long list of persecutions and sufferings thus far endured, including stripes, imprisonments, floggings, shipwrecks, a night and a day in the deep, exhausting journeys, all sorts of perils, hunger, thirst, cold, nakedness and—that burden from which he was never relieved: *"the care of all the churches"* (II Cor. 11:23-28).

Surely the plea of one so utterly devoted to the cause of Christ should have its effect upon the Corinthian believers—and upon us. While "the brethren" went to Corinth with this new letter, Paul remained in Macedonia to let their ministry and his epistle do their work.

"Those parts" which the apostle "went over" at this time must have included a larger area of Macedonia than he had previously visited, for it is evidently while on this journey that he wrote that he had "preached the gospel of Christ" "round about unto Illyricum" and "now" had "no more place in these parts" (Rom. 15:19,23).

193

The apostle had pledged his word to visit Corinth, by the will of God, and we have no doubt that the "three months" in Greece were spent mainly at Corinth, at the home of one of the first converts there—*Gaius* (See I Cor. 1:14 cf. Rom. 16:23).

LETTERS TO GALATIA AND ROME

While we cannot, probably, be entirely certain as to the date of the Galatian epistle, or the place from which it was written, there appear to be some indications that it was at about this time when Paul received word from the churches of Galatia which filled him with astonishment and indignation. The Judaizers had been busy again and had been largely successful not only in bringing the Gentile believers there under the bondage of the law but, as in the case of the Corinthians, in minimizing Paul's apostleship and message. As a result of this "disobedience to the truth" (Gal. 3:1; 5:7) they had lost "the blessedness" they once had known (4:15) so that they "bit and devoured" each other (5:15).

So rapidly had the situation deteriorated in Galatia that Paul immediately penned a letter to them with his own hand, defending his God-given apostleship and re-emphasizing the importance of the special message of grace which the glorified Lord had committed to him. There is more of a tone of extreme urgency in this letter to the Galatians than in any of his other epistles.

One of the indications that the Epistle to the Galatians was written at about this time is its internal similarity to the Roman epistle, both as to doctrine and emphasis.

That *Romans* was written at this time is almost certain, for it was evidently sent from Corinth, where

194

Erastus was the city treasurer (Rom. 16:23 cf. II Tim. 4:20) and Gaius Paul's host (Rom. 16:23 cf. I Cor. 1:14). It was written after Aquila and Priscilla had returned to Rome (Rom. 16:3) and after Paul had "purposed in the spirit" to go to Jerusalem and Rome (Acts 19:21) indeed, when he was about to travel to Jerusalem with the "contribution for the poor saints" there (Rom. 15:25,26).

Writing materials would doubtless be available at the home of Gaius, and Tertius, an amanuensis,[7] was ready to pen the letter at his dictation (Rom. 16:22,23). Haply also, Phoebe, a well known deaconess, or servant, of the church at Cenchrea (the eastern seaport of Corinth) was about to leave for Rome on business at this time. It was doubtless she who carried the letter or at least accompanied those who did. Evidently Phoebe was a woman of some rank, and faithful as a Christian, for the apostle commends her as having been "a succourer [Lit. *one who stands before, a protector*] of many," including himself, and requests the believers at Rome to receive her and to assist her in her business in any way they can (Rom. 16:1,2).

Godly women had a great, if subordinate part in Paul's ministry almost wherever he went. The first convert in Europe, at Philippi, was a woman (Acts 16:14) and the women of the Philippian church had labored with Paul in the gospel (Phil. 4:3) and probably were still doing so at the time he wrote the Philippians from prison in Rome (Phil. 1:3-5). At Thessalonica the believers included "chief [leading] women not a few" (Acts 17:4). At Berea, too, those who believed included "not a

---

7.   A comparison of Romans 16:22 with I Corinthians 16:21, II Thessalonians 3:17 and even Galatians 6:11, indicate that it was not uncommon for Paul to dictate his letters to an amanuensis; indeed that it *was* uncommon for him to do otherwise.

195

few" "honorable women who were Greeks" (Acts 17:12). At Athens one of the only two converts named was a woman (Acts 17:34). At Corinth and Cenchrea there were Priscilla (Acts 18:2,26) and Phoebe (Rom. 16:1) and in his Epistle to the Romans the apostle names several others (Rom. 16).

It is a noteworthy fact that considerably before Paul reached Rome a church had already been established there whose faith was "spoken of throughout the whole world" (Rom. 1:8). Those who suppose these believers were the disciples of circumcision saints who had traveled there from Judaea, should take note that it was *Paul's* gospel, and *not* "the gospel of the kingdom" or "the gospel of the circumcision," that had already begun to reach distant lands and would soon reach out into all the known world (See Rom. 16:25,26; Col. 1:6,23; II Tim. 4:16,17; Titus 2:11).

Doubtless the apostle, in his extensive journeys, gained many helpers who, for business or other reasons, traveled to the metropolis and were used to plant the gospel of the grace of God there. Indeed, the closing lines of his Epistle to the Romans indicates that he already knew a considerable number of the believers there.

BACK THROUGH MACEDONIA TO TROAS

After a three months' stay in Achaia, or Greece, the apostle set out, probably to Cenchrea, to sail across the Mediterranean Sea to Syria, but just as he was about to board ship he learned of a plot by the Jews to capture or kill him and changed his plans so as to return through Macedonia instead (Ver. 3). Whether this new route took him over land or by another ship we do not know, though the latter seems more probable.

196

It appears from Verses 4 to 6 that, to foil the assassins' plot, seven of those who "accompanied" Paul "into Asia" boarded the ship to Troas as scheduled, as though there had been no change in plans, while Paul and his "beloved physician"[8] went north to Macedonia and sailed from Philippi (or Neapolis, its nearby port) to meet the others at Troas.

And here we come upon another one of those symbolic narratives which have become familiar to us in the Book of Acts.

---

8.   The change of person to "us" and "we" in Verses 5 and 6 and to the end of Acts, indicates that Luke had again joined the apostle and doubtless stayed with him until his imprisonment in Rome.

PAUL'S MINISTRY AT TROAS

THE MAN WHO FELL ASLEEP
IN CHURCH

"And we sailed away from Philippi after the days of unleavened bread, and came unto them to Troas in five days; where we abode seven days.

"And upon the first day of the week, when the disciples came together to break bread, Paul preached unto them, ready to depart on the morrow; and continued his speech until midnight.

"And there were many lights in the upper chamber, where they were gathered together.

"And there sat in a window a certain young man named Eutychus, being fallen into a deep sleep: and as Paul was long preaching, he sunk down with sleep, and fell down from the third loft, and was taken up dead.

"And Paul went down, and fell on him, and embracing him said, Trouble not yourselves; for his life is in him.

"When he therefore was come up again, and had broken bread, and eaten, and talked a long while, even till break of day, so he departed.

"And they brought the young man alive, and were not a little comforted."

—Acts 20:6-12

It may be observed that this trip from Philippi to Troas took five days, while a previous trip from Troas to Philippi took only two (Acts 16:11). This could be

198

because they encountered *storm* on this present occasion or otherwise *calm* (equally retarding) or even because they now encountered as a *headwind* the same wind that had previously sped them on their way.

A comparison of Acts 20:7 with I Corinthians 16:2 seems to indicate that already it had become the custom of the believers to meet together on "the first day of the week," rather than on the Sabbath, so that Paul's "custom" of going into the synagogue on the Sabbath days was rather in order that he might minister to them *when they were assembled together*.

Probably the Christian believers met on *our* Saturday night, however, since according to Jewish reckoning sundown on Saturday evening marked the close of the Sabbath and the beginning of the next day. That it was night time is evident from the interesting episode we are now to consider.

It must have been a rare treat to the congregation at Troas to find so many distinguished visitors present as they "came together to break bread." There was a friend from Berea and two from Thessalonica; another from Derbe and two others from their own province. There, also, was the well-known and beloved Timothy, along with Dr. Luke and the Apostle Paul himself (Vers. 4-6).

Of course they asked Paul to be the speaker of the evening, especially since he was "ready to depart on the morrow" (Ver. 7).

What a rare privilege it was to sit at his feet: the former arch-enemy of Christ, now His special representative and a veteran in His service! In all probability he would relate to them how the glorified Lord had stopped him in his wild career, *saving* him, to *"show forth all longsuffering, for a pattern"* to those

199

who should thereafter believe on Him (I Tim. 1:16) and committing to him *"the gospel of the grace of God"* (Acts 20:24).

Though he must leave on the morrow the apostle did not spare himself. He might not see them again, and there was so much to say by way of encouragement and exhortation, instruction and warning!

But who could not listen to such a man preach, even if he "continued his speech until midnight"? Who, in any congregation, could even become drowsy under *his* teaching?

Yet someone *did* fall asleep during that service—someone named *Eutychus*. Of course, he was a "young man." Perhaps he had been very active that day. Besides, there were "many lights" in the place of meeting and evidently a capacity audience, for this young man "sat in a window." All this might well tend to make one's eyes heavy.

Of course Eutychus, sitting where he did, did not mean to allow himself to fall so soundly asleep. Doubtless he fought sleep at first and then merely indulged in a bit of dozing, but before long he had *"fallen into a deep sleep; and as Paul was long preaching, he sank down with sleep"* (Ver. 9).

The results were by no means amusing for, losing his balance, Eutychus fell from his position in the window sill to the ground, three floors below "and was taken up dead"[1] (Ver. 9).

Picture the consternation that must have followed: Paul's preaching interrupted by cries of horror; men

---

1. As a physician, Luke had evidently satisfied himself on this point.

rushing down with lamps or torches; the joy of the night turned into lamentation as they view the bruised and lifeless form of Eutychus lying there on the ground below.

At this point Paul *"fell on him, and embracing him*[2] *said, Trouble not yourselves* [Lit. *'Do not be alarmed'*]; *for his life is in him"*[3] (Ver. 10).

Eutychus means *Fortunate*, and fortunate he was that Paul was the preacher that night, for by the goodness and power of God the apostle restored him to life.

How could they close the meeting now? Yet Paul was to travel on again the next day. Thus we read that he came up again, partook of some refreshments[4] and "talked [*'conversed,'* not *'preached'* as in Verse 7] a long while, even till the break of day."

"And *so* he departed" (Ver. 11). The "so" is emphasized in the Greek to call attention to the happy circumstances attending his departure.

"And they brought [Lit. "took away"] the young man alive, and were not a little comforted" (Ver. 12).

---

2. Rather out of sympathy and affection, than to imitate Elijah and Elisha (I Kings 17:21; II Kings 4:34).

3. There is no contradiction here. As in the cases of Elijah and Elisha, it was Paul's act that, under God, had brought Eutychus back to life.

4. The *breaking of bread* is a familiar Hebraism for *dining together* (see Matt. 14:19; Acts 2:46; *et al*) and does not necessarily refer to the celebration of the Lord's supper. Further the fact that the original word for "eat" in Verse 11 is *geuomai, "to taste,"* would sooner indicate that the Lord's supper is *not* referred to, for the word used in the records of the Lord's supper is not *geuomai,* but *phago,* the more usual word for *eat.* The word *taste* is doubtless used here because, the anxiety being now passed, he *enjoyed* the food. In both Verses 7 and 11 the context must decide whether the breaking of bread refers to the Lord's supper or to a common meal.

THE SYMBOLIC SIGNIFICANCE
OF THIS EPISODE

The striking symbolic significance of this episode is immediately seen when we note the following facts:

1. Paul was the preacher.

2. He continued to preach for a long time.

3. Someone fell asleep under his preaching.

4. The sleeper fell from the third story window to the ground below and was "taken up dead."

5. Paul, under God, restored him to life.

PAUL IS PREACHING TODAY

Christ on earth had sent the twelve to proclaim *"repentance and remission of sins...In His name among all nations, BEGINNING AT JERUSALEM"* (Luke 24:47).

They had begun at Jerusalem, crying to the "men of Israel":

"Repent, and be baptized every one of you in the name of Jesus Christ for the remission of sins..." (Acts 2:38).

Shortly after Pentecost, Peter had said to his Jewish hearers:

"Ye are the children of the prophets, and of the covenant which God made with our fathers, saying unto Abraham, And in thy seed shall all the kindreds of the earth be blessed.

"Unto you first God, having raised up His Son Jesus, sent Him to bless you, in turning away every one of you from his iniquities" (Acts 3:25,26).

202

From the words of our Lord and of Spirit-filled Peter, as well as from the Scriptures written up to that time, it is clear that it was God's revealed purpose to bless the nations *through redeemed Israel*.

Israel as a nation, however, spurned the call to repentance and continued to reject her Messiah, even waging organized war against Him.

It was then that God showed *"the exceeding riches of His grace,"* by *saving* Saul, the leader of the rebellion, and sending him forth with an offer of reconciliation by grace through faith.

Galatians 2:7-9 shows how the twelve, who had been sent to "all nations," now recognized (through their leaders) the change in program and acknowledged Paul as "the apostle of the Gentiles."

The so-called "great commission" had been brought to a standstill by Israel's disobedience. The establishment of the kingdom was to be held in abeyance. God had "concluded them all in unbelief *that He might have mercy upon all"* and Paul was sent forth to proclaim this glad news. To him was committed *"the dispensation of the grace of God"* (Eph. 3:1-3).

PAUL HAS BEEN
PREACHING LONG

Paul has been preaching long—even longer than Moses. Moses preached for about fifteen hundred years; *Paul* has been preaching for more than *nineteen* hundred. The law reigned for about fifteen centuries; *grace* has been reigning for *nineteen* centuries. How great is the longsuffering of God!

203

In I Timothy 1:16 Paul explains:

"Howbeit for this cause I obtained mercy, that in me first [or 'chiefly'] Jesus Christ might show forth all longsuffering, for a pattern to them which should hereafter believe on Him to life everlasting."

In II Peter 3:9 and 15 *Peter* explains that the Lord "is not slack concerning His promise" to judge and reign, "but is *longsuffering* to usward, *not willing that any should perish*, but that all should come to repentance," and bids us "account that":

"The longsuffering of our Lord is salvation; even as our beloved brother Paul also according to the wisdom given unto him hath written unto you."

And *still* the day of wrath has not come! *Still* the message of grace goes forth! *Still* Paul is preaching!

AND THERE ARE MANY LIGHTS

If there is one fact which is recognized by all who have come to rejoice in the message of Paul, it is the fact that it explains so many otherwise difficult passages of Scripture and solves so many otherwise insurmountable problems. Where Paul preaches there are "many lights." Of course! His message was not called *"the secret"* for nothing!

It is indescribably wonderful to have one difficult passage after another become clear as this sacred secret is unfolded; to see light after light go on. Yet the very increase of the light we receive on the Word can lull us to sleep if we are not convicted and exercised by it. And this is just what has happened.

204

THE CHURCH FELL ASLEEP
UNDER PAUL'S PREACHING

Not all at once, to be sure, but one after another, the Church lost hold of those glorious truths which are so distinctively Pauline: The *"mystery"* of the Body of Christ, its heavenly calling and position, the *Rapture*, the blessed hope of our Lord's coming *for us* before He declares war on the ungodly; and even the truth of *justification by faith alone*. All these were let go, one by one until, during the dark ages the Church had fallen into *"a deep sleep"* and, like Eutychus, had *"sunk down with sleep."*

THE CHURCH FELL FROM ITS
POSITION IN THE THIRD LOFT

Paul speaks of having been caught up to the *third* heaven (II Cor. 12:2). This is the highest, as far as Scripture is concerned, and it reminds us that we, who trust in Christ, have been made to sit together with Him "in *heavenly places* [Gr. *epouranious*, the *upper-heavenlies*]" (Eph. 1:20; 2:6) there to be blessed with *"all spiritual blessings"* (Eph. 1:3).

As the Church fell asleep under Paul's preaching the appreciation and enjoyment of all this was lost and the life of the Church was gone. Could it be awakened from this sleep of death? How it needed someone in those dark ages to cry: *"Awake thou that sleepest, and arise from the dead, and Christ shall give thee light!"* (Eph. 5:14).

Eutychus! *Fortunate!*

Surely it was only infinite grace that raised up men like Martin Luther and later John Darby and others to awaken the Church and restore it to life again.

205

PAUL USED TO RESTORE THE
CHURCH TO LIFE AGAIN

Actually, however, it was not Luther or Darby or any of the great men of God since the dark ages, who were used to restore the Church to life, for they preached nothing new. Luther, with his *"grace alone"* and *"the just shall live by faith,"* and Darby, with his proclamation of the *"one body"* and the *"blessed hope,"* were only recovering truths first revealed through Paul.

As it was Paul who was used to restore Eutychus to life, so it is Paul who has been used to restore the Church of this dispensation to life, as men like Luther, Calvin and Darby have been raised up to gradually recover the glorious truths of the Pauline revelation.

One thing remains to complete the picture. Eutychus must be restored to his position in the "third loft." The Church must once more be induced to *occupy* her position in the heavenlies, for there are still thousands of true believers who neither understand nor enjoy their God-given position in the heavenlies in Christ.

Whether Eutychus *did* actually return to the "third loft" again, the Scripture does not clearly state, perhaps lest we should *presume* that the Church will thus return to her God-given place before the dispensation closes.

We *do* know, however, that after it was all over they "brought [i.e., *brought away*] the young man alive, and were not a little comforted" (Ver. 12).

And so—who knows how soon?—the Church which is His Body will be taken away from this scene forever to be with the Lord. *"Wherefore comfort one another with these words"* (I Thes. 4:13-18).

206

In the raising of *Dorcas* (Lit. *Gazelle*) by *Peter*, the emphasis is upon her *activities* and *good works* (Acts 9:36). In the raising of *Eutychus* by *Paul*, no such emphasis is found. He was simply "Fortunate." Thus, symbolically, God's dealings with Israel and with the Body of Christ are compared.

PAUL'S LAST RETURN TO JERUSALEM

FROM TROAS TO MILETUS

"And we went before to ship, and sailed unto Assos, there intending to take in Paul: for so had he appointed, minding himself to go afoot.

"And when he met with us at Assos, we took him in and came to Mitylene.

"And we sailed thence, and came the next day over against Chios; and the next day we arrived at Samos, and tarried at Trogylium; and the next day we came to Miletus.

"For Paul had determined to sail by Ephesus, because he would not spend the time in Asia: for he hasted, if it were possible for him, to be at Jerusalem the day of Pentecost."

—Acts 20:13-16

Paul's seven companions were sent ahead by ship to Assos, while he himself went by foot to meet them. The journey by sea was about forty miles, while that by land was only twenty.

It has been supposed that the apostle adopted this plan that he might enjoy a few more precious hours of fellowship with the disciples at Troas.

The fact that Verse 11 states that he had already "departed," however, and the fact that he chose to travel *alone*, without even Luke (Ver. 14) would seem rather to indicate a desire for *solitude* after the busy time at Troas.

208

Christian fellowship is a blessed experience, but even an apostle would need time for prayer and meditation.[1]

It appears that after taking Paul in at Assos the ship stopped every evening. The reason for this seems quite evident. The summer winds in the Aegean Sea begin blowing from the north early in the morning and die down in the late afternoon.

There has been considerable debate as to whether a regular trading vessel was used on this occasion or whether Paul and his company had engaged a small coast vessel for their private use. Such able expositors as Geikie say they hired their own vessel, while Howson and others insist that this is "surely quite a mistake."

The apparent indications that the vessel was privately engaged are as follows: The ship, if a trader, would have followed her own course. Here, however, she stopped at Assos, apparently only to pick up Paul, and passed by Ephesus simply because Paul was in a hurry and did not wish to stop there. Furthermore, nothing is stated about any other business on this voyage.

Still it seems to us gratuitous to assume from this that Paul and his company had hired the vessel for themselves.

Doubtless this *was* a smaller vessel designed only for use along the coast, for it sailed only from Troas to Patara (Acts 21:1). But it seems too much to assume that because no other business is mentioned it sailed to Assos *only* to pick up Paul. Paul may well have decided to walk to Assos because he knew the vessel was to stop there.

---

1. Especially since the Holy Spirit was witnessing "in every city" that "bonds and afflictions" awaited him, and he feared he would not come this way again (Acts 20:23,25).

209

But even if it did sail to Assos only to take Paul aboard; this still does not prove that it was *privately hired* by Paul and his company, for the captain of a small coastal vessel might well be glad thus to accommodate a company of nine passengers. And as to *sailing by* Ephesus, the text does not state that Paul had determined that the *ship* should do this, but that *he* should do this, i.e., that he would stay aboard rather than disembark there. Indeed, the passage may mean simply that Paul chose a ship in the first place which sailed past Ephesus.

The apostle passed by Ephesus because he hastened to reach Jerusalem by Pentecost and he well knew that he could not appear on the scene among so many converts, friends and co-workers without being detained for a considerable length of time. He would therefore disembark instead at Miletus, some thirty miles further, and from there summon only the elders of the church for a farewell message of encouragement and exhortation. In this way more lasting results might be attained.

WAS PAUL OUT OF THE WILL OF GOD IN GOING TO JERUSALEM?

Perhaps this is the place to consider whether Paul was right or wrong in making this last journey to Jerusalem. This is by no means easy to determine and, depend upon it: those who deal with the subject as though it were a simple matter have given serious consideration to only one side of it—*their* side.

In our research on this subject we were amazed at two things: 1.) the extreme scarcity of comprehensive writings on a subject so manifestly significant, and 2.) the fact that the brief comments in most commentaries on Acts are so one-sided, ignoring the arguments on one side or the other, according to the author's views.[2]

We venture, therefore, to list the main Scriptural arguments on both sides and then see how they may be reconciled.

THE ARGUMENTS FOR PAUL'S GOING TO JERUSALEM AT THIS TIME

These are mostly as follows:

1. Paul's plans were not made "according to the flesh" (II Cor. 1:15-17).

2. Later, standing before the Sanhedrin, and still later, in a letter to Timothy, he declared that from his youth he had served God with a clear conscience (Acts 23:1; II Tim. 1:3).

3. He declared his determination to continue the journey to Jerusalem that he might finish his course and his ministry *"with joy"* (Acts 20:24).

4. When his friends could not dissuade him from his purpose, they said: *"The will of the Lord be done"* (Acts 21:14).

5. After Paul had reached Jerusalem the Lord, rather than rebuking him, *encouraged* him saying: *"Be of good cheer, Paul; for as thou hast testified of me in Jerusalem, so must thou bear witness also at Rome"* (Acts 23:11).

6. Shortly before his death Paul wrote: *"I have fought a good fight, I have finished my course, I have kept the faith,"* (II Tim. 4:7) which, it is alleged, he could

---

2. This is also so with regard to Paul's subjection to Jewish ritualism while at Jerusalem, but this will be considered later.

211

not have said had he been out of the will of the Lord in making this journey to Jerusalem.

But these arguments are not as conclusive as they may seem at first sight. While we agree that it was not the *flesh* that prompted the apostle to go to Jerusalem at this time, it should be observed that in II Corinthians 1:15-17 the apostle does not refer to *all* his plans, or purposes, much less to his purpose to visit Jerusalem for the last time. In this passage he refers to his former plan to visit the *Corinthians* (Ver. 15). It is with respect to the *change* in this plan that he protests: *"Did I use lightness? Or the things that I purpose, do I purpose according to the flesh?"* (Ver. 17).

As to the apostle's assertions that from his youth he had lived before God "in all good conscience," it is certainly clear from his own writings that he was far from perfect and that these statements refer, not to all the details of his life, but rather to his adopted course, in first opposing Christ, then turning to Him and serving Him. Moreover, the fact that he even persecuted Christ with a clear conscience (Acts 26:9) proves that it is possible to do *wrong* with a clear, though warped, conscience.

Numbers 3 and 4 above will be dealt with later, but we pause here to touch briefly upon Numbers 5 and 6.

No one would deny that Paul's *motives* in going to Jerusalem at this time were the highest; that he went with a heart filled with love to Christ and to his kinsmen; risking his very life in going. Is it strange, then, that God should *encourage* him after his noble stand before the angry multitude at Jerusalem and before the Sanhedrin? Would we not *expect* God to do this? This is no proof that Paul was in the directive will of God in going to Jerusalem at this time.

212

Nor does his statement in II Timothy 4:7 prove this. Take the apostle's heated controversy with Barnabas, his insult to the high priest (for which he apologized) and add any other failures you can find in the record; then compare them with the rest of the record and see whether he was not more than justified in declaring: *"I have fought a good fight, I have finished my course, I have kept the faith."* Who of us has done half so well?

THE ARGUMENTS AGAINST PAUL'S GOING TO JERUSALEM AT THIS TIME

These, in turn, are mostly as follows:

1. Paul went to Jerusalem at this time, among other things, *"to testify the gospel of the grace of God"* (Acts 20:24) but long before this God had commanded Paul to *leave* Jerusalem, explaining: *"for they will not receive thy testimony concerning Me"* (Acts 22:18).

2. There is no record that he testified "the gospel of the grace of God" on this visit to Jerusalem. He certainly did not do so by subjecting himself to a Jewish ceremony.

3. There is no record that the Lord Jesus or the Holy Spirit directed Paul to make this visit to Jerusalem (Ctr. Gal. 2:2). If he *had* been so directed, surely it would have been so stated, in view of all the warnings and pleas *against* his going.

4. While on the way, he received several warnings *from the Spirit* as to what would befall him if he went up to Jerusalem (Acts 20:23; 21:10,11) and it is distinctly stated that the disciples at Tyre *"said to Paul through the Spirit, that he should not go up to Jerusalem"* (Acts 21:4).

213

5. He was taken from Jerusalem to Rome as *"the prisoner of Jesus Christ for you Gentiles"* (Eph. 3:1). He was also a prisoner *for* Christ, but in *this* connection he was the prisoner *of* Christ for the sake of the Gentiles.

PAUL'S SPIRIT AND THE HOLY SPIRIT

An important question to be taken into consideration here is just how much the Holy Spirit and how much Paul's own spirit was involved in this episode.

Five times in the record the word *spirit* (Gr. *Pneuma*) is used, and we believe that in each case it is clear whether Paul's spirit or the Holy Spirit is referred to.

In Acts 19:21 we read that *"Paul purposed in the spirit...to go to Jerusalem."* Now this phrase "in the spirit" is familiarly used of man's own spirit[3] and had there not been a point to prove no one, probably, would ever have questioned the natural interpretation, that Paul resolved in his spirit to go to Jerusalem.

In this connection it should not be overlooked that the passage distinctly states that it was *Paul* who *purposed* to go to Jerusalem. If God had purposed his going, it would have been said that the Holy Spirit *led* or *instructed* him to go.

This, of course, is not to deny that the term "in the spirit" is used to show that it was the highest part of Paul's being, that part which held communion with God, that moved him to go.[4]

In Acts 20:22 the apostle says of himself: *"And now, behold, I go bound in the spirit unto Jerusalem,"* i.e., he

---

3. See Acts 18:5,25; I Corinthians 5:3; II Corinthians 2:13, all of which, like 19:21, contain the definite article in the original.

4. But even the believer's *spirit* may err, as implied in I Thessalonians 5:23.

felt himself bound to go. That his own spirit is referred to here is evident from the fact that he *then* proceeds to say that *"the Holy Ghost* [Gr. *the Spirit, the Holy]"* witnesses in every city that bonds and afflictions await him (Ver. 23).

A considerable majority of translations render the word spirit with a small "s" in both Acts 19:21 and 20:22 as the natural meaning of the original. That this is correct is further confirmed by the fact that unquestionably the Holy Spirit is referred to in all three of the warnings and exhortations *not* to go to Jerusalem. If the above two passages, then, *also* referred to the Holy Spirit we would be confronted with the contradictory situation of the Holy Spirit influencing him both to go and not to go.

We have just seen that Paul himself declared that "the Holy Spirit" had warned him of the results if he went to Jerusalem at this time. The other two passages are Acts 21:4, where the disciples at Tyre *"said to Paul through the Spirit, that he should not go up to Jerusalem"* and Acts 21:10,11, where *"Agabus...took Paul's girdle, and bound his own hands and feet, and said, Thus saith the Holy Ghost, So shall the Jews at Jerusalem bind the man that owneth this girdle, and shall deliver him into the hands of the Gentiles."*

There can be no question that Luke and Paul's other companions, as well as "they of that place," viewed Agabus' prophecy as a warning from God as to what would befall Paul if he persisted in his purpose to go to Jerusalem, for they *all* besought him—*with tears*—"*not* to go up to Jerusalem," and it was only *"when he would not be persuaded"* that they said: *"The will of the Lord* [i.e., His *permissive* will] *be done"* (Vers. 12-14).

215

THE SOLUTION

Having examined the foregoing passages on both sides of the question we are in a better position to find the solution to the problem. Certainly we can see that to say lightly either that Paul was wholly right or that he was wholly wrong; either that he was *in* or *out* of the will of God in the matter, is to take a shallow view of a complex problem. Human nature and human experience are not so simple as all that.

There is no indication in the record that Paul was in the *directive* will of God in going to Jerusalem, yet it is evident also that he was not *consciously* out of God's will in going; indeed, he felt himself bound, by the highest part of his nature, to go.

The apostle had three reasons for going to Jerusalem at this time: 1.) *"to minister unto the saints"* (Rom. 15:25) 2.) *"to worship"* (Acts 20:16; 24:11) and 3.) *"to testify the gospel of the grace of God"* (Acts 20:24). The first two were to foster better relations between the Jewish believers and the Gentile churches and to show both believers and unbelievers at Jerusalem that he did not despise the law of Moses. The third reason, however, was the most important.

We view the whole scene as follows:

Years before, upon his first return to Jerusalem after his conversion, the Lord had said to him:

"Make haste, and get thee quickly out of Jerusalem: for they will not receive thy testimony concerning Me" (Acts 22:18).

At that time Paul had even debated the question with the Lord. These people, he argued, knew how he had led them in the persecution against Christ; how he had imprisoned and had beaten in every synagogue those who believed on Christ, and had consented and helped in the stoning of Stephen. Surely they would listen to *him* and his testimony might well turn them from their enmity to trust in Christ. But the Lord knew better and replied summarily:

"Depart: for I will send thee far hence unto the Gentiles" (Acts 22:21).

Yet, though sent to the Gentiles with glorious good news, the apostle's heart kept bleeding for his beloved people, whom he had led in rebellion against Christ. In Romans 9:1-3 he writes of his *"great heaviness and continual sorrow"* over their condition, and solemnly swears before God that if it were possible he could wish *himself* accursed for them, and a few lines farther on he writes fervently that his *"heart's desire and prayer to God for Israel is, that they might be saved"* (Rom. 10:1).

Not only did the apostle pity his headstrong kinsmen; he felt responsible for having led them, some years back, in their opposition to Christ. Also, he felt responsible to *the Lord* for having stirred up all this hatred against *Him*.

Thus it was that even though the Holy Spirit bore witness in every city that bonds and afflictions awaited him if he went to Jerusalem, he still felt *"bound in the spirit"* to go; he felt that he *must* go to finish his appointed course and his ministry.[5]

---

5. A footnote in the *Scofield Reference Bible* (pg. 1178) suggests that Paul had the "law-bound Jewish *believers*" in mind when he spoke of "testifying the gospel of the grace of God." This seems improbable to us since he had already "communicated" his message to those at Jerusalem (Gal. 2:7-9) and had even "disputed" with them about it so that a testimony to *them* about the gospel of grace would not be required to finish his course. It was the Jewish multitude and their leaders to whom he had not yet been able to give this testimony.

The declaration of the disciples at Tyre is, of course, the strongest argument of those who contend that Paul was wholly wrong and out of the will of God in going. These disciples evidently had the gift of prophecy. They "said to Paul *through the Spirit*, that he should *not* go up to Jerusalem" (Acts 21:4).

The Greek word for *"not"* here, however, is not *ou* but *me*. It is *subjective* rather than *objective*, dealing with thoughts and feelings rather than with facts, as *ou* does. While *ou* denies a thing directly and absolutely, *me* does so according to judgment, preference, etc. This is why *me* is sometimes used as a conjunction: "lest," "that...not," etc.

The Spirit's word through the Tyrean disciples, then, was not a *command* but rather advice and a warning that he should not go up to Jerusalem, i.e., lest he suffer the afflictions predicted.

The greatest test, probably, came when at Caesarea the prophet Agabus,[6] in a dramatic and impressive warning, predicted the apostle's arrest and imprisonment at Jerusalem, causing both his companions in travel and his Caesarean friends to beseech him, weeping, not to persist in his purpose (Acts 21:10-12).

Once more his response clearly indicates that he did not consider this a condemnation of his action but rather a test of his faithfulness (Ver. 13).

Thus while Paul was not *directed* to go to Jerusalem on this occasion (as he had been on another, Gal. 2:2) and indeed was warned of bonds and afflictions if he went, he still did so out of a sense of faithfulness to his Lord, and God used it to give Israel one more impassioned plea from the lips of one who had been

---

6. Already known as a true prophet (Acts 11:27,28).

warned not to go to them; who had been told that they would not listen; who stood before them now in chains, relating the story of *his* conversion, if, perchance, it might lead to *theirs*.

After this he was taken to Rome to become "the prisoner of Jesus Christ for [the] Gentiles" (Eph. 3:1). We are nonplussed, we must confess, to find that so few commentators have grasped the significance of this phrase. It does not say that Paul was a prisoner *for* Christ (though this is also true). It does not say he was a prisoner of the Jews or of the Romans. It says he was the prisoner *"OF Jesus Christ, FOR you Gentiles,"* i.e., Jesus Christ was holding him in prison for the sake of the Gentiles, not as punishment, of course, but because his heart kept turning back to his kinsmen according to the flesh; to those for whose apostasy he held himself so largely responsible.

This solution, we believe, is consistent with the whole record and those who accuse us of exalting Paul above Christ should bear witness that we thus "magnify his office" without exalting him.

PAUL'S FAREWELL TO THE EPHESIAN ELDERS

"And from Miletus he sent to Ephesus, and called the elders of the church.

"And when they were come to him, he said unto them, Ye know, from the first day that I came into Asia, after what manner I have been with you at all seasons,

"Serving the Lord with all humility of mind, and with many tears, and temptations, which befell me by the lying in wait of the Jews:

"And how I kept back nothing that was profitable unto you, but have showed you, and have taught you publicly, and from house to house,

"Testifying both to the Jews, and also to the Greeks, repentance toward God, and faith toward our Lord Jesus Christ.

"And now, behold, I go bound in the spirit unto Jerusalem, not knowing the things that shall befall me there:

"Save that the Holy Ghost witnesseth in every city, saying that bonds and afflictions abide me.

"But none of these things move me, neither count I my life dear unto myself, so that I might finish my course with joy, and the ministry which I have received of the Lord Jesus, to testify the gospel of the grace of God.

"And now, behold, I know that ye all, among whom I have gone preaching the kingdom of God, shall see my face no more.

"Wherefore I take you to record this day, that I am pure from the blood of all men.

"For I have not shunned to declare unto you all the counsel of God.

"Take heed therefore unto yourselves, and to all the flock, over the which the Holy Ghost hath made you overseers, to feed the church of God, which He hath purchased with His own blood.

"For I know this, that after my departing shall grievous wolves enter in among you, not sparing the flock.

"Also of your own selves shall men arise, speaking perverse things, to draw away disciples after them.

"Therefore watch, and remember, that by the space of three years I ceased not to warn every one night and day with tears.

"And now, brethren, I commend you to God, and to the word of His grace, which is able to build you up, and to give you an inheritance among all them which are sanctified.

"I have coveted no man's silver, or gold, or apparel.

"Yea, ye yourselves know, that these hands have ministered unto my necessities, and to them that were with me.

"I have showed you all things, how that so laboring ye ought to support the weak, and to remember the words of the Lord Jesus, how He said, It is more blessed to give than to receive.

"And when he had thus spoken, he kneeled down, and prayed with them all.

"And they all wept sore, and fell on Paul's neck, and kissed him,

"Sorrowing most of all for the words which he spake, that they should see his face no more. And they accompanied him unto the ship."

—Acts 20:17-38

If perchance the reader has passed over the above passage from Acts to get to our comments on it, we suggest turning back to read every word of it, for here we have the inspired record of one of the most touching incidents in the apostle's life: his farewell to the Ephesian elders. No discourse in Acts is so full of tender solicitude for his helpers in the work, along with jealousy for the purity of his God-given message, as this parting exhortation to those among whom he had labored longer than in any other city. This is the first time, too, that we read of warm manifestations of love toward Paul. Hitherto Luke, by the Spirit, has told us much about the hate and opposition of his enemies, but nothing of the affection and devotion of the Galatians (Gal. 4:14,15) the Thessalonians (I Thes. 3:6) the Philippians (Phil. 1:25,26; 4:15,16) and others.

Now we can thank God for the plot on his life as he was about to sail direct to Syria (20:3) for had he not been forced to change his plans he could never have made this farewell address to the Ephesian elders, and this precious gem would never have been placed in the crown of inspired truth.

It is important to note that the apostle sent to Ephesus for the *elders* of the church alone. He wished to speak especially to *them* regarding the work in Asia. Thus the address has special significance to pastors and leaders in Christian work. As the apostle reviews his ministry among them we do well to ask ourselves whether we measure up. As he warns and exhorts we do well to take thoughtful heed.

PAUL REVIEWS HIS MINISTRY IN EPHESUS

There must have been much excitement and joy among the leaders of the church at Ephesus when they received the message that their beloved Paul, whom they had not seen since the great uprising over Diana, was at Miletus and waiting to speak with them. Doubtless they came with all haste and, as soon as possible, gathered around him to hear what it was he wished to say.

"Ye know," he began, *"from the first day that I came into Asia, after what manner I have been with you at all seasons"* (Ver. 18).

He had served his Lord humbly, as His bondslave,[7] with many tears and testings which befell him principally by the lying in wait of the Jews. Thus the plot of Acts 20:3 was but one of many such plots. Everywhere he went his life was in danger. Sometimes the pressure became so great that he burst forth in tears of exasperation and anxiety.

Meantime he had faithfully ministered to their spiritual needs, keeping back "nothing that was profitable" to them. Considering, indeed, the *capacity* of his hearers, but never his own advantage, he taught them all that was good for them, not shunning to declare to them "all the counsel of God"[8] (cf. II Cor. 4:2; I Thes. 2:4).

Alas, how many men of God there are today who do "keep back" truths which would be most profitable to their hearers; who avoid declaring all the counsel of God, lest they lose a few speaking engagements, a comfortable position or a bit of human applause. Such *cannot* say to *their* hearers, as the apostle could to his:

"Wherefore I take you to record this day, that I am pure from the blood[9] of all men"[10] (Ver. 26).

But not only had the apostle been consistent in his conduct and faithful in his ministry; he had put all his energy into it, giving of himself above measure, like a man running to win a race.

---

7. This is the root of the word "serving."

8. As far as it had been revealed to him, of course, for there was still more to be revealed (See Acts 26:16; II Cor. 12:1).

9. This is a Hebrew idiom disavowing responsibility for the failure of others.

10. The word "men" is not in the original. The next verse shows that the apostle meant all *concerned*, all who had come under his teaching.

He had taught them not only "publicly," but also "from house to house" (Ver. 20). He did not, like so many modern pastors, neglect family visitation. He knew the value of personal contact, and we may be assured that the believers at Ephesus learned some of their most precious lessons and that many were even saved, as Paul dealt with them in their own homes.

Of course the apostle kept no regular hours. *"By the space of three years,"*[11] he says, *"I ceased not to warn every one night and day,"* and that, *"with tears,"* so anxious was he lest his words might be in vain (Ver. 31). In the light of this let us, who are in places of spiritual leadership, ask ourselves how many tears of anxiety or solicitude *we* have shed for those whose spiritual welfare God has entrusted to us.

But above all this, so far was the apostle from seeking material gain from his labors, that he could stretch forth his hands before them and remind them that *they themselves* knew how those hands had provided not only for his own needs, but also for the needs of those who were with him[12] (Ver. 34).

Paul had written to the Corinthians reminding them that it is only *right* that the congregation should see to the financial support of its pastor (I Cor. 9:7-14) since the true pastor gives far, far more than he receives; indeed, he had stressed the point that "so hath the Lord *ordained*, that they which preach the gospel should live of the gospel" (Ver. 14).

---

11. The three years including *three months* at the synagogue (19:8) *two years* at the school of Tyrannus (19:9,10) and a *"season"* after the departure of Timothy and Erastus (19:22).

12. Paul seems always to have had a band of helpers with him, aiding him in the discharge of the many duties in which he was involved by the care of all the churches. .

But now he was addressing *pastors*, explaining how sometimes they must cheerfully forego these prerogatives and reminding them of his own example of financial self-reliance (Vers. 34,35).

In this connection the apostle reminds them of certain "words of the Lord Jesus" which were known to them but are not recorded in any of the four Gospels:

"It is more blessed to give than to receive" (Ver. 35).

How true is this declaration by our Lord, yet how little is it believed! If pastors really believed it they would the more "gladly spend and be spent" for their congregations. If their hearers believed it they would provide more generously for both the worker and the work.

The apostle did not say all this in a spirit of pride but with evident deep humility, yet his words indicate a consciousness of complete and unflinching fidelity to his God-given ministry. Thrice he says, *"Ye know....I take you to record....Ye yourselves know"* (Vers. 18,26,34). And his assertions *must* have been true or he would not have been able to make such an appeal to those with whom he had lived and worked so intimately for three years. Indeed, the affectionate and tearful response of his hearers prove them true.

WHAT THE APOSTLE HAD PREACHED

Some who have gone to dispensational extremes, reading that Paul had preached repentance and the kingdom of God, immediately conclude that the apostle must have had some special temporary ministry, connected with Israel and the Messianic kingdom until after the close of Acts when the mystery was revealed to him.

This is incorrect, for the apostle had by this time already written to several of the churches about various phases of the mystery, even though *all* its glories had not yet been revealed (Rom. 11:25; 16:25; I Cor. 2:7; 15:51-53; I Thes. 4:15-18, etc.).

In Verse 24 of our passage the apostle makes it clear that the particular ministry he had received of the Lord Jesus was *"to testify the gospel of the grace of God."* This was *his special ministry.* But this does not mean that he would not *confirm* what Peter and the twelve had taught about the Messiahship of Christ. Could anyone suppose that those who persisted in *denying* that the crucified Jesus was the true Messiah could possibly *trust* Him as their personal Savior? Assuredly not! And thus it was that Paul sought first to convince the Jews everywhere that "Jesus *is* the Christ."

So it is also that in the passage before us he declares that he had testified to both Jews and Greeks, *"repentance toward God, and faith toward our Lord Jesus Christ"* (Ver. 21).

Now it is quite true that as *repentance* was *the* message of John the Baptist, Christ and the twelve, so *grace* is *the* message for today. But this does not mean that repentance has no place today. Repentance is not *penitence;* much less is it *penance.* It is rather a change of mind and attitude. Grace had been *Paul's* special message up to this time yet repentance was a *part* of that message, as was also faith toward the Lord Jesus Christ.

As to his preaching "the kingdom of God" (Ver. 25) he still speaks of "inheriting" the kingdom of God in Ephesians 5:5 and of his "fellow workers unto the kingdom of God" in Colossians 4:11, both of which passages were written considerably after the close of Acts.

It must be remembered that this term, unlike "the kingdom of heaven,"[13] is a very broad one. We find it used in both the opening and closing verses of the Acts and in each case the context must be kept in view.

When our Lord, before His ascension, taught the eleven "the things pertaining to the kingdom of God" (Acts 1:3) He dealt with the *earthly establishment* of that kingdom, which the apostles hoped for and which Peter was soon to offer to Israel (Acts 3:19-21). But when Paul, in bondage in Rome, preached the kingdom of God (Acts 28:31) he would, of course, tell what had become of the offer of its establishment on earth, and explain how this was now being held in abeyance (Cf. Rom. 11:25-27).

Above all let us observe carefully that *"the* ministry" which Paul had "received of the Lord Jesus," was the proclamation of *"the gospel of the grace of God"* (Ver. 24). It was by preaching this message that he hoped to finish the course which he had begun so long ago.

WHAT THE FUTURE HELD
IN STORE FOR HIM

There was no turning back for the apostle. He would continue, "bound in the spirit,"[14] to Jerusalem, even though the Holy Spirit had been witnessing all along the way that "bonds and afflictions" awaited him there.

All of us who have been called into places of service for the Lord would do well to meditate often on the next

---

13. Found only in Matthew.

14. This term is an idiom meaning to feel one's self responsible. The "spirit" here, as we have shown, is his own, not the Holy Spirit, which is distinguished from Paul's spirit in the next verse by the addition of the word "Holy" and (in the original) by the familiar repetition of the definite article: *"the* Spirit, *the* Holy."

verse, in which Paul expresses his attitude toward the sufferings which would inevitably overtake him as he pursued his journey to that caldron of hate where the Lord had been rejected and crucified.

To describe it he uses the most familiar of all his metaphors: the footrace. He can allow his mind to dwell on nothing except the *race* and the finishing of his course. None of the alarming predictions divert him from his purpose. He does not even consider his own life to be of any account, that he might successfully finish his course.[15]

The apostle seemed convinced that he would never again see the Ephesian elders. Whether or not this knowledge was absolute, he certainly contemplated no further ministry among them. Whether or not he may after all have revisited Asia under the conditions referred to in II Timothy 1:15; whether he may even have been permitted to carry out his purpose to journey to Spain (Rom. 15:24) will be discussed in a later chapter, but it is evident that he did not expect the brethren at Ephesus to see his face again.

What the future ultimately held in store for the faithful apostle was the prize to which he alludes in Verse 24. He had indeed run to "obtain" (I Cor. 9:24) and had not run "in vain" (Phil. 2:16). As he finished his "course" years later, he stood ready to receive "a crown" (II Tim. 4:7,8).

THE CALL TO FAITHFULNESS

We turn now from what the future held in store for Paul to what the future held in store for the church at Ephesus.

---

15. The words "with joy" are omitted in some MSS.

"Grievous wolves" would enter from without, "not sparing the flock" (Ver. 29). And, what is always more disconcerting, apostates would arise *from within*, "speaking perverse things, to draw away disciples after them" (Ver. 30). How naturally ready unstable believers are to follow such, may be gathered from what had taken place at Corinth, where so many sought to follow Apollos—who even *refused a following!* In the case of the Ephesian church, whose elders Paul was now addressing, we are given ample confirmation of the truth of his warning. It was not long before Hymenaeus and Alexander had "made shipwreck" of the faith and had become blasphemers (I Tim. 1:19,20). And this Hymenaeus, along with another, Philetus, succeeded in "overthrowing the faith of some" (II Tim. 2:17,18). Indeed, in his last letter the apostle had to write to Timothy: *"This thou knowest, that all they which are in Asia[16] be turned away from me"* (II Tim. 1:15).

Paul well knew that such things would take place; he knew that the world, the flesh and the devil would conspire together to overthrow what he had so tirelessly labored to build. Thus it is that he exhorts them:

"Therefore watch, and remember, that by the space of three years I ceased not to warn everyone night and day with tears" (Ver. 31).

Christian leaders do well to take this exhortation deeply to heart. Churches, however true to the Word and to Christ, do not naturally remain that way; they naturally depart from the faith and its Author. Indeed, this is true of every one of us individually. Not one of us

16. It is granted that the "all" here may refer to a certain company which Timothy would recognize, or to the believers in Asia *as a body*. In any case it is evident that there was serious and widespread defection.

dare trust himself. Each must look to God continually for grace to remain true, for the destructive influences, within as well as without, are strong. Thus it is that the apostle here states that he had "ceased not to warn *every one*"[17] and thus it is that he exhorted the elders of the Church: *"Therefore watch"* (Ver. 31) and *"Take heed therefore unto yourselves, and to all the flock, over the which the Holy Ghost hath made you overseers"* (Ver. 28).

In view of his departure from them, and in view of the spiritual perils that threatened, the apostle now concluded his exhortation by commending them to God and His Word,[18] but more particularly to *"the word of His grace, which,"* he said, *"is able to build you up, and to give you an inheritance among all them which are sanctified"* (Ver. 32).

"The word of His grace" was, of course, the particular message which Paul had been commissioned to proclaim. It was the message for the dispensation now dawning, and it was *this message* that God would use to establish them in the faith, especially as its glories were further revealed to Paul and through him in his epistles.

How similar is this benediction to that found in a letter the apostle had so recently written:

"Now to Him that is of power to stablish you according to my gospel, and the preaching of Jesus Christ according to the revelation of the mystery, which was kept secret since the world began" (Rom. 16:25).

It is because the Church has failed to follow these instructions for her own spiritual health and growth

---

17. See also Colossians 1:28.
18. There is no thought of apostolic succession. The apostle does not commit them to Timothy but "to *God* and *the word of His grace.*"

that she is so weak and ill today. May God awaken His people to these truths and cause them to return in faith to the *one* great body of truth which alone can establish them and build them up spiritually: *"the word of His grace"; "the preaching of Jesus Christ according to the revelation of the mystery."*

THE PARTING

The parting scene is almost too sacred to intrude upon.

Having finished his discourse the apostle knelt down on the shore with his beloved co-workers for a parting prayer. Luke has not recorded the prayer for us. Perhaps this would have been impossible anyway, for presently there was a mutual outbreak of grief as all present "wept sore" and "fell on Paul's neck, and kissed [Lit. ardently kissed] him, sorrowing most of all for the words which he spoke, that they should see his face no more" (Vers. 36-38).

Actually they should have sorrowed most of all at his prediction that apostates would arise from among themselves, but this must have been difficult for them to take in under the circumstances, and their love for Paul and their sorrow at the thought of seeing his face no more showed how much his ministry and message had meant to them.

It is touching to see the grief-stricken group accompany the apostle to the waiting ship, there clinging to him until it became necessary for him to tear himself away from them.[19]

---

19. The words "gotten from," in 21:1 mean, literally, "torn away" or "pulled away."

231

THE TEARS OF PAUL

Other writers, notably Dean Howson, have observed that the tears which Paul shed during his ministry for Christ had, like those of his Savior, manifested three aspects of his nature, and that we find all three of them in this one passage in Acts.

Our Lord while on earth had shed tears of *suffering and anguish* at the cross (Heb. 5:7) tears of *pastoral solicitude* as He wept over Jerusalem (Luke 19:41) and tears of *natural affection* as He wept with the bereaved at Lazarus' tomb (John 11:35).

In this respect Paul reflected the nature of his Master and Lord as indicated in the very passage we have been considering.

First, he speaks of his *"many tears"* occasioned by "the lying in wait of the Jews" (Ver. 19). These were tears of *suffering and anguish*, wrung from his eyes by the bitter, constant, relentless opposition of the Jews to his ministry. His life, as we have seen, was in constant danger as they plotted against him, stirred up the masses against him or sought to ambush him. He had to stand his ground, flee for his life or hide from his pursuers, as circumstances (and sometimes the Lord) indicated. He had to make quick decisions, alter important plans, leave young converts and devoted friends again and again because of the violent opposition of his kinsmen. All this told on his nervous system so that he frequently burst into tears simply because the pressure was too great.

But like his Lord too, he shed tears of *pastoral solicitude*. "I ceased not to warn everyone night and day," he says, *"with tears"* (Acts 20:31). Little wonder

232

his ministry was so effective! He *wept* as he dealt with his children in the faith about their lives and doctrine— he wept lest his warnings fall on deaf ears.

But he also wept tears of *natural affection*. While it is true that it is said of the Ephesian elders that "they all wept sore" (Ver. 37) who will question that Paul wept with them? It was *his love* for them that had won their hearts, and now with them he shed tears of natural human affection.

Paul's last journey to Jerusalem has both its comparisons and its contrasts with our Lord's journey thence to suffer and die.

Our Lord, of course, went to Jerusalem to die for the sins of others, while Paul went because, having led his nation in opposition to Christ, he now felt responsible to witness to them of Christ. Also, Christ went to Jerusalem in the *directive* will of God, while Paul did not. But his sufferings at Jerusalem, like those of Christ, were predicted beforehand. Also, Paul, like his Lord, was surrounded by sorrowing friends on his way to Jerusalem. He, like Christ, was himself distressed at the prospects of his suffering (Acts 21:13; Rom. 15:30,31 cf. John 12:27). Like his Lord, the apostle also found himself the center of Jewish enmity and like his Lord he had to hear them cry: *"Away with such a fellow from the earth: for it is not fit that he should live"* (Acts 22:22).

233

THE GATHERING STORM

FROM MILETUS TO CAESAREA

"And it came to pass, that after we were gotten from them, and had launched, we came with a straight course unto Coos, and the day following unto Rhodes, and from thence unto Patara:

"And finding a ship sailing over unto Phenicia, we went aboard, and set forth.

"Now when we had discovered Cyprus, we left it on the left hand, and sailed into Syria, and landed at Tyre: for there the ship was to unlade her burden.

"And finding disciples, we tarried there seven days: who said to Paul through the Spirit, that he should not go up to Jerusalem.

"And when we had accomplished those days, we departed and went our way; and they all brought us on our way, with wives and children, till we were out of the city: and we kneeled down on the shore, and prayed.

"And when we had taken our leave one of another, we took ship; and they returned home again.

"And when we had finished our course from Tyre, we came to Ptolemais, and saluted the brethren, and abode with them one day.

"And the next day we that were of Paul's company departed, and came unto Caesarea: and we entered into the house of Philip the evangelist, which was one of the seven; and abode with him.

"And the same man had four daughters, virgins, which did prophesy.

"And as we tarried there many days, there came down from Judaea a certain prophet, named Agabus.

"And when he was come unto us, he took Paul's girdle, and bound his own hands and feet, and said, Thus saith the Holy Ghost, So shall the Jews at Jerusalem bind the man that owneth this girdle, and shall deliver him into the hands of the Gentiles.

"And when we heard these things, both we, and they of that place, besought him not to go up to Jerusalem.

"Then Paul answered, What mean ye to weep and to break mine heart? for I am ready not to be bound only, but also to die at Jerusalem for the name of the Lord Jesus.

"And when he would not be persuaded, we ceased, saying, The will of the Lord be done."

—Acts 21:1-14

THE JOURNEY TO TYRE

Leaving Miletus, the apostle and his company sailed "with a straight course" to nearby Coos or Cos, famous then, as now, for its wines, fruits and silks. Here they evidently stayed overnight, proceeding on "the following day" to world-renowned Rhodes.

This famous city, named after "the island of roses" on which it was situated, was one of the busiest harbors on the archipelago. And there, some 340 years before, had been erected one of "the seven wonders of the world," a great bronze statue of Apollo which stood 105 feet high. Some historians say that the great Colossus stood astride the harbor, but this is questioned by

235

others. About 224 B.C., however, an earthquake hurled it into the sea, where it remained a mass of bronze until about 656 A.D., when the Saracens took possession of the island and sold the metal to a Jewish dealer who employed 900 camels to carry it away.

At the time when Paul entered the harbor, if historians are correct, the harbor was still strewn with pieces of the Colossus, only parts of the two legs still standing on their bases. Perhaps he recalled the fate of the god Dagon and smiled as he viewed the wreckage.

The text does not say that the party stayed overnight at Rhodes, and it is possible that the ship went right on to Patara the same day. Doubtless they sailed only by day on this part of the journey, but the prevalence of the northwest wind in the Aegean Sea would speed them along. Dr. Clarke, in a firsthand report, says of this: "It is surprising for what a length of time, and how often, the NW rages in the Archipelago. It prevails almost unceasingly through the greater part of the year" (Vol. III, pg. 380).

Patara, a harbor on the coast of Lycia, was evidently the ship's destination, but here the apostle and his company were fortunate enough to find another ship just ready to sail across the Mediterranean to Tyre. Nothing is said here about staying overnight. We do not find the phrase "the next day" or "the day following." Rather, the record, especially in the original, gives the impression that no time was lost. Evidently they changed ships *immediately* and set sail *that night* for Tyre, about 400 miles across the sea.

Now with all canvas spread and a northwest wind helping, they need not fear sailing by night. "Even the timidity of ancient navigation," says Clarke, "did not refuse, with a fair wind, to pass by night over this safe and unobstructed piece of water."

The phrase, "When we had discovered Cyprus," is expressive in the original. It indicates that they were sailing fast; that Cyprus loomed suddenly into view and then disappeared as quickly out of sight again. Doubtless the apostle thought with joy of his namesake as he passed the island.

Soon they landed at Tyre, where "the ship was to unlade her burden" (Ver. 3). At this time Tyre was in the state of decline from her glory in the days when such dire prophecies were made against her, to her desolation at the time of their fulfilment.

Luke's account of the entire voyage, from Troas to Tyre, gives the impression that the weather had all along been highly favorable. Moreover, the advantage of finding a ship at Patara waiting to sail had not only relieved Paul of his anxiety about reaching Jerusalem in time for Pentecost, but had given him considerable time to spare.

"Finding disciples,"[1] therefore, the company "tarried there seven days" (Ver. 4) evidently the length of time it would take for the ship, a large sea-going vessel, to unload her cargo and reload.

THE SPIRIT'S WARNING
NOT TO GO TO JERUSALEM

Here, as we have seen, the disciples "said to Paul through the Spirit, that he should not go up to Jerusalem" (Ver. 4).

---

1. The original indicates a search. Probably Paul did not know any believers at Tyre, though they doubtless had heard much about him.

As we have pointed out, it was not mere concern for Paul's welfare that constrained these disciples to urge him not to continue on his way to Jerusalem; they spoke *"by the Spirit."* We have also shown that the phraseology, in the Greek, does not indicate a direct prohibition, but rather a *warning* and a *plea*. It is probable, further, that Paul understood that this warning was from the Spirit, for he had already said: *"The Holy Ghost witnesseth in every city, saying that bonds and afflictions abide me"* (20:23).

His responses to such pleas and warnings indicate strongly that he did not regard them as a divine prohibition against his going to Jerusalem, but considered them rather as a challenge and a test of his faithfulness (See 20:24; 21:13).

Thus, while the apostle's motives and purposes were noble indeed, it cannot be said that he was in the directive will of God in going to Jerusalem. Surely the Spirit's persistent warnings *against* going to Jerusalem were not to be construed as His leading to go there.

THE FAREWELL AT TYRE

The account of the farewell at Tyre is particularly touching. Evidently the disciples here had not known Paul personally, so that the parting scene would not be the same as that at Miletus, for example. But the remarkable fact is that in these few days Paul had already found such a place in their affections that all together they accompanied him and his party to the ship to say farewell. The addition of the "wives and children" here makes the group specially picturesque and touching.

Before parting, the whole company kneeled down on the shore to pray; Paul, his eight companions and the Tyrean believers, perhaps all of them pouring out intercessory supplications for each other. The children would never forget it!

But sailing-time at length arrived and Paul and his company had to say farewell, board ship and sail away, as their new-found friends returned sorrowfully to their homes.

AGABUS' PROPHECY

Proceeding on their way the apostle and his companions stopped at Ptolemais to greet "the brethren" there, staying with them for one day,[2] and then continued on to Caesarea, where Paul spent his last days of freedom. Their host there was the well known Philip, like Paul a Helenist, and therefore probably more sympathetic to Paul's cause than the Hebrew believers were.

Philip had originally been one of the seven treasurers who had had oversight of "the daily ministration" in Pentecostal days when the believers at Jerusalem had had "all things common" (See Acts 6:1-5). Since that time, however, the Jerusalem church had been scattered by a "great persecution" and Philip had been used rather as an evangelist (See Acts 8:4-40). But while Philip was perhaps no longer actively a treasurer of the Church at Jerusalem, the fact that in addition to being called "Philip the evangelist" here, he is also designated as "one of the seven," may well imply that he still had enough association with, or knowledge of, financial matters in the Church at Jerusalem to have relieved Paul of the necessity of personally delivering the "collection" he had gathered for its poor.

---

2. Evidently the length of time their ship remained in port.

This Philip also had four daughters which had given themselves to God's service as phophetesses (21:9). There was nothing wrong, of course, in women prophesying in those days, for Joel had specifically predicted with regard to Pentecost: *"Your daughters shall prophesy,"* (Acts 2:17) and in the light of the Spirit's witness "in every city" along Paul's journey that "bonds and afflictions" awaited him at Jerusalem, it is not to be doubted that these damsels added their Spirit-inspired testimony to those already given.

But the most impressive and solemn warning of all was yet to be conveyed by Agabus, a known and trusted prophet who had, years before, predicted the great famine which was to impoverish the Judaean saints. At that time he had been instrumental in procuring the first Gentile contribution for the poor believers of Judaea. This time, however, he came to deliver a dramatic warning as to what would befall the apostle if he persisted in his purpose to go to Jerusalem.

The feeling which led to the murderous plot against Paul's life recorded in Acts 23:12, could hardly have been a secret to a prophet living in Judaea. And now having learned, either supernaturally or by report,[3] about the apostle's approach, Agabus goes down to Caesarea to warn him, evidently finding him with a company of his associates and friends. Adopting the symbolic manner of many Old Testament prophets, he approaches the apostle and takes off the girdle by which his robe is held together, using it to bind his own hands and feet, and saying:

"So shall the Jews at Jerusalem bind the man that owneth this girdle, and shall deliver him into the hands of the Gentiles" (Ver. 11).

---

3. There would have been plenty of time for such a report to reach him (See Ver. 10).

Now it is certain that this passage, read simply and naturally, could be interpreted in no other way than as a warning against Paul's proceeding further to Jerusalem. That Agabus indeed spoke as a prophet of God is proven, not only by the literal fulfilment of his prophecy in Acts 11, but also by the literal fulfilment of *this* prophecy here.

The question, of course, is whether the Spirit thus warned him to *deter* him from his purpose or to *prepare* him for the ordeal. We believe the former is the case. Has it ever been God's way to prepare His servants for testings by *warning* them about them? Has He not rather done this by *encouraging* them as to His faithfulness? Certainly this is so in the case of Paul himself (See 18:9; 23:11; 27:23-25).

Certainly all those present understood Agabus' prophecy as a warning to Paul that he should not proceed, for both his co-workers, including even Luke, and the believers at Caesarea began to plead with him, with tears, to abandon his purpose (Vers. 12,13).

If Paul had the hate of the Jews and the dislike, or at least suspicion, of many of the believers at Jerusalem, he surely also had the ardent love of a host of saints who appreciated his ministry as the apostle of grace, for wherever he paused to say farewell there were touching demonstrations of affection toward him.

Paul's response to the pleas of his friends reveals something of the greatness of the man and of his motives. With a heart bleeding for his kinsmen and with a deep sense of obligation toward the Christ he had taught them to hate, he was not able to view Agabus' warning in the same way as did his friends. He was no fanatic or would-be martyr; he was a veteran in persecution, with scars to show, yet he was by no means a stoic. Rather, he had a sensitive, affectionate nature, and the tearful appeals of his companions and friends were crushing him and caused him to exclaim:

"What mean ye to weep and to break mine heart? for I am ready not to be bound only, but also to die at Jerusalem for the name of the Lord Jesus" (Ver. 13).

If any fault can be found with the great apostle for persisting in his purpose to go to Jerusalem at this time, surely no one can question the loftiness of his motives, nor the depth of his devotion to Christ. Those who charge him with consciously, willfully disobeying God in this matter, should search their hearts to see if their own motives are nearly so high or their devotion nearly so deep.

Finally all present ceased pleading with the apostle, saying: *"The will of the Lord be done."* In the light of the context it is, of course, erroneous to conclude from this that Paul's friends now saw Paul's purpose to be in accord with the directive will of God. They rather spoke of God's *permissive* will, resigning themselves to what was seen to be inevitable.

PAUL'S LAST VISIT TO JERUSALEM

AT THE HOME OF MNASON

"And after those days we took up our carriages, and went up to Jerusalem.

"There went with us also certain of the disciples of Caesarea, and brought with them one Mnason of Cyprus, an old disciple, with whom we should lodge.

"And when we were come to Jerusalem, the brethren received us gladly."

—Acts 21:15-17

The feast now at hand, the apostle and his company had to leave Caesarea for Jerusalem. This is the first time we read of their "carriage," or "baggage," perhaps because this was the last lap of their journey, to be undertaken on foot, and this baggage contained the precious "collection" for the Jewish saints.

The group now formed a small caravan. Besides the eight brethren who had accompanied Paul there were also "certain of the disciples of Caesarea" who went along and, perhaps, Mnason, an early believer, a native of Cyprus with whom Paul and his company were to lodge at Jerusalem.[1]

---

1. Some texts read *"bringing us to one Mnason,"* instead of *"brought with them one Mnason,"* but this rendering may be begotten of an imagined difficulty, for if there was time for Agabus to come down from Jerusalem to warn Paul of the dangers there, why could not Mnason have come down to offer him lodging in case he persisted in his purpose?

This was important now. Suitable lodging would at best be difficult to find in Jerusalem at feast time and Mnason's hospitality would minimize the inevitable danger to Paul's life. Moreover the brethren from Caesarea would serve as a kind of escort.

In Jerusalem, evidently at Mnason's home, "the brethren" held an informal and hearty welcome for the party. It is evident that these brethren, however, did not include James and the elders, for Paul and his associates visited them "the day following" (Ver. 18).

WITH JAMES AND THE ELDERS

"And the day following Paul went in with us unto James; and all the elders were present.

"And when he had saluted them, he declared particularly what things God had wrought among the Gentiles by his ministry.

"And when they heard it, they glorified the Lord, and said unto him, Thou seest, brother, how many thousands of Jews there are which believe; and they are all zealous of the law:

"And they are informed of thee, that thou teachest all the Jews which are among the Gentiles to forsake Moses, saying that they ought not to circumcise their children, neither to walk after the customs.

"What is it therefore? the multitude must needs come together; for they will hear that thou art come.

"Do therefore this that we say to thee: We have four men which have a vow on them;

"Them take, and purify thyself with them, and be at charges with them, that they may shave their heads:

and all may know that those things, whereof they were informed concerning thee, are nothing; but that thou thyself also walkest orderly, and keepest the law.

"As touching the Gentiles which believe, we have written and concluded that they observe no such thing, save only that they keep themselves from things offered to idols, and from blood, and from strangled, and from fornication."

—Acts 21:18-25

THE STATE OF THE CHURCH
AT JERUSALEM AT THIS TIME

It is with sadness that we view the condition of the Church at Jerusalem at this time.

First, we are told that Paul and his company "went in unto James"—"and the elders were *present*" (Ver. 18).

We have already seen how Peter was the Christ-appointed leader of the Messianic Church in those early days when "they were all filled with the Holy Ghost" (See Matt. 16:19; Acts 1:15; 2:14; 2:37; 5:29; etc.). We have seen too, how James, "the Lord's brother" (not even one of the twelve) gradually gained the ascendancy over Peter, probably because of his physical relationship to our Lord. Thus we find Peter reporting to "James and to the brethren" in Acts 12:17. Later Paul mentions James alone as present with Peter at Jerusalem during an earlier visit there (Gal. 1:19). Next we find Peter merely testifying at the council at Jerusalem, while James presides and brings the council to a close with the words: *"Wherefore, I decide"* (Acts 15:19). Still later, at Antioch, we see Peter intimidated by "certain [who] came from James," so that he

245

separates himself from Gentile believers with whom he has been enjoying fellowship (Gal. 2:11,12). And now Paul and his companions go in unto James, and so final is his authority that the record states merely that "the *elders* were *present*" (Acts 21:18). At the council, some fourteen years previous, *"the apostles and elders"* had gathered together to discuss Gentile liberty from the law (Acts 15:6). *Now* there is no trace of evidence that any of the apostles are even present; the record mentions only *"James and the elders."* If any of the twelve apostles *are* to be included among the "elders," but are not even designated as apostles, we have still further evidence of the secondary character of their position at this time. James, whose very name means "Supplanter," has wholly taken over Peter's position.

In commenting on the Jerusalem council later, Paul had called "James, Cephas and John" (with James at the head) those "who *seemed* to be somewhat" and "who *seemed* to be pillars," pointing out that "the gospel of the circumcision" had been committed *"to PETER"* (Gal. 2:6-9).

This elevation of James over Peter and the eleven, whom our Lord had appointed, is evidence of the spiritual decline among the Judaean believers after the raising up of Paul and it has an important bearing on the passage we are now to consider.

A COOL RECEPTION

As Paul saluted James and the elders there was a superficial show of harmony, but the elements of suspicion and discord lurked beneath. It had not been James who had opened his home to Paul. He had not been among those who had gathered to welcome the

246

great apostle on the previous night. And his party had not made things easy for Paul in late years.

But now perhaps the atmosphere would be cleared as Paul related to them "particularly," i.e., *in detail,*[2] "what things *God* had wrought among the Gentiles by his ministry." It must have been thrilling to hear the great apostle tell of idols cast away, sinful books burned, wicked practices abandoned and Christ received and glorified in city after city, the delegates from the various churches doubtless presenting their gifts at this time; an immense amount, and a sacrificial proof of their affection toward their brethren in Judaea.

The response? "They glorified the Lord, and said"—quickly changing the subject to a matter that could only embarrass the apostle. The record does not say one word about their agreeing to help the Judaean believers understand Paul and his God-given ministry, nor one word about their inviting *him* to tell them what God had wrought through him, nor even one word about their thanking him and the Gentile churches for so generously keeping their promise of some years back (Gal. 2:10)—and nothing would have fallen more naturally within the scope of Luke's account, had it taken place.

Instead they pointed out "how many thousands" (Lit. *myriads*, or *tens* of thousands) of believing Jews there were, all of them "zealots[3] for the law," and urged upon him that since these had been informed that he had apostatized from Moses, he ought to silence the rumor by publicly taking part in a Nazarite vow.

---

2. This may further indicate the unfavorable attitude of those present toward his ministry.

3. The word, in the original, is a noun.

As we read the record we do not receive the impression that these men were completely candid, for what greater zealot for the law was there than James himself, and was it not a group who "came from James" who had caused Peter to separate himself from the Gentile believers? (Gal. 2:12). If these myriads of Jewish believers had come to believe that Paul had apostatized from Moses, they had done so under the leadership of James and his party.

James and the elders were using an old familiar device in labeling *others* zealots and declaring: "They are all saying this about you," but refraining from telling Paul how they themselves felt about it.

In the words of John Kitto, "It is disappointing... to find the apostle's glorious recital of gospel triumphs, and the elders' apparently hearty responsive thanksgiving, immediately followed by a proposition of expediency, with a view to conciliate unworthy prejudices, based on false representation" (*The Apostles and Early Church*, pg. 304).

Years before, at the great Jerusalem council, Peter had stated that *God* had put "no difference" between them and the Gentiles, purifying the Gentiles' hearts by faith. He had further urged his brethren not to place a yoke upon the neck of the Gentile disciples which neither the Jewish fathers nor their children had been able to bear (Acts 15:9,10). He had even gone so far as to say: "But we believe that through the grace of the Lord Jesus Christ *we* shall be saved, even as *they*" (Ver. 11).

As a result of this magnificent testimony James, Peter, John and the whole church had given solemn and public recognition to Paul as the apostle of the uncircumcision and the apostle of grace (Acts 15:23-29; Gal. 2:7-9). The church at Jerusalem should have gone on from there, as Peter *did* (II Pet. 3:15-18) and should now have accepted Paul in accordance with that agreement. But under James and his party they had declined and gone backward, rather than forward, spiritually. Geikie says of this: "...whereas some time ago, only a portion of these were extreme in their Jewish ideas (Acts 15:1,5) all were now fanatically zealous of the law. So rapidly had the extreme party in the nation spread their bitterly irreconcilable Judaism..." (*New Testament Hours*, Vol. III, pg. 375).

COULD PAUL HAVE ERRED
BY SUBMITTING TO JAMES?

Before going into a detailed examination of James' proposal[4] and Paul's acceptance of it, we must find a Scriptural answer to the above question. Mark well, we do not yet ask whether the apostle *did* err in acquiescing, but whether, in the light of other Scriptures, it is even *possible* that he could have done so.

We pose this question because there are many who, viewing the apostle's godly, faithful life; hearing him say: *"Be ye followers of me,"* etc., and rejoicing in his glorious message of grace, subconsciously entertain the notion that he *could not* have erred so grossly and, in answer to those who feel he *did*, reply that if this is so, the famed apostle was actually one of the greatest hypocrites in Scripture and not worthy of a hearing.

This whole subject is admittedly a difficult one—so difficult that the writer, for one, has never once heard a comprehensive sermon on it, and has been unable to find a single book dealing with all of the Scriptures involved.

---

4. Assuming that James was the spokesman for the elders.

Many speakers and writers have, on the basis of a few passages, declared that Paul was right, or that he was wrong, in involving himself in Judaism at this time, but few indeed have gone into the subject at all comprehensively. This is why we first inquire whether, in the light of other passages of Scripture, it is even *possible* that he might have erred here.

Surely no believer would deny that Paul's life as a Christian is probably the greatest example of human devotion and faithfulness to Christ in all history. Indeed, who of us can even begin to measure up?

As to some of his inspired statements concerning himself, however, much more is often read into these statements than they actually say. His "follow me" is used at least once with regard to his *teaching* and otherwise with regard to *certain details or characteristics* in his behavior, or to his *adopted course*.

One of the strongest statements in this category is found in Philippians 4:9, where he says:

"Those things, which ye have both learned, and received, and heard, and seen in me, do; and the God of peace shall be with you."

But let us not read more into this than it actually says. A glance at the preceding context will reveal that the apostle did not intend to set himself up as the standard of perfection; though he had, to be sure, set the Philippians a noble example. Indeed it is in this same letter that, telling the Philippian saints of his longings and aspirations, he assures them: *"Not as though I had already attained, either were already perfect"* (3:12) adding that he must *forget* those things which are behind, looking only *ahead* and straining for the prize. In doing *"this one thing,"* he calls upon them to be followers together of him (Phil. 3:10-17).

Paul would have been the last person to claim perfection, as is evident from his testimony in Romans 7, and those who tell *us* to "get out of the seventh of Romans into the eighth," should observe that Paul himself wrote these two chapters at *the same sitting*; that the same one who declared: *"There is therefore now no condemnation to them which are in Christ Jesus,"* also humbly confessed:

"For I know that in me (that is, in my flesh) dwelleth no good thing: for to will is present with me; but how to perform that which is good I find not" (Rom. 8:1; 7:18).

But, says some objector, if he could so sternly rebuke Peter and the Galatians for going back into legalism and then, without some special reason, go back into it himself, he was such a hypocrite that I cannot be impressed by his writings.

Why not? Have you forgotten to search your own heart? Does the deep devotion of the Apostle Paul make you less understanding of him if he lapses? Furthermore, he *wrote* by the *inspiration of God*.

Moses sinned in many ways; do you refuse to believe *his* writings? David committed both adultery and murder; do you refuse to read his Psalms? The prophets, one after another, failed; do you distrust their predictions? Peter denied his Lord and later played the hypocrite at Antioch; do you question the truth of his epistles? Of course not—because these men, though themselves failing creatures, *wrote by divine inspiration*. Thus God would keep us from trusting in man and lead us to trust in *His Word alone*.

But Peter was rebuked for his failure at Antioch; would not God have rebuked Paul if he were similarly guilty? In the first place, no careful student of the record

251

would say that Paul was "similarly guilty" in agreeing to offer the sacrifices of the Nazarite. Peter went back on the light he had received, *"fearing them which were of the circumcision"* (Gal. 2:12). Paul, on the other hand, became involved in this vow out of a burning love to his kinsman whom he hoped would thereby be won to listen to his testimony about Christ.

But did not the Lord *commend* him in Acts 23:11, when He stood by him and said: *"Be of good cheer, Paul: for as thou hast testified of Me in Jerusalem so must thou bear witness also at Rome"?* No, at least He did not commend him *for taking part in the Jewish vow.* He rather *comforted* Paul in this case, understanding his great love for Israel and for Himself, and his deep sense of responsibility for having led Israel in their rebellion against Christ.

But did not the great apostle, in the very face of martyrdom, say: "I have fought a good fight, I have finished my course, I have kept the faith" (II Tim. 4:7)? Of course! Read the record of his faithful, tireless service for Christ. Go through the long, but far from complete, list of his sufferings for Christ in II Corinthians 11. Note how his prison epistles show us even more of the glories of Christ and His grace, and take us even farther into the heavenlies than do the epistles written before this visit to Jerusalem. Consider all this, together with much more that might be said about his life and teachings, and then ask whether this lapse can cancel all that out. Indeed, who, in all history has had nearly so much reason to say: *"I have fought a good fight"* or: *"I have kept the faith"?*

By way of illustration, there may be a time, or several times, in the life of a consecrated servant of God when his sincere love for a friend and his earnest desire to see him saved, may lead him into some course of action not in God's will, and may even temporarily dull his perception as to God's will. If this takes place you will be unjust to charge him with unfaithfulness or with flagrant rebellion against God—especially if you yourself do not have half so much love for God or for *your* friends.

THE REPORT CONCERNING PAUL
WAS IT TRUE OR FALSE?

The report which, according to James, had found general credence among the Jewish believers of Judaea, was that Paul had taught all the Jews living among the Gentiles "to apostatize[5] from Moses, saying that they ought not to circumcise their children, neither to walk after the customs."

Now this charge was rather complicated by prejudice, as such charges often are. As it stood it was false. Paul had started no rebellion against Moses or the law. To say that the law was fulfilled by Christ is not to deny but to *confirm* its claims.

But the apostle *did* teach that the law had been fulfilled in Christ and that it was *therefore* unnecessary to observe its ceremonial rites—and he taught this not only to the Gentiles but also to the Jews which were among them.

"After the reading of the law and the prophets" in the Pisidian synagogue, the rulers asked Paul for a "word of *exhortation*." In response the apostle *gave*

---

5. This is the very Greek word used in Acts 21:21. While it sometimes means simply "to depart," James probably used it here in the sense of apostasy from the Word of God through Moses.

them a word of exhortation with respect to each. With respect to the law he exhorted them not to trust in it, but to trust in Christ, saying:

**"Be it known unto you therefore, men and brethren, that *through this man is preached unto you the forgiveness of sins:*

"And by Him all that believe are justified from all things, from which *ye could not be justified by the law of Moses"* (Acts 13:38,39).

Certainly there were Jewish believers among the Galatians and they were included in the number of those to whom the apostle wrote:

"...false brethren...came in privily to spy out *our liberty* which we have in Christ Jesus" (Gal. 2:4).

"...*I through the law am dead to the law...*" (2:19).

"Are ye so foolish? having begun in the Spirit, are ye now made perfect by the flesh?" (3:3).

"...the law was our schoolmaster...But after that faith is come, *we are no longer under a schoolmaster"* (3:24,25).

"...*How turn ye again to the weak and beggarly elements, whereunto ye desire again to be in bondage?*

"*Ye observe days, and months, and times, and years.*

"*I am afraid of*[6] *you, lest I have bestowed upon you labor in vain"* (4:9-11).

"Stand fast therefore in the liberty wherewith Christ hath made us free, and be not entangled again with the yoke of bondage.*

---

6. *About.*

"Behold, I Paul say unto you, that if ye be circumcised, Christ shall profit you nothing"[7] **(5:1,2).**

"...they constrain you to be circumcised; only lest they should suffer persecution for the cross of Christ.

"...they...desire to have you circumcised, that they may glory in your flesh.

"But God forbid that I should glory, save in the cross of our Lord Jesus Christ, by whom the world is crucified unto me, and I unto the world" **(6:12,13,14).**

The Galatian congregations were, of course, largely made up of Gentiles, but the apostle did not single the Gentiles out as he wrote about circumcision, so that the principle certainly applied also to those already circumcised and had its bearing on any contemplated circumcision of their children.

Nor can it be said that in the Galatian letter the apostle argued only against seeking to be *justified* by the law, for he clearly warns those *already* justified against becoming "entangled" again by submitting to one of its rites, warning them that submission to one implies the responsibility to obey all (See Gal. 5:1,3). And in this connection he had warned them that *"a little leaven leaveneth the whole lump"* (5:9).

Next consider the Corinthian church. It was begun with a group from the synagogue, including the household of Crispus, the chief ruler of the synagogue and, later, Sosthenes, the next chief ruler (Acts 18:8,17; I Cor. 1:1).

To these Jews "which were among the Gentiles," he wrote:

---

7.   Not *actually*, of course, but *logically*.

"For by one Spirit are we all baptized into one body, whether we be Jews or Gentiles..." (I Cor. 12:13).

"Wherefore henceforth know we no man after the flesh..." (II Cor. 5:16).

To them he wrote that the law was *"the ministration of death"* and *"the ministration of condemnation"* (II Cor. 3:7,9). Nor did the apostle here refer only to the ten commandments, for in saying that all this had been "abolished" he clearly referred to the *whole* law (cf. Ver. 13 with Ex. 34:32,33).

And to both the Jewish and Gentile believers at Corinth he had written:

"...I am jealous over you with godly jealousy: for I have espoused you to *one husband*, that I may present you as a chaste virgin to Christ.

"But I fear, lest by any means, as the serpent beguiled Eve through his subtlety, so your minds should be corrupted from *the simplicity that is in Christ"* (II Cor. 11:2,3).

And only recently he had written to the believers at Rome—and especially to the *Jewish* believers among them—in the same vein:

"...ye also are become *dead to the law...that ye should be married to another...*" (Rom. 7:4).

"But now *we are delivered from the law, that being dead wherein we were held; that we should serve in newness of spirit, and not in the oldness of the letter"* (Ver. 6).

Indeed, if Paul had not taught the Jews among the Gentiles to give up Judaism, what right did he have to rebuke Peter for reverting to it while visiting with the Gentiles at Antioch? Peter, remember, had been *"living after the manner of Gentiles, and NOT as do the Jews"* while there at Antioch. And *"the other Jews"* among them had been doing the same, until "certain came from James." *Then* Peter and the other Jewish believers began living "as do the Jews" again and were rebuked by Paul for their dissimulation (See Gal. 2:11-14).

We cite these passages, and could cite others, only to show that while Paul had not, to be sure, *apostatized* from Moses, he *had* taught the Jews among the Gentiles that the law had been fulfilled in Christ and that *therefore* they were to enjoy freedom from its yoke, so that the current reports about the apostle were not exactly "nothing" as James intimated (Ver. 24). Indeed, of those who contend that the report was *entirely without foundation*, we know of none who face up to the facts.

JAMES' PROPOSAL

James' proposal, evidently agreed upon beforehand, must be carefully considered in the light of its background.

The Jewish church had become numerically powerful in Jerusalem and Judaea. Since the scattering of Acts 8:1 the rulers of Israel had lost Saul of Tarsus, the flaming leader of their rebellion against Christ, and had themselves become less aggressive. The result was that great numbers had returned to Jerusalem until, some ten years later, not only was there a "multitude" of believers in the city, but they had attained so favorable a position that the Church could hold the great council of Acts 15 with no one to molest. And now, another

257

thirteen or fourteen years later, there are evidently greater numbers than ever[8] (Acts 21:20).

But the council at Jerusalem, while it had closed the mouths of the Judaizers as far as public opposition to Paul's message of grace was concerned, had by no means won them to the attitude which Peter had displayed in his noble declaration of Acts 15:8-11. Instead they had dogged Paul's footsteps wherever he had gone, seeking to undermine his ministry among the Galatians, the Corinthians and the Gentile believers in general. Indeed, Peter himself, along with other Jewish believers, including even Barnabas, had nearly caused serious division in the church at Antioch under the influence of "certain [that had come] from James" (Gal. 2:12,13).

And now do James and the elders make their proposal to Paul to help *him*, or because *they* are embarrassed by his presence in Jerusalem at this time? If their desire is truly to help, *they* are in the position to do so now, but this does not appear to be the case, for, without offering to endorse his ministry or to stand by him in any way, they urge *him* to go through a Jewish ritual to appease those who have been informed (partly in truth) that he is leaving Judaism.

The multitude, they say, will certainly "come together" when they hear that Paul has arrived. Something, then, must be quickly done, *by Paul*, in a *public* way, to convince them that they have been misinformed; that the apostle is a good Jew, faithfully observing the ordinances of the law.[9]

---

8. Granted that many of the believers present in Jerusalem at this time had come from distances, the great majority would still have been from Jerusalem and Judaea.

9. The words *"walkest orderly and keepest the law"* can mean nothing less than *faithful observance* of the law.

Their proposition, therefore, was this: *Paul* himself was evidently not under a vow at this time, but *they* had four men who were, and Paul could join *publicly* with them in their vow by purifying himself and paying for the sacrifices marking the consummation of their vow—a considerable amount, since two doves or pigeons, one he-lamb, one ewe lamb and a ram had to be offered for *each* of the four (Num. 6).

This procedure was evidently not uncommon at that time. Indeed, Josephus tells how Agrippa I courted Jewish favor by thus financing Nazarite vows (Ant. XIX, 6,1).

James and the elders evidently wished Paul to leave with *them* any questions he might have about this, urging him: *"Do therefore this that we say unto thee"* (Ver. 23). And to induce him further to yield, they reminded him that they had "written and concluded that [the Gentiles] observe no such thing"[10] (Ver. 25).

WOULD IT BE RIGHT OR WRONG
TO YIELD?

Thus the apostle was urged to endorse the action of four Jewish zealots in taking a Nazarite vow, by financing, not one, but *five* bloody sacrifices *for each*. And he was urged to do this to prove that he was a faithful observer of the law. Would it be right or wrong of him to yield?

As we examine all the Scriptures involved we can come to but one conclusion: It would be wrong.

---

10. *R.V.* omits this part of the verse. The context seems to favor *A.V.*, but if *R.V.* is correct it would then seem to indicate that James and the elders were putting stronger *pressure* on the apostle.

Much is said about the two programs that run side by side through the latter part of Acts. We have no objection to the term "side by side," if only it is understood that it was not God's purpose for both programs to continue *with equal force* during those years. Just as the new program gradually emerged, the old was gradually to pass away. There was to be a *transition* from the one to the other. Peter's part in the conversion of Cornelius and his household, his words in Acts 15:8-11 and the decision of the Jerusalem council alone had indicated that even on the part of the Jewish believers there was to be a gradual liberation from the law. The breaking down of "the middle wall of partition" was to affect those on both sides.

But had not Paul written the Corinthians that every man should abide in his own calling, and that the circumcised should not become uncircumcised? (I Cor. 7:18). First, the apostle here does not refer to doctrinal positions which men might hold, but to *physical circumstances* in which they are found, including slavery, virginity, married life, etc. Now there were evidently some Jewish converts that had become so extreme in their feelings about circumcision and the law, that they had sought, by surgical operations, to become "uncircumcised." The Greek word "*epispaomi*," unlike the usual word for uncircumcision, is a surgical term meaning "to draw over." Thus the passage has nothing to do with Jews remaining in Judaism.

But had he not also written: *"And unto the Jews I became as a Jew, that I might gain the Jews; to them that are under the law, as under the law, that I might gain them that are under the law; to them that are without law, as without law, (being not without law to God,*

but under the law to Christ,) that I might gain them
that are without law"*? (I Cor. 9:20,21).

This passage is thought by some to contain the full
justification of Paul's involvement in Judaism at this
time. They suppose that it means that he alternately
placed himself in subjection to the law and at liberty
from it as he labored, now with Jews and then with
Gentiles.

Those who interpret this passage in this way to
defend Paul's action at Jerusalem should take care
that they do not charge him with worse than a lapse in
faithfulness. We can understand how the apostle, like
all other men of God, should stumble and fall, but the
above interpretation of I Corinthians 9:20 would make
Paul guilty of *habitual duplicity*.

In the first place, the apostle labored with Jews
and Gentiles most of the time. In practically all of
the churches he founded there were Jews at first; then
Gentiles were added. Now suppose he placed himself
under the law in order to win the Jews, and then, later,
these same Jews learned that among the Gentiles he
cast off the yoke and taught that the ceremonies of
Judaism were "nothing"; what would they—what *could*
they think of him?

We believe that the passage in I Corinthians 9
simply means that, sympathetically, he placed himself
mentally in the position of those with whom he dealt.
He did not go back into Judaism while among Jews, but,
recognizing their prejudices, he refrained from doing
what might offend them—so that he might gradually
teach them the same truths he had taught the Jews at
Pisidian Antioch: justification from all things *by faith
in Christ, apart from the law* (Acts 13:38,39).

261

In the next verse in I Corinthians 9, the apostle says: *"to the weak became I as weak."* Does this mean he actually became *weak*? Of course not. It means he *sympathized* with the weak, dealing with them gently and not showing off his strength. In the same way he became *"as* a Jew" to the Jews and *"as* under the law" to those who were under it.[11]

As we have said, the two programs in later Acts were not to continue with equal force. The old was permitted to continue for a time, only because men are slow to learn and customs of long standing are difficult to throw off. But that the apostle sought to show "the Jews which [were] among the Gentiles" the *finished* work of Christ and their liberty in Christ, along with the Gentiles, is evident from the fact that at Antioch he, along with Peter, had lived "after the manner of Gentiles" and had rebuked Peter for reverting to Judaism for fear of those of James' party (Gal. 2:14).

How could either Peter or Paul have practiced the popular interpretation of I Corinthians 9:20,21 here at Antioch anyway, with *both* Jews and Gentiles present? In such cases the fruits of duplicity would surely be reaped! And note further that Paul rebuked Peter on this occasion, not for crossing a Jewish-Gentile line the wrong way or at the wrong time, but for *going back on light received* (Gal. 2:15-19). Peter had learned by a special vision and by the conversion of Cornelius that God had made no difference between Jew and Gentile and he had publicly stated this, and more, at the council at Jerusalem. Now, by separating the Jews from the Gentiles at Antioch, he was building again that which

---

11. Some MSS even add the words *"not being myself under the law"* here (See I Cor. 9:20, R.V.).

262

he had destroyed, and thus making himself a transgressor (Gal. 2:18).

Thus it is not enough to argue that there was one program for the Jew and another for the Gentile, during the latter part of Acts, for it was on the basis of revealed *truth* as to Old Testament rites that Paul fought for Gentile liberty from them, and it was on the basis of revealed truth also that the Jewish program was gradually to be abandoned (Acts 15:8-11; Heb. 10:1-39; etc.). Therefore, one who sought now to place himself under the law was condemned, not because he violated a program, but because he disobeyed *the truth* (See Gal. 3:1; 5:7).

As Paul now agreed to take part with unbelieving priests and Levites in offering burnt offerings, sin offerings and peace offerings, all of which had been fulfilled in Christ, he would surely be helping to keep Jewish believers under bondage from which the Gentiles had been freed and which even Peter had described as a yoke too heavy to bear (Acts 15:10). In the light of all the Scriptures on the subject, it is surely more tenable to hold that he lapsed here than that this was his policy.

But had he not on a previous occasion, taken a vow and hastened to keep a feast at Jerusalem? Was the apostle out of the will of God on this occasion too? In answer we say, examine the record and observe the circumstances: In the only recorded case where a congregation in a synagogue, "desired him to tarry longer time with them" he "consented not" because he hastened because it was his desire "by all means" to reach Jerusalem by feast time (Acts 18:20,21). And then the Spirit draws a veil about the apostle's activities. What feast it was he wanted to keep, we are not told.

Nor are we told whether he reached Jerusalem in time, or how he was received. Indeed, it is only *implied* that he arrived at Jerusalem at all.[12]

Certainly we are not informed, either by Paul himself or by Luke, what good reason there was for taking the vow or why it was so necessary that he keep a Jewish feast at Jerusalem. We can only conclude that his "great heaviness and continual sorrow" over Israel kept turning his heart back to Jerusalem and impelled him to take even this course to win them if possible.

But what about his circumcision of Timothy and the baptisms he administered? Were not both of these connected with the law? Here we must again emphasize the transitional character of the latter part of Acts. Without considering again the circumstances surrounding Timothy's circumcision, this, like Paul's baptisms, was done before he had even written his first epistle and while he was still receiving revelations, one after another, from the glorified Lord. And when he does look back, years later, on the Corinthian baptisms administered by him, he thanks God that he did not baptize more, adding: *"For Christ sent me not to baptize, but to preach the gospel....For the preaching of the cross...is the power of God"* (I Cor. 1:14-18).

As to James' proposal that Paul prove to the "zealots for the law" that he himself was a faithful observer of the law, the fact is that only a few days later Paul testified: *"I...WAS zealous[13] toward God, as ye all are this day"* (Acts 22:3). And later again he testified before Felix:

---

12. It merely states that he had "gone up, and saluted the church" (Acts 18:22).

13. Here too the original word is a *noun*: "I was a *zealot*."

"But this I confess unto thee, that *after the way which they call heresy,* so worship I the God of my fathers, believing all things which are written in the law and in the prophets" (Acts 24:14).

The apostle *could not,* then, have been a faithful observer of the law. Why should he now seek to prove that he was? Why should he try to prove to the Jews that he "walked orderly and kept the law" when he *certainly* had not done so among the Gentiles?

He had come to Jerusalem to bring an offering to the poor saints there and to "testify the gospel of the grace of God." There is no record that the offering was gratefully received, and surely he could not "testify the gospel of the grace of God" by offering blood sacrifices. But even the sacrifices were not actually offered. So far from James' plan succeeding, a great commotion and Paul's arrest "when the seven days were almost ended," prevented him from having any part in the offering of the proposed sacrifices.

THE APOSTLE YIELDS

"Then Paul took the men, and the next day purifying himself with them entered into the temple, to signify the accomplishment of the days of purification, until that an offering should be offered for every one of them."

—Acts 21:26

Thus Paul, as the representative of the four Nazarites, entered into the temple to announce to the priest that after seven days' purification the prescribed sacrifices should now be offered.

It is strange to see Paul yielding to James and going back again to what he had only recently called "weak and beggarly elements."

265

What all his own reasons were for doing so we do not know. It cannot be said that, being at Jerusalem, he submitted to the authority of the circumcision apostles, for there is no evidence that any of them were there— indeed, the evidence rather indicates that they were *not* present at the meeting.

Yet, he later testified before the Sanhedrin: *"I have lived in all good conscience before God until this day"*[14] (Acts 23:1). Doubtless he reasoned that the charge made against him was untrue, that he was here on Jewish ground and that joining in the vow might induce the Jews to give him a hearing. Also, had he not at great labor and through long months organized the collection of the great offering which they had now brought to their Jewish brethren? Must this all go in vain? What would the churches say if, after sacrificing so heavily of their means, the plan miscarried? Such would be the thoughts running through his mind, and so complex can spiritual problems become.

As we know, the plan miscarried anyway, for the object of the course he took was altogether frustrated by the uprising that took place just before its completion, with the added result that his public ministry was brought to a close, at least for the present, and he was led away as *"the prisoner of Jesus Christ for [the] Gentiles"* (Eph. 3:1). This, we take it, was not done as a *punishment*, but rather as a means to keep him *"the apostle of the Gentiles,"* regardless of how keenly he might feel obligated to the Jews.

---

14. He may well, however, have referred to *his adopted course*, first in *persecuting* Christ and then in *proclaiming* Him.

THE UPROAR AT JERUSALEM

"And when the seven days were almost ended, the Jews which were of Asia, when they saw him in the temple, stirred up all the people, and laid hands on him,

"Crying out, Men of Israel, help: This is the man that teacheth all men everywhere against the people, and the law, and this place: and further brought Greeks also into the temple, and hath polluted this holy place.

"(For they had seen before with him in the city Trophimus an Ephesian, whom they supposed that Paul had brought into the temple.)

"And all the city was moved, and the people ran together: and they took Paul, and drew him out of the temple: and forthwith the doors were shut.

"And as they went about to kill him, tidings came unto the chief captain of the band, that all Jerusalem was in an uproar:

"Who immediately took soldiers and centurions, and ran down unto them: and when they saw the chief captain and the soldiers, they left beating of Paul.

"Then the chief captain came near, and took him, and commanded him to be bound with two chains; and demanded who he was, and what he had done.

"And some cried one thing, some another, among the multitude: and when he could not know the certainty for the tumult, he commanded him to be carried into the castle.

"And when he came upon the stairs, so it was, that he was borne of the soldiers for the violence of the people.

"For the multitude of the people followed after, crying, Away with him.

"And as Paul was to be led into the castle, he said unto the chief captain, May I speak unto thee? Who said, Canst thou speak Greek?

"Art not thou that Egyptian which before these days madest an uproar, and leddest out into the wilderness four thousand men that were murderers?

"But Paul said, I am a man which am a Jew of Tarsus, a city in Cilicia, a citizen of no mean city: and, I beseech thee, suffer me to speak unto the people.

"And when he had given him license, Paul stood on the stairs, and beckoned with the hand unto the people. And when there was made a great silence, he spake unto them in the Hebrew tongue, saying,"

—Acts 21:27-40

PAUL SEIZED IN THE TEMPLE

The thousands of pilgrims who traveled to Jerusalem on its principal feast days would, of course, be those which were most zealous of the law and the traditions of the fathers. Also, of the unbelieving Jews who resided in Jerusalem there would probably be few left who would recognize Paul, for it was now more than twenty-five years since he had been in the public eye in Israel, as the leader of the great persecution against Christ.

Thus it was "the Jews which were of Asia" who started the great uprising against Paul in Jerusalem.

It was as the seven days of purification were about to be accomplished that these zealots saw him in the temple and raised a cry against him. They had recognized Trophimus of Ephesus with him in the city and now supposed that he had brought "Greeks[1]...into the temple" to demonstrate his contempt for Israel, the law and the temple.

That Paul's ministry had been widely discussed—and misrepresented—is evident from the cry: *"Men of Israel, help! This is the man that teacheth all men everywhere against the people, and the law, and this place"* (Ver. 28).

This was practically the same charge upon which the Sanhedrin, along with Saul, had stoned Stephen to death years before (Acts 6:13). Now the apostle hears the same charge of blasphemy hurled at him. The charge was, of course, utterly untrue, as was the additional charge that he had polluted the temple by bringing Greeks inside, yet it was bound to stir the people up to indignation.

Excavations of the Palestine Exploration Society (Report for 1871, pg. 132) have brought to light a slab of stone with an inscription, deciphered by M. Clermont Ganneau, which illustrates the horror with which the Jews looked upon the profanation by Gentiles of that inner portion of the temple grounds sacred to Jews alone. The inscription reads:

"No man of alien race is to enter within the balustrade and fence that goes round the temple. If any one is taken in the act, let him know that he has himself to blame for the penalty of death that follows."

---

1. The four men for whom Paul was now about to offer sacrifices may have been with him and mistaken for Greeks.

Such a cry, then, raised against one who had been so long and so widely slandered, had an immediate effect.

Whether Alexander, the Ephesian Jew (Acts 19:33,34; II Tim. 4:14,15) had anything to do with this uprising we are not told, but the pattern followed closely that of the uprising at Ephesus some years previous.

Suddenly the whole city was in commotion, the people running together and dragging[2] Paul out of the temple and closing the great doors to prevent further desecration. Holding him illegally, they began to beat him and were about to kill him when something occurred to stop them.

Overlooking the temple grounds was the "castle" of Antonia, the barracks of the Roman soldiers who kept order in Jerusalem. No more had the tumult started down below than a report of it was relayed to "the chief captain of the band,"[3] probably by sentries on duty. Immediately the chief captain, Claudius Lysias, with a detachment of soldiers, ran down to investigate and restore order.

With this the Jews "left beating of Paul" (Ver. 32). Once more the apostle owed his safety from violence to intervention by civil authorities.

PAUL AND LYSIAS

Supposing that Paul was responsible for the uprising, the chief captain took him into custody, commanding his soldiers to bind him with "two chains."[4] Already Agabus' prediction was being fulfilled (See Vers. 10,11).

---

2. Gr. *Helko*

3. "Chief captain," Gr. *chilliarch*, "captain over a thousand"; "Band," Gr. *speira*, one of the ten divisions of a legion, or about 600 men.

4. Probably to two soldiers, at the wrists (cf. 12:6).

But the confusion was so great that it was impossible for Lysias to get at the root of the trouble. As it had been at Ephesus, "some cried one thing, some another" (cf. Ver. 34 with 19:32). Lysias therefore "commanded him to be carried into the castle," and Paul actually *had* to be *carried* up the stairs by the soldiers, so great was "the violence of the people." Meantime one consistent cry alone rose above the angry tumult; the same cry which had been heard at the trial of the Lord Jesus:

"Away with him!" All this before the apostle had even been heard. So unreasonable and vicious can religious bigotry cause men to be.

One would suppose that having just been rescued from a severe beating by men intent on killing him, and hearing even now the wild clamor for his life, the apostle would be more than grateful to be taken to a place of shelter and safety, but not so. He, apparently, was the only cool person in all that multitude. Moreover, his heart bled for those whose blind, bitter hatred of Christ was but the reflection of his own former feelings, when he had led his nation in a brutal war against Messiah.

Thus it was that the apostle, now to be led into the castle, respectfully asked the chief captain in Greek: *"May I speak unto thee?"* The fact that Paul addressed him in Greek surprised the chief captain, who had supposed him to be an Egyptian with whom Rome had previously had trouble. And here Paul demonstrates his breeding and aristocratic consciousness. With calm dignity he identifies himself, pressing home to Lysias the fact that he is a citizen of Tarsus, "no mean city,"[5] and requesting an opportunity to speak to the people.

---

5. One highly honored by the Roman government.

271

This tactful approach, together with his bearing under such circumstances evidently struck Lysias, so that he granted him permission to address the furious throng.

But now Lysias is in for another surprise, for Paul turns at the top of the stairs to address the multitude, not in Greek, which all could understand, but in *Hebrew!* In his alertness and presence of mind, the apostle had at least two reasons for this.

First, to conciliate the Jews. They would expect him to address them in Greek; instead he does so in the language which none but the Circumcision could understand and which was associated in their minds with all that was sacred in the Judaism they fought for. This would speak to them of loyalty to God's law rather than apostasy from it (See 22:2).

Secondly, he did *not* wish *Lysias* to understand. To Lysias he had just said: "I am...a Jew of *Tarsus*...a citizen of *no mean city*" (Ver. 39) but to the Jews he now says in Hebrew: "I am verily...a Jew, born in Tarsus...*yet brought up in this city*..." (22:3). To them he places Tarsus in the background and places the emphasis upon Jerusalem. Also, it would be better if Lysias did not hear how he had persecuted many of his kinsmen "to the death" or he might prejudice the captain against him.

How graciously God had overruled! An uprising had hindered Paul from offering the sacrifices he was about to make, which would largely have nullified his testimony. And now, on account of that same uprising, he is given an opportunity to address his countrymen in greater numbers than could have been arranged in any other way. Such a meeting could never have been called, nor could any building have held so great a multitude.

How else could so many Jews from Jerusalem and of the dispersion have been gathered together to hear a final testimony to Christ? And what circumstances would be better calculated to gain their most profound attention? This was his opportunity. Could he turn them to Christ and proclaim to them "the good news of the grace of God"?

As the apostle "beckoned with the hand unto the people" with that characteristic gesture which more than once gained him the attention of his audiences (See Acts 13:16 and 26:1) the multitude "made a great silence" (Ver. 40). Yet, here was a vast audience which would put to a test the power of that voice already strengthened by much public speaking.

PAUL'S DEFENSE BEFORE THE MULTITUDE

HE RECOUNTS THE STORY OF HIS CONVERSION

"Men, brethren, and fathers, hear ye my defense which I make now unto you.

"(And when they heard that he spake in the Hebrew tongue to them, they kept the more silence: and he saith,)

"I am verily a man which am a Jew, born in Tarsus, a city in Cilicia, yet brought up in this city at the feet of Gamaliel, and taught according to the perfect manner of the law of the fathers, and was zealous toward God, as ye all are this day.

"And I persecuted this way unto the death, binding and delivering into prisons both men and women.

273

"As also the high priest doth bear me witness, and all the estate of the elders: from whom also I received letters unto the brethren, and went to Damascus, to bring them which were there bound unto Jerusalem, for to be punished.

"And it came to pass, that, as I made my journey, and was come nigh unto Damascus about noon, suddenly there shone from heaven a great light round about me.

"And I fell unto the ground, and heard a voice saying unto me, Saul, Saul, why persecutest thou Me?

"And I answered, Who art thou, Lord? And He said unto me, I am Jesus of Nazareth, whom thou persecutest.

"And they that were with me saw indeed the light, and were afraid; but they heard not the voice of Him that spake to me.

"And I said, what shall I do, Lord? And the Lord said unto me, Arise, and go into Damascus; and there it shall be told thee of all things which are appointed for thee to do.

"And when I could not see for the glory of that light, being led by the hand of them that were with me, I came into Damascus.

"And one Ananias, a devout man according to the law, having a good report of all the Jews which dwelt there,

"Came unto me, and stood, and said unto me, Brother Saul, receive thy sight. And the same hour I looked up upon him.

"And he said, The God of our fathers hath chosen thee, that thou shouldest know His will, and see that Just One, and shouldest hear the voice of His mouth.

"For thou shalt be His witness unto all men of what thou hast seen and heard.

"And now why tarriest thou? Arise, and be baptized, and wash away thy sins, calling on the name of the Lord."

—Acts 22:1-16

The Book of Acts contains no less than three accounts of Paul's conversion. The first is a simple narration of the story by Luke in Chapter 9, but the other two are apologetic in character, as Paul defends himself, first before the multitude here at Jerusalem and then before Agrippa.

Tactless preachers, who hinder their usefulness by blunt outspokenness which is more apt to offend than to convince, would do well to study this address by the Apostle Paul. The remarkable fact about it is, not that he failed to persuade his hearers, but that in his God-given skill to adapt himself to his audience, he was able to keep them listening with rapt attention as long as he did. Certainly we have here one of his most remarkable addresses, for its sympathy and tact, its sincerity and honesty and its persuasive force.

The apostle's gesture had quieted the tumult, his use of the Hebrew had gained for him a breathless silence, and now his words are calculated to conciliate his hearers and draw them into sympathy with himself and his point of view.

He addresses them respectfully as "brethren and fathers," thus claiming kinship with them. He had told the Roman Lysias that he was a "Jew of Tarsus... *no mean city*" (21:39) but to this audience he points out that while he had been "*born* in Tarsus," he was "*brought up in this city* [*Jerusalem*]" (22:3). Tarsus

275

falls into the background and Jerusalem is given prominence. Indeed, he was "taught," or trained, in the "perfect," or exact "manner" in which the fathers had observed the law (cf. Gal. 1:14) "at the feet" of no less a rabbi than Gamaliel, "a doctor of the law," held "in reputation among all the people"[6] (5:34). Surely, then, his present course could not have been lightly adopted as the result of some idea of his own.

He shows that he understands perfectly this outburst of zeal for God and His law: "I...was[7] zealous [Lit. a zealot] toward God, as ye all are this day" (Ver. 3 cf. 21:28). Indeed, he had outdone them in his determination to stamp out what he had considered a heresy.

In his reference to his training at the feet of Gamaliel he hints that he was a Pharisee, but he does not *say* so, lest the Sadducees, including most of the priesthood, start the uproar all over again. But he does openly appeal to the testimony of the high priest and "all the estate of the elders"[8] as to his commission to have the believers at Damascus punished. And here again, adroitly, he tells them that he *"received,"* not "desired" as in 9:1,2, letters of authorization to Damascus. This would demonstrate the confidence which the Hebrew leaders had placed in him. And these letters, he says, were addressed to the "brethren" at Damascus, a term he does not, in this address, use even of his fellow-believers in Christ.

---

6. Indeed, still considered one of the greatest rabbis Israel ever produced.

7. Note how skillfully he implies that he is no longer such (cf. Gal. 1:14) while Acts 21:20 informs us that even the Jewish *believers* in Judaea were still zealots for the law.

8. Evidently a larger body than the Sanhedrin (though including it) and identical with "all the senate of the children of Israel" in Acts 5:21.

276

To show further that he had not merely been an opinionated young man trying to start something new, he stresses the miraculous in his conversion. He points out, as Luke's account does not, that it was "about noon" when "a great light," brighter than the midday sun, shone round about him and that he "could not see for the glory of that light." And at this, he says: "I fell to the ground." He had been *humbled* by God, not puffed up by a little knowledge. It was nothing less than a miraculous and divine revelation that had led him to change his course and to say to the One whom he had so bitterly persecuted: *"What shall I do, Lord?"*[9]

The cause of the great uprising that followed Paul's address should be kept in mind as we read this part of the narrative. The multitude raised no commotion as the apostle related how he had found Jesus to be the Messiah. Tens of thousands in Jerusalem believed this and the rest tolerated it (See 21:20). What enraged them was Paul's preaching of the *finished* work of the *now-risen* Christ and the consequent replacement of law by grace sufficient for uncircumcised Gentiles as well as Jews (21:28). This was the issue even among the *believers* at Jerusalem (See 21:20,21).

And this is still the great issue today. "Christianity" as an offshoot of Judaism, with believers in Christ under the law, is tolerated, but *true* Christianity, with its freedom from the law and its riches of grace cannot be countenanced! Even some leaders of Fundamentalism pronounce it anathema. This, the glorious all-sufficiency of Christ, is what Satan hates and opposes most bitterly.

---

9. There is no contradiction between Acts 9:7 and 22:9. Paul's companions *heard* the voice, but did not hear "the voice of Him that spoke to me," i.e., they did not understand anything being said.

It was at the very time of Paul's conversion that the Lord Himself had commissioned Paul to go to the Gentiles (26:17) and Ananias too had been told that Paul was "a chosen vessel" to bear Christ's name "before the Gentiles..." (9:15) but, tactfully, the apostle here saves any mention of the Gentiles until the account of his return to Jerusalem. Acts 22:21,22 show clearly enough why it was wise to refrain, as long as possible, from saying what was almost certain to arouse the anger of his hearers again.

In his reference to Ananias the apostle again demonstrates his superb tact. The account in Acts 9 depicts Ananias as a "disciple" in close communion with Christ, but here Paul does not even mention (though he implies) his faith in Christ. Instead he refers to him as *"a devout man according to the law"* and *"having a good report of all the Jews which dwelt there"* (Ver. 12) which was also, of course, true. This would give them a feeling of kinship with Ananias and would assure them that *he* would not have fellowship with a blasphemer, nor even with a former persecutor, except upon clear evidence that *God* had changed his heart.[10]

Further pursuing his conciliatory approach, the apostle recalls how Ananias had called him *"Brother Saul"* and had declared: *"The God of our fathers* hath chosen thee...."* And now is the time to explain that he was the chosen vessel to usher in a new dispensation, for Ananias had been instructed to inform him that he had been chosen of God 1.) to *"know His will,"*[11] 2.) to

---

10. Ananias' objections to visiting Paul confirms this to be true (See Acts 9:13,14).

11. This could not refer to His will *for Paul*, for why should he be "chosen" to know that? Who else should it be revealed to? Clearly it refers to the will of God spoken of in Ephesians 1:9,11; 5:17, His will, or program, in view of Israel's rejection of Christ.

"see that Just One," Christ, 3.) to *"hear the voice of His mouth"* and 4.) to *"be His witness"* of what he had *"seen and heard."*[12]

But now once more he approaches a dangerous point. *To whom* was he to bear witness of what he had seen and heard? As we have already seen, it was mainly to the Gentiles. How dexterously he touches upon this here, using the phrase *"unto all men"!*

Finally he relates how Ananias had instructed him:

"And now why tarriest thou? arise, and be baptized, and wash away thy sins, calling on the name of the Lord" (Ver. 16).

We have already discussed the baptism of Paul (see notes on Acts 9) but there are a few additional points that should be stressed here.

First, it is evident that Paul was thoroughly converted on the road to Damascus, yet *at that time* water baptism was still required for salvation (Mark 16:16) thus he was called upon to "wash away his sins" by water baptism, not that water in itself could wash away sins, but as an expression of faith. When God said water baptism was necessary to salvation faith would respond *by being baptized.*[13]

Second, this passage bears witness to the fallacy of the "watery grave" theory of our immersionist brethren. We do not—nor did they then—bury people in water. Does the reader suppose that in the cases of Cornelius, Lydia, the Philippian jailor and in Paul's case here, they just happened to have vessels large enough to hold sufficient water to *bury* people in? Certainly there is no

---

12. See the author's book entitled: *Moses and Paul*, pgs. 20-28.
13. See the author's chapter on *The Principles and Dispensations of God*, in his book *Things That Differ*.

indication in any of the above cases that they went out and got the equipment or conducted the applicant to any place where they might find such facilities. This crude theory of burial in water comes from the false notion that Romans 6:4 and Colossians 2:12 refer to *water* baptism.[14]

Water baptism is a natural symbol for *washing*, or *cleansing* as this passage and many others indicate (cf. Mark 7:1-5 where *baptizo* is twice rendered *wash* and where it is used alternately with *nipto*, another word for *wash*; also Hebrews 9:10, where the original word is *baptismos*).

Third, it should be observed that Paul here relates what took place *at the time of his conversion*. He was converted under the dispensation when water baptism was required and, symbolically, he was baptized to wash away his sins, but later, using the very same word rendered "wash" here (Gr. *apolouo*) he had written to the Corinthians:

"And such were some of you: *but ye are washed*, but ye are sanctified, but ye are justified, in the name of the Lord Jesus, and *by the Spirit of our God"* (I Cor. 6:11).

And still later he was to write to Titus:

"Not by works of righteousness which we have done, but according to His mercy He saved us, by the washing of regeneration, and the renewing of the Holy Ghost" **(Titus 3:5).**

Though the apostle's address is not yet finished, this concludes the account of his conversion. Before leaving it we again point out that whereas the twelve had "seen and heard" Christ only in His ministry *on earth*

---

14. For a fuller discussion of this subject see *Real Baptism*, by Charles F. Baker.

and were commissioned to be witnesses of these things (Acts 4:20) Paul had seen and heard Him in His glory "far above all" and had been commissioned to bear witness to this and to other revelations he was still to receive of and from the glorified Lord (26:16). Indeed, the closing words of this address at Jerusalem deal with one of these revelations.

UNTO THIS WORD

"And it came to pass, that, when I was come again to Jerusalem, even while I prayed in the temple, I was in a trance;

"And saw Him saying unto me, Make haste, and get thee quickly out of Jerusalem: for they will not receive thy testimony concerning Me.

"And I said, Lord, they know that I imprisoned and beat in every synagogue them that believed on Thee:

"And when the blood of Thy martyr Stephen was shed, I also was standing by, and consenting unto his death, and kept the raiment of them that slew him.

"And He said unto me, Depart: for I will send thee far hence unto the Gentiles.

"And they gave him audience unto this word, and then lifted up their voices, and said, Away with such a fellow from the earth: for it is not fit that he should live.

"And as they cried out, and cast off their clothes, and threw dust into the air,

"The chief captain commanded him to be brought into the castle, and bade that he should be examined by scourging; that he might know wherefore they cried so against him."

—Acts 22:17-24

Paul's purpose in addressing the multitude at Jerusalem was not merely to tell them the story of his conversion. There was more to be said and he must come to the point.

Cautiously he explains how, *after* his conversion and commission to tell *"all men"* what he had seen and heard, he returned again to *Jerusalem* and went to the *temple* to *pray*. And it was there, in the House of God, while engaged in prayer, that, in a trance,[15] the Lord bade him hasten to leave Jerusalem, since they would not receive his testimony concerning Him. We know from the record in Acts 9 that his very life was in danger at that time (Ver. 29) but it would not be wise to bring this up here. Rather, the apostle shows how he longed to stay and labor with his people by recalling how he had argued the case with the Lord Himself, citing the fact that these people knew how he had imprisoned and beaten those who had believed on Christ and how he had even had a part in Stephen's death, guarding the clothes of those who stoned him, so that surely they would listen to *his* testimony.

How unjust and untrue, he implies, is the charge that he has been *against* the people, *against* the law and *against* the temple! Yet, in his references to his persecution of believers in Christ and the stoning of Stephen we find a noble example of one seeking to make public reparation for public sin, largely blaming *himself* for their unbelief.

But he recalls how the Lord would not *permit* him to stay, commanding him summarily:

"Depart: for I will send thee far hence unto the Gentiles" (Ver. 21).

---

15. Gr. *ekstasis*, a carrying outside of one's self.

Surely this could not refer to some particular journey which Paul was to take, but to the field of labor which henceforth was to be his. Certainly the multitude understood it so.

Thus the apostle acknowledges that the Lord Himself had instructed him to *leave* Jerusalem; that they would not listen anyway, yet here he was pleading with them—and under such circumstances! Could he offer greater proof of his love for them?

Indeed, the apostle would have gone on to cap his address with a proclamation of God's grace (See 20:24) and a plea to his hearers to accept that grace, but this is another one of the interrupted addresses of the Book of Acts. They did not permit him to finish.

He had avoided mentioning the Gentiles until now, deferring this until he had first showed the Jews how he loved *them* and how only at the divine command, specific and repeated, had he left the favored people to go to the Gentiles. But they "gave him audience" only "unto this word" and then, as when fire is set to an explosive, they burst forth in a demonstration of uncontrolled rage that immediately terminated the apostle's address.

They should have been interested in the salvation of the Gentiles (See Gen. 22:18; Isa. 56:6-8) but their intense national pride had blinded them to all else the apostle had said, so that they cried: *"Away with such a fellow from the earth: for it is not fit that he should live!"* And "as they cried out" they "cast off their clothes[16] and threw dust into the air."

---

16. I.e., their outer garments. The apostle well knew what this meant. They were prepared to stone him if only the chief captain would hand him over to them (See 22:20).

Gentiles! So *this* was to be the climax! *Now* he had gone too far! Imagine this apostate from the law, this traitor to his nation, alleging a vision from heaven and a trance in the temple as his defense in flinging open the doors of divine worship to these "sinners of the Gentiles," these dogs of the uncircumcision! They would not hear another word. This man must be put to death.

Alas, Paul's hopes and prayers regarding Jerusalem had not been realized. His "heart's desire and prayer to God...that they might be saved" (Rom. 10:1) had not been fulfilled. He had not been permitted to proclaim "the gospel of the grace of God" (Acts 20:24) to them. He had not been "delivered from those who did not believe in Judaea," nor had the sacrificial ministration from the Gentile churches been "accepted of the saints" there (Rom. 15:30,31). If they accepted the *money* (which we are not told) it had certainly not served to bring them closer to their Gentile brethren in Christ.

If the unbelieving Jews were Paul's bitter enemies then "James and the elders," along with any of the twelve apostles who were present, were his very doubtful friends. Neither now, nor later, do we find one of them standing at his side, even though James, Cephas and John had officially and publicly acknowledged him, some years back, as the apostle of grace and the apostle to the Gentiles.

Indeed, the compromise which James and his party had persuaded Paul to make had produced nothing— but this uproar—while *they* stayed in the background.

Yet the apostle had acted only out of love for his kinsmen and his Lord, and it was thus, in the providence of God that Israel received one final touching testimony to Christ from the lips of one who had even been instructed to leave them to their fate.

Surely Isaiah's inspired prediction had been amply fulfilled:

"But to Israel He saith, *All day long have I stretched forth my hands unto a disobedient and gainsaying people"* **(Rom. 10:21).**

But now the apostle was to face another test. His address, delivered in Hebrew, had borne the air of a confidential communication to the Jews alone, with the result that Lysias and his soldiers could only listen with vain curiosity and perhaps impatient suspicion. And now, at this renewed and persistent uproar, Lysias evidently suspected that Paul *was* guilty of some grievous crime.

He therefore commanded that the apostle be brought into the castle to be "examined by scourging" (Ver. 24). This was far more brutal than our so-called "third degree." It was a series of whippings inflicted to extort an admission of crime.

PAUL AGAIN ASSERTS HIS RIGHTS AS A ROMAN CITIZEN

"And as they bound him with thongs, Paul said unto the centurion that stood by, Is it lawful for you to scourge a man that is a Roman, and uncondemned?

"When the centurion heard that, he went and told the chief captain, saying, Take heed what thou doest; for this man is a Roman.

"Then the chief captain came, and said unto him, Tell me, art thou a Roman? He said, Yea.

285

"And the chief captain answered, With a great sum obtained I this freedom. And Paul said, But I was free born.

"Then straightway they departed from him which should have examined him: and the chief captain also was afraid, after he knew that he was a Roman, and because he had bound him.

"On the morrow, because he would have known the certainty wherefore he was accused of the Jews, he loosed him from his bands, and commanded the chief priests and all their council to appear, and brought Paul down, and set him before them."

—Acts 22:25-30

The apostle was by now a battle-scarred warrior for Christ. Already he had suffered "stripes above measure." "Of the Jews" he had "five times received...forty stripes save one."[17] "Thrice" he had been "beaten with rods," by the Roman lictors (See II Cor. 11:23-25). Now it was to be the Roman whip.

But as they bound him to the whipping post, with "thongs,"[18] doubtless having stripped him to the waist (cf. 16:22) he asked the centurion who stood by: *Is it lawful for you to scourge a man that is a Roman—and umcondemned?"*

Note the emphasis here. A twofold illegality had been committed.

If it was—and it *was*—a violation of Roman law to scourge a Roman citizen, how much more flagrant a violation to scourge him without even a hearing!

---

17. Forty were not permitted, lest the victim die.
18. Lit. straps. The word is thrice rendered "latchet" with reference to the straps of our Lord's sandals (Mark 1:7; Luke 3:16; John 1:27).

The effect of Paul's quiet question was instantaneous! The centurion into whose hands the brutal examination had evidently been entrusted, went immediately to the chief captain and exclaimed: "What are you about to do? This man is a Roman!"

This brought the chief captain himself to the scene with the astonished inquiry: *"Art thou a Roman?"* He had been surprised to hear him speak Greek; then again to hear him speak Hebrew. Now was he a Roman citizen too? Paul's brief, perhaps curt reply, *"Yes,"* may have expressed censure of the captain's hasty action.

Embarrassed, Lysias becomes friendly, even confidential with Paul, explaining how it cost him a great sum of money to become a Roman citizen.[19] But Paul, still pressing his advantage, answered simply: *"But I was born [a Roman]."*

With this, *all* those who had stood ready to "examine" him "departed straightway." No one wanted to be involved. And the chief captain, who had given the original order for the scourging, "was afraid."

Not far from this spot the Lord Jesus Christ had been scourged by the Romans, yet Paul now could and did claim exemption as a Roman citizen. Indeed the record of the Acts depicts him, on several occasions, standing on his rights as a Roman. There were several reasons for this but the *dispensational* significance

---

19. Some feel that Lysias brought up this matter, doubting that a poor Jew could possibly have been a Roman citizen. We reject this because 1.) Paul was plainly not the type to bluff for temporary advantage and thus risk greater punishment, 2.) Roman citizenship was conferred upon many poor people for varied reasons and 3.) We do not believe Paul was poor at this time, as we will show when we deal with his financial status at this period of his ministry.

is perhaps most important, for the Spirit would thus emphasize the Gentile character of his apostleship and ministry.

This faithful servant of God had earnestly testified to the chosen people as "a Jew" (Ver. 3) and they had gone about to slay him. But when he represented himself to the Gentiles as "a Roman" (Ver. 25) his word was instantly accepted and he was treated with respect.

But there is a further dispensational lesson for us here. Paul, the former enemy of Christ, now reconciled by grace and standing here as "a Jew" and "a Roman" in one "man," is the natural representative of the Church of this present dispensation, the "one new man," composed of Jews and Gentiles reconciled to God in one body by the cross (See Eph. 2:14-16). That this dispensation had dawned and the "one Body" was being formed, is evident from what he had already written to the Corinthians and the Romans (See I Cor. 12:13,27; Rom. 12:5).

Paul's magnificent self-composure in all this had again, under God, placed him and his cause in an advantageous position. Indeed, Lysias would have been glad if, like the Philippian magistrates, in similar embarrassment, he could have let the apostle go with an apology,[20] but Jerusalem was not Philippi. Down there was the angry multitude, clamoring for the apostle's execution. At least Paul's protest would stiffen the chief captain's determination to see justice done.

Still in the dark as to the Jews' complaint against Paul, Lysias "loosed him from his bands"[21] (Ver. 30) the

---

20. See notes on Acts 16:35-40.

21. A different word than "bound" in Verse 25. It was not illegal to hold a Roman prisoner in chains (See 26:29; Col. 4:3; II Tim. 2:9).

next day and called for a meeting of the Sanhedrin, setting Paul before them, that formal charges might be made against him.

Probably this session was not held in the regular chambers of the Sanhedrin, or Roman soldiers would not have been allowed inside, nor in the castle, for Lysias, and his soldiers, later had to go "down" to it (See 22:30; 23:10). Perhaps it was held in some neutral place.

The fact that a mere "chief captain" over a thousand Roman soldiers could summon the Jewish Sanhedrin to a meeting indicates how subservient Israel, and even its Supreme Court, had become to Rome.

PAUL BEFORE THE SANHEDRIN

"And Paul, earnestly beholding the council, said, Men and brethren, I have lived in all good conscience before God until this day.

"And the high priest Ananias commanded them that stood by him to smite him on the mouth.

"Then said Paul unto him, God shall smite thee, thou whited wall: for sittest thou to judge me after the law, and commandest me to be smitten contrary to the law?

"And they that stood by said, Revilest thou God's high priest?

"Then said Paul, I wist not, brethren, that he was the high priest: for it is written, Thou shalt not speak evil of the ruler of thy people.

"But when Paul perceived that the one part were Sadducees, and the other Pharisees, he cried out in the council, Men and brethren, I am a Pharisee, the son of a Pharisee: of the hope and resurrection of the dead I am called in question.

"And when he had so said, there arose a dissension between the Pharisees and the Sadducees: and the multitude was divided.

"For the Sadducees say that there is no resurrection, neither angel, nor spirit: but the Pharisees confess both.

"And there arose a great cry: and the scribes that were of the Pharisees' part arose, and strove, saying, We find no evil in this man: but if a spirit or an angel hath spoken to him, let us not fight against God.

"And when there arose a great dissension, the chief captain, fearing lest Paul should have been pulled in pieces of them, commanded the soldiers to go down, and to take him by force from among them, and to bring him into the castle.

"And the night following the Lord stood by him, and said, Be of good cheer, Paul: for as thou hast testified of Me in Jerusalem, so must thou bear witness also at Rome."

—Acts 23:1-11

A CHANGE IN ATTITUDE

Paul has now evidently abandoned all hope of receiving justice at the hands of his countrymen, for his attitude and conduct toward even the members of the Sanhedrin now changes abruptly.

Only yesterday he had addressed the multitude as "Men, brethren, *and fathers*," speaking to them in the most conciliatory manner.

Now, on trial before the Sanhedrin, *he* opens the proceedings himself, addressing them as "Men and brethren," thus placing himself on the same level with them and, fixing his eyes intently upon them, avows that *he*—could *they* say as much?—has lived in all good conscience before God until this day.

When the high priest commands those standing by to smite him on the mouth for this he answers with a stinging rebuke, and when reprimanded for *that*, he explains that he had not realized that it was the high priest who had given the order to strike him, but he does not apologize to the high priest or take back one word of what he has said.

Indeed, he goes even farther, deliberately dividing the Sanhedrin by "crying out" that *he* is a *Pharisee*.

But let us begin at the beginning. Actually the Sanhedrin could have no final authority in this case. They had not assembled to consider some charge made against Paul by the Jews. It was Rome who had taken Paul into custody for an apparent breach of the peace and Lysias, the chief captain, had merely asked the Sanhedrin to hear him so that *he*, the chief captain, might ascertain the cause of the uprising and decide whether a formal charge could even be brought against him.

Paul, quick to take this in, began addressing *them*, not waiting for them to arraign him in formal trial. He had more reason to expect justice from Rome.

This alone might anger the high priest, but what Paul said, and the manner in which he said it, enraged him. Addressing them as his equals (Ver. 1, ctr., 4:8; 7:2) the apostle fixed his eyes on them with searching gaze[1] and cast reflections on their integrity by earnestly asserting that *he* had lived "before God in all good conscience...until this day"[2] (Ver. 1).

This the high priest could not endure, betraying his true character by commanding those who stood by to smite Paul on the mouth. How true the saying: "The more liberty taken by despots, the less they allow their subjects."

---

1. Some suppose that the apostle merely strained to see the jurors because of defective eyesight, but the word *atenizo* is used rather in the sense that we give it here (See Luke 22:56; Acts 3:4,12; 11:6; 13:9; etc.).

2. In the light of Romans 7:15-25 and the Scriptures as a whole, he could not have been referring to all the details of his conduct, but to *his adopted course*, in first persecuting Christ, then serving Him and proclaiming His saving grace among the Gentiles.

This brutal insult, illegally ordered by a judge, drew from Paul the indignant accusation that he was a "whited wall," i.e., a hypocrite (cf. Matt. 23:27) to sit there as a judge, yet command the defendant to be smitten contrary to the law.

Fault has been found with the apostle for not showing the same humility as had his Lord when similarly outraged. In this connection it should be observed that our Lord had come to earth especially to take the blame and bear the penalty for the sins of others and particularly for His people, Israel, while on this occasion Paul faced Israel's rulers after their final demonstration of apostasy against Messiah. The actions of both our Lord and Paul on these two occasions are therefore representative; the one of God's mercy to Israel, the other of His judgment upon them.

The apostle's answer to those who upbraided him for rebuking the high priest, has been understood by some as sarcasm. How, they ask, could Paul have failed to recognize the president of the Sanhedrin? He must, therefore, have meant: "I did not know that one who would do this could possibly be the high priest."

We do not accept this interpretation, however. Apart from a consideration of the exact wording in the original here, it is doubtful that Paul's words could have been intended as a sarcastic rebuttal. In the first place, it would not be like Paul to "speak evil of dignitaries." Second, Israel's high priests, at this time of her history, were appointed with gross irregularity, partly due to national apostasy from God's commands and partly to Rome's intrusion, so that one illegitimate high priest after another held office and the council was even presided over, at times, by substitute "high priests."[3] Under these circumstances—and Paul having been in Jerusalem but a few days—it is quite understandable that he would not recognize the high priest.

Others take Paul's "wist not" to mean: "did not take into consideration." Paul's words would then be a confession that he had spoken hastily, failing to take into consideration the dignity of Ananias' office. But in addition to this being a strained rendering of the original, it is logical that in such a case Paul would have apologized *to the high priest.*

Had the apostle known that it was the high priest who had ordered him smitten he would have refrained from rebuking him in view of the command in Exodus 22:28. But having done so he merely explained how this had come about and retracted neither his rebuke nor his prediction. The more shame that the *high priest* should be guilty of so brazenly violating the basic rules of justice.

Paul's words, then, were representative of God's attitude toward Israel and her rulers at that time, and indeed if history is correct Paul's prediction was soon fulfilled, for not long after Ananias was slain by an assassin.

It is possible that an outrage so undeserved rankled the Pharisees too, coming as it did from the high priest. It must be remembered that whereas the Pharisees were the more popular and the more numerous in Israel, the Sadducees were the more rich and powerful, and the high priestly party were of this sect (see Acts 4:6; 5:17).

---

3. Lightfoot refers to this very high priest as "a man who had the semblance of the high priest's office without the reality."

Now the Pharisees were the "strict" sect (Acts 26:5) and while their deep prejudices sometimes warped their sense of justice, they could not approve the Sadducees' crude and flagrant disregard for even the form of justice, nor appreciate their high-handedness.[4]

Paul knew too that there was a deep doctrinal division between the Pharisees and the Sadducees and, taking advantage of the situation, he cried out: *"Men and brethren, I am a Pharisee, the son of a Pharisee;*[5] *of the hope and resurrection of the dead I am called in question"* (Ver. 6) thus directing the jurors' attention to a subject on which he knew the Pharisees would be on his side. This maneuver had an instantaneous effect. Almost immediately *"there arose a dissension between the Pharisees and the Sadducees"* and *"the multitude was divided"* and *"there arose a great cry; and the scribes that were of the Pharisees' part arose and strove"* for the apostle's acquittal, till the *"dissension"* was so *"great"* that the chief captain became concerned *"lest Paul should have been pulled in pieces of them"* and sent his soldiers down to take him from them by force. Thus Paul was brought again under the jurisdiction—and protection—of the Roman government.

What a change from the respectful, sympathetic, conciliatory approach of yesterday to the "rough-and-tumble" tactics of today! To extricate himself from the legal power of an apostate Sanhedrin, he grasps the initiative and *keeps* it, addressing *them* before he is even accused, rebuking a jurist for ordering an illegal

---

4. For a comparison of the Pharisees' and Sadducees' conduct in this connection, see John 7:51; 11:47-50.

5. Some of the best MSS have "Pharisees," making him the offspring of a *line* of Pharisees.

abuse and crying out that he is a Pharisee, so as to divide and confound them.

The apostle's declaration has been challenged, though, on two counts: Was it quite truthful of him to say that he *still was* a Pharisee and that it was concerning the hope of the resurrection that he had been called in question?

The answer to the first objection is that he had qualified his declaration clearly enough. It was with regard to the doctrine of the resurrection that he was a Pharisee, just as with regard to the doctrine of the believer's eternal security we might say: "I am a Calvinist." The apostle's statement was in no way misleading for his hearers understood perfectly that he was not now associated with the organized body of Pharisees.

As to the second objection, Paul was indeed getting down to the *basic* reason why the Jews hated him so bitterly—and here is an important dispensational lesson to learn.

The circumcision apostles and the multitudes of Jewish believers at Jerusalem had for years believed and proclaimed the resurrection of Christ, yet the unbelieving Jews, even now, tolerated them. Why this great outcry against Paul. Ah, it was because he had, by revelation, preached the resurrection of "the Seed of David" in a new light as the basis for a proclamation of *freedom from the law and salvation by grace to Jew and Gentile alike* (See II Tim. 2:7-9; Rom. 4:22-25; 10:9; etc.). This was what they so bitterly opposed.

More than this, Paul's affirmation before the Sanhedrin was more than a subtle stroke to cause division and save his own skin; it was a declaration of the basis for accepting or rejecting Christ.

THE LORD ENCOURAGES PAUL

The trying experiences through which the apostle had gone in the past weeks and especially the last two hectic days, may well have left him exhausted and downcast. What would be the final outcome of this uprising against him? Would Lysias free him or would there be more trouble about it? If Lysias did acquit him what would he do then, how could he escape from Jerusalem alive? What about his plan to carry the gospel to Rome; would this now be prevented? The outlook was dark.

It was that night, as thoughts such as these troubled the weary apostle that—*"the Lord stood by him."* How beautiful! It does not appear that any of his companions were with him nor, evidently, did the church at Jerusalem or its leaders do anything to help him. He was alone. But *"the Lord stood by him, and said*:

"Be of good cheer, Paul: for as thou hast testified of Me in Jerusalem, so must thou bear witness also at Rome" (Ver. 11).

Many difficulties might still lie ahead and the road might be long, but he *would* reach Rome with the gospel. Ah, *this* is how God prepares His servants to pass through ordeals! How serene the scene has suddenly become! A raging tempest just behind him; an unknown plot to murder him just ahead, but *he* can rest in the care of Him "who worketh all things after the counsel of His own will."

Let us not read more into this passage than it says, however, or construe it as an endorsement of *all* Paul had done at Jerusalem. Whatever his failures there, he had nobly testified of Christ, and he is now given divine

297

assurance that opportunity will be granted him to do the same at Rome.

This is not the only crisis in which Paul was given supernatural encouragement. He had been thus sustained in the dangerous days at Corinth (18:9,10) and would be again in the fearful storm on the way to Rome (27:22-24) and at his first appearance before Caesar (II Tim. 4:16,17).

A CONSPIRACY UNCOVERED

"And when it was day, certain of the Jews banded together, and bound themselves under a curse, saying that they would neither eat nor drink till they had killed Paul.

"And they were more than forty which had made this conspiracy.

"And they came to the chief priests and elders, and said, We have bound ourselves under a great curse, that we will eat nothing until we have slain Paul.

"Now therefore ye with the council signify to the chief captain that he bring him down unto you tomorrow, as though ye would enquire something more perfectly concerning him: and we, or ever he come near, are ready to kill him.

"And when Paul's sister's son heard of their lying in wait, he went and entered into the castle, and told Paul.

"Then Paul called one of the centurions unto him, and said, Bring this young man unto the chief captain: for he hath a certain thing to tell him.

"So he took him, and brought him to the chief captain, and said, Paul the prisoner called me unto him, and prayed me to bring this young man unto thee, who hath something to say unto thee.

"Then the chief captain took him by the hand, and went with him aside privately, and asked him, What is that thou hast to tell me?

"And he said, The Jews have agreed to desire thee that thou wouldest bring down Paul tomorrow into the council, as though they would enquire somewhat of him more perfectly.

"But do not thou yield unto them: for there lie in wait for him of them more than forty men, which have bound themselves with an oath, that they will neither eat nor drink till they have killed him: and now are they ready, looking for a promise from thee."

—Acts 23:12-21

THE PLOT TO AMBUSH PAUL

"And when it was day...."

How the apostle would need the assurance received from the Lord only last night!

No more had the sun risen than the most determined attempt upon Paul's life so far was launched as more than forty zealots conspired together to take the law into their own hands and assassinate him.

Doubtless they justified themselves for this, feeling they were carrying out the will of God. It looked as if Paul might go free, and should the uncircumcised Romans be allowed to obstruct the just punishment of a traitor against the law?[1]

Thus they bound themselves with a solemn oath, declaring that they would "neither eat nor drink till they had killed Paul" (Ver. 12). Indeed, their report of

---

1. Thus has the Roman church again and again absolved its subjects from allegiance to civil rulers, ignoring the Spirit's declaration that *"every soul"* should be *"subject unto the higher powers,"* since *"the powers that be,"* whether good or bad, *"are ordained of God"* and whoever *"resisteth the power, resisteth the ordinance of God"* (Rom. 13:1,2).

this to the leaders of the Sanhedrin shows the intensity of their bitterness, for they said, literally: *"We have cursed ourselves with a great curse"* (Ver. 14).

It was to the Sadducean party of the Sanhedrin that they revealed their plan (Ver. 14 cf. 5:17) urging them to persuade the rest of the council (Ver. 15). It was a bold plan, by which the assassins were placing their own lives in jeopardy, not only of starvation but of the Roman sword. The chief captain would not, they were sure, deny the Sanhedrin an opportunity to enquire further into Paul's case, especially since he, the chief captain, had failed to obtain the desired information from the session held on the preceding day. The council, therefore, was to request Paul's presence for such further investigation, and the forty-odd assassins would waylay him and slay him as he was being escorted to the council chamber.

The agreement of the leaders of the Sanhedrin to take part in this plot (Ver. 20) shows the depth of infamy to which cultured and religious people can sink (cf. Matt. 26:4; Acts 6:11; etc.) and the very fact that the assassins could go to the chief justices of Israel's Supreme Court, divulge their plot to them and seek their complicity in it, indicates how notorious was their contempt for the law they pretended to uphold. Once again Paul was in peril by his own countrymen.

In the apostle's experiences on this occasion we see again the dispensational trend so evident in the Book of Acts. Twice, on previous occasions, Peter had been miraculously delivered from prison as angels appeared to open the doors (Acts 5:19; 12:7-10). Indeed, Paul himself had seen prison doors fly open and his fetters fall miraculously off some years before at Philippi, but now, when such a miracle would seem to serve so great a purpose, no miracle takes place. God has "stretched forth His hands" long enough to this "gainsaying people"; why increase their condemnation by allowing them to close their eyes to still further evidence?

But this trend is further seen in the fact that during Peter's imprisonment in early Acts, the whole Judaean Church prayed "without ceasing" for him. But now, though the number of Hebrew believers had multiplied into "myriads" and the Jewish Church had become strong in Jerusalem, there is not a single hint that any of them—even of their leaders—did one single thing to help Paul.

THE PLOT DISCOVERED

Ah, but God, while not directly intervening, was *overruling*. He who had "stood by" Paul to reassure him last night was standing by today to see His promise through.

The apostle had a sister, whose son, in the providence of God, was in Jerusalem at this time. Whether he *lived* there with his mother is not known, but if so it may indicate that they were not believers, since Paul had not lodged with them on this visit, nor do we read that he had any contact with them.

The apostle did have believing relatives in Rome (Rom. 16:7,11) but there is no indication that any of his immediate family were saved, nor any reason to assume they were, for truth does not run in families.

Perhaps the lad, like so many others, was in Jerusalem only for the feast days, but the point is that God had just the right person there at just the right time to hear about the plot on Paul's life.

Whether the lad was sympathetic to Paul's cause or not, this was his own flesh and blood and he could not allow him to be thus slain in cold blood. Moreover, the record indicates that he was still very young, so that he would not soon be suspected of treachery, either by Paul or by Lysias.

The apostle, being still an uncondemned prisoner, was evidently detained under only a moderate form of military custody, for it appears that his nephew had free access to him (Ver. 16 cf. 24:23; 27:3; 28:16,30).

The calm presence of mind and level-headedness with which Paul received and acted upon the lad's report was characteristic of him. God had assured him that he *would* reach Rome, but he did not therefore dismiss the report as representing no threat to his safety. He realized that while God is sovereign, human responsibility and effort form part of His plans (cf. Acts 27:24,31). Calling one of the centurions, therefore, he said, simply: *"Bring this young man[2] unto the chief captain, for he hath a certain thing to tell him"* (Ver. 17).

The centurion then conducted the lad to Lysias with his message from "Paul the prisoner," a designation henceforth to become familiar to many. The chief captain hereupon "took him by the hand" to more private quarters and there asked what it was he had to say.

The manner in which Lysias received the lad would seem to indicate further the lad's youth and Lysias' sympathetic interest in Paul.

The lad related with some feeling the facts he had learned about the plot, beseeching the chief captain: *"Do not thou yield unto them, for there lie in wait for him of them more than forty men"* (Ver. 21).

---

2.   Gr. *neanias*, youth.

THE PLOT THWARTED

"So the chief captain then let the young man depart, and charged him, See thou tell no man that thou hast showed these things to me.

"And he called unto him two centurions, saying, Make ready two hundred soldiers to go to Caesarea, and horsemen threescore and ten, and spearmen two hundred, at the third hour of the night;

"And provide them beasts, that they may set Paul on, and bring him safe unto Felix the governor.

"And he wrote a letter after this manner:

"Claudius Lysias unto the most excellent governor Felix sendeth greeting.

"This man was taken of the Jews, and should have been killed of them: then came I with an army, and rescued him, having understood that he was a Roman.

"And when I would have known the cause wherefore they accused him, I brought him forth into their council:

"Whom I perceived to be accused of questions of their law, but to have nothing laid to his charge worthy of death or of bonds.

"And when it was told me how that the Jews laid wait for the man, I sent straightway to thee, and gave commandment to his accusers also to say before thee what they had against him. Farewell.

"Then the soldiers, as it was commanded them, took Paul, and brought him by night to Antipatris.

"On the morrow they left the horsemen to go with him, and returned to the castle:

"Who, when they came to Caesarea, and delivered the epistle to the governor, presented Paul also before him.

"And when the governor had read the letter, he asked of what province he was. And when he understood that he was of Cilicia;

"I will hear thee, said he, when thine accusers are also come. And he commanded him to be kept in Herod's judgment hall."

—Acts 23:22-35

Even a casual reading of those passages in the New Testament which deal with officers in the Roman Army must impress upon our minds the commendable qualities of character which they, as a class, possessed. Perhaps the discipline of their military training brought out these good traits. The centurion at Capernaum, the centurion at the cross, Cornelius and Julius, the centurion of Augustus' Band, are some examples that stand out in our minds.

Lysias, the chief captain at Fort Antonia, was another who, heathen though he was, possessed qualities of character which stand out in striking contrast to the evil treachery of the religious leaders of Israel.

Already we have seen his justice and even kindness to Paul; and if, in the excitement of the uprising, he had committed an illegality in binding Paul for scourging, it was doubtless only because he had assumed that one in Paul's position would have claimed his Roman citizenship immediately had he been a Roman.

The fact that Lysias took Paul's nephew "by the hand" would indicate further that beneath the soldier's rough exterior there was a kind and gentle heart.

305

At the same time the chief captain exercised the official caution appropriate to his position. First, he heard the lad "privately." Then he dismissed him without indicating what action he would take, merely cautioning him: *"See thou tell no man that thou hast showed these things to me"* (Ver. 22).

Then, too, Lysias acted with the dispatch of a well-trained army officer. He was responsible, not only for the safety of a Roman citizen, but also for the protection of the public peace. Convinced that the lad had told the truth and realizing that something like this was just what some Jewish zealots were likely to do, he issued immediate orders to two of his centurions to assemble two hundred regular infantry (probably heavily armed) along with seventy cavalry and two hundred spearmen.[3] The total army of four hundred seventy men would thus be prepared to meet various forms of attack, and their departure was delayed until nightfall (9 P.M.) so that none could pursue until the city gates were opened again at six o'clock in the morning. By that time they would be nine hours' march away.

The large number of soldiers engaged to conduct Paul to Caesarea may indicate how dangerously unsettled the situation was at Jerusalem, but on the other hand Lysias, whose sympathies by this time were clearly with Paul, may have given him this large escort to raise his prestige and at the same time show the Jews how he would protect a Roman citizen from their hostility.

How graciously God had overruled the designs of Paul's enemies—not by some miraculous demonstration, but by the most natural chain of circumstances.

---

3. The translation here is probably correct. The exact term in the original is "right hand graspers," doubtless referring to those who hurled spears with the right hand.

306

How the Lord's "Be of good cheer" must have rung in his ears as just after nine that very evening he was on his way to Caesarea with an escort fit for a king! And imagine the chief priests' chagrin when, instead of obtaining permission to bring Paul in for further questioning, they were turned away with the curt response: "I have sent him to the governor at Caesarea; you are to go and make your complaint against him there"!

Lysias' letter to Felix demonstrates further his character and ability as a Roman officer, though in it he yields to the natural human inclination to protect himself from blame and place himself in the best possible light before Felix—even to some misrepresentation of the facts.

Addressing Felix as "Your Excellency," the chief captain correctly places Paul's case in a favorable light and that of his accusers in an unfavorable one, while at the same time changing a few facts to his own advantage.

Lysias' statement that he had already commanded Paul's accusers to appear before Felix, was doubtless legitimate. It is easily possible that the chief priests had already requested Paul's presence for a further hearing (Ver. 21) and that Lysias had given them his reply, but in any case he must have done so before his letter could be read by Felix.

Marching through the night, Lysias' troops conducted Paul safely to Antipatris, some forty miles distant, doubtless waking the townsfolk all along the way. Having brought him thus far the four hundred infantry and spearmen marched back to Jerusalem leaving the cavalry to convey the apostle the rest of the way to Caesarea. There was no need to leave the Castle of Antonia too lightly manned.

307

It would appear from the record that the cavalry doubtless after a period of rest, pressed on to make the remaining twenty-five miles to Caesarea that same day, reaching the city while it was still daylight.

What must have been the thoughts and feelings of the Caesarean believers as the weary cavalcade rode into the city with *Paul* in their midst! Only a few days ago Agabus had warned him of the dangers at Jerusalem, predicting that he would be delivered into the hands of the Gentiles, and they all, along with Paul's own companions, had pleaded with him not to go (21:8-12). Now already Agabus' prediction had been fulfilled and their fears were realized. And what thoughts must have filled *Paul's* heart and mind! But God was in it all, for in this way Paul was to bear the name of Christ before "kings," as predicted in Acts 9:15, and fulfill a still greater ministry among the Gentiles.

If Paul's would-be assassins held true to their oath they must all have died of starvation, but Lightfoot shows from the Talmud that such vows could be easily annulled.

When the soldiers had presented Paul and the letter from Lysias to Felix, the governor enquired what province the prisoner came from. Learning that he was a Cilician, Felix then promised him a full hearing[4] when his accusers should arrive, and kept him meantime in Herod's praetorium.

---

4.   It is doubtful that Felix' territory could have included Cilicia, but since this was not a *neighboring* province and the uprising had taken place in Judaea, Felix doubtless felt justified in taking the case.

PAUL BEFORE FELIX

TERTULLUS' ACCUSATION

"And after five days Ananias the high priest descended with the elders, and with a certain orator named Tertullus, who informed the governor against Paul.

"And when he was called forth, Tertullus began to accuse him, saying, Seeing that by thee we enjoy great quietness, and that very worthy deeds are done unto this nation by thy providence,

"We accept it always, and in all places, most noble Felix, with all thankfulness.

"Notwithstanding, that I be not further tedious unto thee, I pray thee that thou wouldest hear us of thy clemency a few words.

"For we have found this man a pestilent fellow, and a mover of sedition among all the Jews throughout the world, and a ringleader of the sect of the Nazarenes:

"Who also hath gone about to profane the temple: whom we took, and would have judged according to our law.

"But the chief captain Lysias came upon us, and with great violence took him away out of our hands,

"Commanding his accusers to come unto thee: by examining of whom thyself mayest take knowledge of all these things, whereof we accuse him.

"And the Jews also assented, saying that these things were so."

—Acts 24:1-9

The Jews lost no time in pursuing the man who had thus far eluded their grasp. It was only five days after Paul's departure from Jerusalem that Ananias and the elders[1] appeared at Caesarea to prosecute him. This may be ascertained from the fact that this was the twelfth day since his *arrival* at Jerusalem (Ver. 11) and he had been in Jerusalem for about seven days (21:27; 22:30; 23:11,12).

It must have been unusual for the high priest in person to attend trials at Caesarea, nearly seventy miles distant, but he had a personal interest in the prosecution of the man who had called him a "whited wall."

The judge before whom they were to make their complaint was anything but a man of justice or integrity. Historians tell us that he was a former slave, elevated to his present position as governor of Judaea only through the influence of his brother Pallas, a favorite of the Emperor, but was recalled and tried at Rome for maladministration, finally to be acquitted by Nero only, again, because of his brother's intercession. Josephus tells of his injustice and cruelty and Tacitus says that "in the practice of all kinds of lust and cruelty he exercised the power of a king with the temper of a slave" (*Hist.* V, 9). This all agrees with what the Scriptures tell us about him.

Many commentators believe that Tertullus, the counsel for the prosecution, was an Italian lawyer, engaged by the Jews because of his knowledge of Roman law and for the effect his procurement might have upon the Roman governor. If this is so—and it may well be—the Scripture does not make this plain nor make any point of it, for Tertullus stands here

---

1. Or "certain elders."

310

representing Israel and Israel's attitude toward Christ and His servant Paul.

In accordance with Roman law, the charges against Paul were not heard until Paul had been "called forth" to meet his accusers "face to face" (Ver. 2; 25:16). Then the orator, Tertullus, presented the formal complaint before Felix.

Tertullus' extravagant flattery of the wicked Felix stands in sharp contrast both to his vicious and unscrupulous attack upon Paul and to Paul's thoughtful and factual response. He would not have dared to praise Felix for integrity, justice or benevolence, or the looks on the faces of the Jewish elders (who thoroughly detested Felix) might have betrayed his insincerity and angered the governor, so he lauded him instead for the "quietness" which Judaea, in some measure, had enjoyed under his reign, and the "excellent measures" instituted by his "providence"—a term usually reserved for the gods and the Emperor. For all this Tertullus assured him of the uninterrupted and universal gratitude of the Jews (Ver. 3).

Long years before Moses had declared, by inspiration of God, that if Israel rebelled against Him:

"The stranger that is within thee shall get up above thee very high; and thou shalt come down very low.... he shall be the head, and thou shalt be the tail" (Deut. 28:43,44).

This process was rapidly taking place as the chosen people declined in power before the ascendancy of Rome. Even a few years previous, at their rejection of Christ, the Council had largely taken matters into their own hands and had *driven* Pilate to do what they wished, as "the voices of them and of the chief priests prevailed, and Pilate gave sentence that it should be as they required" (Luke 23:23,24). Now they come with abject flattery to a ruler they despise, careful not to be "tedious," to him and beseeching him out of his "clemency" to hear them a "few words" (Vers. 2-4).

The strategy which the prosecution employed is not hard to discern.

First, they made three charges against him: one of *sedition*, against Roman law, another of *heresy*, against Hebrew law, and a third of *sacrilege*, against both.

Paul was "a pest," "a plague,"[2] Tertullus declared, stirring up sedition "among all the Jews throughout the world." Apart from the base untruth of this charge it would be of interest to enquire since when the Jews had become such patriotic Roman subjects! Who could deny that the chief priests themselves would have been genuinely pleased to have anyone stir up opposition to Rome "among all the Jews throughout the world"?

Then, too, Paul was supposed to have been "a ringleader of the sect of the Nazarenes."[3] This charge came nearest to the truth, though Paul was something higher than the "ringleader" of a "sect." He merely proclaimed the truth about Christ and this was supposed to be heresy against the law of Moses which, in turn, Rome had pledged itself to respect.

Finally, Paul was charged with having "gone about to profane the temple." This accusation was, of course, utterly false, but it was calculated to weigh heavily with

---

2. The word is a noun in the original, *"fellow"* having been supplied by the translators in A.V.

3. A contemptuous term for believers in Christ. The word "sect" here is *hereseos*, or "heresy" as in Verse 14.

312

Felix, since it was to Rome's advantage to preserve inviolate the sanctity of the temple.

But the Jews' strategy went farther than the formal charges,[4] involving the propriety of Lysias' having sent Paul to Felix for a Roman trial. In another brazen departure from the truth Tertullus declared that the Jews had apprehended Paul and would have judged him according to their law, but that Lysias had come and "with great violence" had taken him out of their hands, commanding them to make their complaints before Felix.

This, of course, was flatly contradictory to Lysias' report and an obvious attempt to turn the tables on him, making *him* the disturber of the peace, so that Felix might be induced to give Paul back into their hands—and that the assassins might yet have their opportunity to strike.

Finally, Tertullus suggests that Paul be examined by torture,[5] whether or not Felix delivers him into their hands, indicating further that their motive in all this was purely revenge.

Before leaving Tertullus we may observe an example of the human trait of twisting the truth to one's own advantage. By now we have had three conflicting accounts of what happened in the uprising at the temple.

---

4. The passage from the word "whom" in Verse 6 to "unto thee" in Verse 8 is omitted from some of the earliest MSS but not from the Syriac, which antedates our oldest MSS. From the context, also, it appears to belong to the text.

5. *Anakrino* is used forensically of a searching examination by torture (See John 19:1 cf. Luke 23:14; Acts 22:24,29; etc.). Since the Greek relative is in the singular Tertullus could not have been suggesting such an examination of the Jews, nor, in the context, could he have meant that Lysias should be thus examined. The "whom," then, refers to Paul.

The first is Luke's account in Acts 21 to 23, inspired by the Holy Spirit and therefore correct:

Certain Jews had "stirred up all the people" against Paul and had "laid hands on him" (21:27). Having "dragged him out of the temple" they "went about to kill him" (Vers. 30,31). Then "when they saw the chief captain and the soldiers they left beating Paul" (Ver. 32).

Lysias then took the apostle into custody and "demanded who he was and what he had done" but "could not know the certainty for the tumult" (Vers. 33,34). Later, therefore, Lysias "bade that he should be examined by scourging" only to discover that he was about to illegally scourge a Roman citizen (22:24,25). Finally, he had commanded the Sanhedrin to meet and decide on a charge or charges against the apostle, but this too had proved inconclusive as Lysias was again forced to rescue Paul from their hands as they fought among themselves and almost pulled him to pieces (22:30-23:10).

In Lysias' letter to Felix, however, the facts are strangely altered to his own advantage. Explaining how the apostle had been seized by the Jews and might have been killed by them, he continues: "Then came I with an army[6] and rescued him, *having understood that he was a Roman*" (23:27). This last was, of course, untrue, for Lysias had not learned that Paul was a Roman citizen until he had already given orders to examine him by scourging (22:24-28). This was simply a shrewd attempt on Lysias' part to obviate, if possible, having to face a charge of illegal conduct toward a Roman.

Lysias gives the impression, further, that *having brought Paul before the Hebrew council*, he had learned

---

6. Or "my troops."

314

what they had against him when, as a matter of fact, Lysias had failed to learn anything from this investigation, for the judges had fought so fiercely among themselves that he had been obliged to send troops down to rescue Paul a second time (23:10). But it would not be wise to let Felix know that he had been frustrated in his attempts to learn what the Jews had against Paul.

But now the Jews' account of the incident, as related by Tertullus, is different again. *He* says, with reference to Paul: *"Whom we took, and would have judged according to our law, but the chief captain Lysias came upon us, and with great violence took him away out of our hands"* (24:6,7). "And the Jews also assented, saying that these things were so" (Ver. 9).

According to their testimony everything had gone smoothly and they were just about to give Paul a fair trial when Lysias "came upon them" and "with great violence took him away"! This was a more brazen misrepresentation than anything Lysias had written, for not only were they about to kill Paul when Lysias rescued him, but they had almost torn him to pieces a second time and had finally taken part with more than forty assassins in a vicious plot to do away with him (21:31; 23:10,12,20,21). Indeed, it was Lysias who had *commanded them* to give Paul a hearing and *they* had then fought so among themselves that Paul's very life had again been endangered (22:30; 23:7-10).

PAUL'S DEFENSE

"Then Paul, after that the governor had beckoned unto him to speak, answered, Forasmuch as I know that thou hast been of many years a judge unto this nation, I do the more cheerfully answer for myself:

315

"Because that thou mayest understand, that there are yet but twelve days since I went up to Jerusalem for to worship.

"And they neither found me in the temple disputing with any man, neither raising up the people, neither in the synagogues, nor in the city:

"Neither can they prove the things whereof they now accuse me.

"But this I confess unto thee, that after the way which they call heresy, so worship I the God of my fathers, believing all things which are written in the law and in the prophets:

"And have hope toward God, which they themselves also allow, that there shall be a resurrection of the dead, both of the just and unjust.

"And herein do I exercise myself, to have always a conscience void of offence toward God, and toward men.

"Now after many years I came to bring alms to my nation and offerings.

"Whereupon certain Jews from Asia found me purified in the temple, neither with multitude, nor with tumult.

"Who ought to have been here before thee, and object, if they had ought against me.

"Or else let these same here say, if they have found any evil doing in me, while I stood before the council,

"Except it be for this one voice, that I cried standing among them, Touching the resurrection of the dead I am called in question by you this day."

—Acts 24:10-21

316

The simple, dignified manner in which Paul opened his defense before Felix stands out in sharp contrast to Tertullus' false and servile flattery. Having received the governor's signal to offer his reply, the apostle began by saying simply and truthfully, that it pleased him to be heard by one whose unusually long tenure of office in Judaea had given him so much experience in its affairs.

Similarly the apostle's plea was based solely on simple facts, simple logic and the justice of his cause, as he dealt fully with the charges made against him.

First, there was one basic fact which Felix could easily "ascertain"[7] for himself. It was now but twelve days since Paul had come to Jerusalem. This, as Felix knew, was the beginning of the Feast of Pentecost, and it would help to establish his argument that he had come "to worship," or "worshipping" (Ver. 11). Under James' persuasion he had, of course, become more deeply involved in Judaism than he had intended, but the issue now was only whether or not he was guilty of the charges of sedition, heresy and sacrilege.

Granted, the feast time might have been chosen as an opportune time to stir up sedition, but he effectively disposes of such a possibility by pointing out that they had not found him disputing or stirring up the people, either in the temple or in the synagogues or anywhere in the city (Ver. 12).

This at the same time exposed another flaw in Tertullus' accusation. Tertullus might accuse him of stirring up insurrection "throughout the world," but Felix was governor of *Judaea* and the question was what he had done at *Jerusalem* during the past days. As to

---

7. Not "understand," as in A.V.

the rest, the apostle answered simply: *"Neither can they prove the things whereof they now accuse me"* (Ver. 13).

But the apostle answers the charge of heresy with still greater effectiveness and embarrassment to his opponents.

"This I confess,"[8] he says, "that after the way which *they* call heresy, so worship I the God of my fathers, believing all things which are written in the law and in the prophets" (Ver. 14). His faith in Christ was not apostasy from the Old Testament Scriptures but *obedience* to them. *They* were the heretics for refusing to believe the Scriptures and for rejecting their own Messiah. Even the finished work of Christ, which Paul had been proclaiming, was no contradiction to the Old Testament but rather the culmination of its message and program. The doctrine of justification by faith in Christ alone did not make the law void; it *established* the law and offered the *only* basis upon which God could be just in justifying sinners (See Rom. 3:24-26,31).

But the apostle is not yet through with his answer. He will place his accusers with their backs against the wall.

"Believing all things which are written in the law and in the prophets," he says: *"[I] have hope toward God, which they themselves also allow, that there shall be a resurrection of the dead, both of the just and unjust"* (Vers. 14,15).

It should be observed that a few days previous, before the Sanhedrin, he had made an issue of the Sadducean denial of the resurrection and had exposed the disunity among Israel's rulers. He might have done

---

8. The Greek word used here does not mean *to admit guilt*, but *to speak freely*.

this again before Felix but refrained, doubtless out of respect for his nation and for the testimony he and they could both give before Felix. Since the majority in the Sanhedrin and the vast majority of the Jews believed in the resurrection; since this was the traditional Hebrew faith and the teaching of their Scriptures, he could truthfully say: "which they themselves also allow," leaving them to face secretly the embarrassing fact that the heretics were to be found among *them*, his accusers, and at the same time leaving them speechless lest they expose before Felix the deep discord that prevailed among them. *He* believed the Old Testament Scriptures as to the resurrection, while some of *them*, even their chief priests, did not—and will *they* now charge *him* with heresy?

But while the apostle had demonstrated to them the weakness of their position, he was not even yet through answering the charge of heresy. Using the very truth which some among them denied, he would press home *their* guilt, probing their consciences still more deeply.

Proceeding with his defense, the apostle declares that it is *because* there will be a resurrection both of the just and unjust; *because* all will have to face God some day, that *"I exercise myself, to have always a conscience void of offence toward God, and toward men"* (Ver. 16).

Less than a week before he had told the Sanhedrin, with searching gaze, that he had been living "in all good conscience before God," for which the high priest had commanded those who stood by to "smite him on the mouth" (23:1,2). Now, before Felix, where the high priest cannot do the same, Paul again presses home the matter of conscience.

There was a significant reason for this. The great issue between Israel and Paul was no longer theological, but *moral*. They had by now been surrounded by overwhelming proofs that Jesus *was* "the Christ, the Son of God," but in spite of it all they still stubbornly rejected Him. They were violating their consciences and closing their eyes to the truth.

This is largely so with those who oppose the Pauline message today. They have been faced with facts so undeniable and surrounded with proofs so overwhelming that they can no longer answer us by the Scriptures, yet they continue to stage a delaying action against this great truth and oppose, in various ways, those who proclaim it. As with the religious leaders of Paul's day, it is no longer a question of theological interpretations, but of *conscience*. Such should ask themselves how they will answer to Him before whom all of us shall one day give an account.

And now the apostle touches upon one of the most important reasons he had come to Jerusalem, i.e., *"to bring alms to my nation, and offerings"*[9] (Ver. 17). This fact could be fully substantiated and was in itself an answer to all three charges made against him.

Furthermore, it was certain Jews from *Asia* who had originally charged him with wrongdoing, though they had found him "purified in the temple, neither with multitude, nor with tumult." Why, then, were they not here before Felix to make their complaint? Could there be a clearer proof of the weakness of their case than their absence from this trial?

And those who *had* made formal charges before Felix had no personal knowledge of wrongdoing in the

---

9.   An examination of the occurrences of the Greek *prosphora*, and especially of its verb, *prosphero*, will show that the word "offerings" here by no means necessarily refers to sacrificial offerings, but to offerings of any kind.

apostle, otherwise he argued, "let these same here say if they have found any evil doing in me while I stood before their council" (Ver. 20) boldly challenging them to state before the governor the results of that trial.

And to further press home to *them* the bankruptcy of their cause, he brings up again the matter which had stirred up such fierce animosities among them at his trial in Jerusalem that they might have killed him had not the Roman soldiers rescued him.

He brings the matter up as sort of an acknowledgement, but one that effectively closes their mouths, saying: *"Except it be for this one voice [utterance], that I cried standing among them, Touching the resurrection of the dead I am called in question by you this day"* (Ver. 21).

ALL CHARGES REFUTED

Thus the apostle answered his accusers step by step so effectively that it put *them* on the defensive and, indeed, closed their mouths completely.

As to the charge of *sedition*: It was only twelve days since he had arrived at Jerusalem. Half that time he had been engaged in fulfilling a Jewish ritual and the other half he had been in Roman custody. Furthermore, his known conduct had disproved this charge, nor was their an iota of testimony or evidence that he had engaged in sedition.

As to *heresy*: He had never swerved from faith in the writings of Moses and the prophets. The heretics were to be found among *them*.

As to *sacrilege*: He had come to bring alms and offerings to his nation; why would he profane their temple? Indeed, his enemies had found him "purified" in the temple, "neither with multitude nor with tumult."

The Jews from Asia had no case against him, else they would have been present to testify against him. Neither did the rulers at Judaea have a case against him or they would have accepted his challenge to tell what evil doing they had found in him.

ACTION DEFERRED

"And when Felix heard these things, having more perfect knowledge of that way, he deferred them, and said, When Lysias the chief captain shall come down, I will know the uttermost of your matter.

"And he commanded a centurion to keep Paul, and to let him have liberty, and that he should forbid none of his acquaintance to minister or come unto him."

—Acts 24:22,23

Felix, both because of his position as governor of Judaea and because his wife was a Jewess, had "a more perfect knowledge of that way" than to be convinced that the charges made against Paul were true. Moreover, none of them had been substantiated by firsthand testimony. Yet he did not dismiss the case but only "deferred" it pending Lysias' arrival to testify.

Whether Felix actually had any intention of calling for Lysias, so as to learn "the uttermost" of the matter, is doubtful. There is no record that he ever did send for him; indeed, it seems quite evident from what *is* recorded that he detained the apostle for less honorable reasons.

He had learned that Paul had come to Jerusalem with large sums of money. Could he get some of it? Would Paul's friends perhaps, be willing to pay well for his release? At any rate he would see that they were permitted to visit him without restriction.

Thus the apostle was placed in *custodia militaris*,[10] with special instructions to the centurion "that he should forbid none of his acquaintance to minister or come unto him" (Ver. 23).

Had the Jews not pressed the case against Paul to begin with, he would doubtless have been liberated, but the Lord would now keep him as His prisoner for the Gentiles (Eph. 3:1).

PAUL BEFORE FELIX AND DRUSILLA

"And after certain days, when Felix came with his wife Drusilla, which was a Jewess, he sent for Paul, and heard him concerning the faith in Christ.

"And as he reasoned of righteousness, temperance, and judgment to come, Felix trembled, and answered, Go thy way for this time; when I have a convenient season, I will call for thee.

"He hoped also that money should have been given him of Paul, that he might loose him: wherefore he sent for him the oftener, and communed with him.

"But after two years Porcius Festus came into Felix' room: and Felix, willing to show the Jews a pleasure, left Paul bound."

—Acts 24:24-27

---

10. There were three forms of custody for uncondemned prisoners under Roman law 1.) *custodia publica*, or confinement in the public jail, 2.) *custodia militaris*, or military custody, under a soldier or soldiers responsible with their lives for the prisoner's safe keeping, and 3.) *custodia libera*, or free custody under the supervision of some notable person. The first was the most severe and the third so mild that the accused could go free at the custodian's assurance that he would appear for trial. The second is evidently the one which, on several occasions, applied in Paul's case.

It will be observed that the text says that "after certain days...Felix *came* with his wife Drusilla." Literally, the term is *"having arrived."*

This harmonizes with historical accounts which indicate that it was about this time that the wicked Felix, with the aid of Simon, a magician from Cyprus,[11] succeeded in enticing the beautiful Drusilla away from Azizus, king of Emesa, whom she had some six years previous, married at the age of fourteen. Now about twenty, she already had an infamous past. She was the daughter of Herod Agrippa I (of Acts 12) the sister of Herod Agrippa II (of Acts 26) and was a little girl at the time her father had accepted worship as a god and had been suddenly stricken dead (Acts 12:22,23).

This Drusilla was "a Jewess" (Ver. 24) and, upon her "arrival" with Felix, would naturally be interested in Paul's case. She had doubtless heard of him since childhood and would wonder why he had so suddenly turned to the Christ whom he and his nation had despised and rejected, and why he now served Him with such passion. At any rate, upon Felix' arrival with Drusilla, he sent for Paul and heard him,[12] not concerning the accusations recently made against him, but "concerning the faith in Christ" (Ver. 24).

Nearly all the circumstances now were vastly changed. This was not a trial but a private interview with two exalted but guilty wretches, and it was his solemn responsibility to witness before them in such a manner that their souls might, if possible, be rescued from death. And who can fail to admire both the moral

---

11. Supposed by some to be the *Simon Magus* of Acts 8.
12. The implication seems clear that Felix, with Drusilla *now present*, heard Paul.

courage and the tact with which the apostle met this responsibility?

Addressing the one person who, humanly speaking, had the power to liberate him, Paul began by speaking of *righteousness*, which Felix had habitually ignored, of temperance (or self-control) which he had signally failed to exercise, and of *judgment to come*, from which there was neither escape nor appeal.

The apostle could have used a different approach, to be sure, perhaps winning Felix as a friend of his cause and gaining his own freedom, but Paul was a man quite unlike his accusers, who would "compass sea and land to make one proselyte" (Matt. 23:15). He had stated that it was his aim "to have always a conscience void of offence toward God, and toward men" (Ver. 16) and now he was proving it. What Felix—and Drusilla—*needed* was *regeneration*, and this could never be the result of friendly persuasions regarding the merits of the "cause" he represented. He must reach their *consciences;* he must show them their guilt, their peril, their need. And this the apostle did, until Felix was terrified.[13]

Yet the apostle did all this in a way so tactful that the governor could have no reason to be offended.[14] Though Felix was guilty of the vilest sins and the blackest crimes, including private murder and public massacre, the apostle did not accuse or berate him. He would let the Spirit and Herod's own conscience do that. Instead he spoke of *"righteousness"*—in the abstract; the nature of righteousness, the requirements of righteousness, righteousness as related to our fellowmen and to

---

13. Gr. *emphobos*.
14. Paul's God-given wisdom in addressing individuals and audiences so diverse in character and background, over so wide a ministry, would make a study in itself.

God—and God's own essential and infinite righteousness. Then he proceeded to discuss a subject which followed in natural and logical sequence: the *"self-control"* which man is obligated to exercise in view of the requirements of righteousness. Though the guilty governor knew little of self-control he could hardly take offence, for such subjects were freely discussed in all the schools of philosophy. Yet the *truth* was boring deep into his conscience as he was, perhaps for the first time, confronted by his *sin*.

But the apostle, to be faithful, must go still farther than this. He must show Felix and his Jewish paramour the *urgency* of their need. Thus he proceeded to a subject not discussed by the philosophers of the day, but only in the Hebrew Scriptures: the *"judgment to come."* Felix had already learned of the apostle's convictions as to this, for his declaration that there would be "a resurrection...both of the *just* and *unjust*" (Ver. 15) carried the direct implication that those thus raised would be called to account before God. But now the apostle pressed this truth home, doubtless by citing passages from the Holy Scriptures, until the governor became so alarmed that he suddenly cut the interview short, saying: *"Go your way for now; when I find an opportunity I will call for you."*

Some have carelessly concluded that Paul was preaching "kingdom" truth here, that this address was not compatible with "the gospel of the grace of God." But such overlook the fact that we have here another of the interrupted discourses of the Book of Acts. What Paul had been saying formed the introduction to the gospel of the grace of God, for still today, no man truly proclaims grace who does not proclaim it against the background of the righteous wrath of God against sin. Any who may question this should consider prayerfully such passages as Ephesians 2:1-10 and the early chapters of Romans.

Paul had hoped that, having shown Felix his need, he could now show him God's gracious *provision* for that need, but the governor would listen no further. Here he stands in sharp contrast to the Philippian jailor who, trembling also, asked:

"Sirs, what must I do to be saved?" (Acts 16:29,30) with the result that he was gloriously saved. But Felix, trembling, sent the man of God away, promising to hear him further when he should find an opportunity. In this he has had multitudes of followers who, convicted by the Spirit of their sin and need, have resisted instead of yielding, hoping for another chance.

The depth of human depravity is seen in the fact that though Felix did call for Paul again, many times, he actually did so in the hope that he would be offered a bribe to release Paul. So had he hardened his conscience. As the wretch calls for Paul increasingly and communes with him, we can almost hear him subtly hinting, promising, threatening—but all to no avail. Paul would not stoop to means so dishonorable to gain his release, neither would he permit his dearest friends to do so for him.

And so two long years slowly passed by with Paul still in custody at Caesarea. Yet the long hours, with the disappointment of delay, must have been measurably shortened by refreshing visits from Philip and the Caesarean brethren. Perhaps, also, Luke was still on hand, along with Aristarchus (Acts 24:4 cf. 27:2). Then too there must have been many Hebrew believers in the vicinity who showed compassion on him in his bonds (Heb. 10:34).

Thus did God care for Paul and give him opportunity for fellowship, prayer, meditation on the Word and—rest. Yet, while we have no record of any converts gained while at Caesarea, or of a single letter he wrote from there, it is inconceivable that he should remain largely idle for two whole years. Doubtless he carried on a wide ministry all the while.

After two years, in which Felix conversed with the apostle many times, he was still as unscrupulous as ever. Vacating his office in favor of Porcius Festus, he still left Paul bound though it was customary on such occasions to release uncondemned prisoners. He did this to "show the Jews a pleasure" (though he hated them roundly) for, if history is correct, he was being called to account by Nero for maladministration of his government, and he would need as much Jewish friendship as he could win. Thus he sacrificed an innocent man's liberty at the altar of his own selfishness. Nor was he the first Roman provincial ruler to cater to the citizens of turbulent Judaea. At their clamor Pilate had given Jesus into their hands (Luke 23:22-24). Herod Agrippa I had killed the Apostle James and "because he saw it pleased the Jews, he proceeded further to take Peter also" (Acts 12:1-3). Here Felix leaves Paul bound to win the Jews' favor (24:27) and in a short time his successor, Festus, will similarly seek to sacrifice Paul's rightful interests for Jewish favor (25:9).

PAUL'S FINANCIAL STATUS AT THIS TIME

It is quite evident that Paul was not financially straitened during this period of his ministry. He had brought with him at least eight others from Greece (20:1-5) mostly by ship. He had agreed to bear the cost of no less than twenty sacrificial offerings required to complete the vows of four Nazarites (21:23,24 cf. Num. 6). His treatment at the hands of both Lysias and Felix indicates that they did not consider him a poor Jew. Poor men have seldom received much attention in civil courts and this was notoriously so in Paul's day, yet he, though not released, was treated with marked respect from Jerusalem to Rome. Lysias became friendly with him, Felix with Drusilla gave him at least one private audience, Agrippa and Bernice desired to see him, Felix hoped for a bribe from him and a rich Roman official would scarcely look for a small gift—and as we proceed to the end of Acts it will still be evident that Paul had, or had at his disposal, some considerable amount of money.

How to account for this is not so simple a matter. Surely he would not have agreed to the diversion of any of the funds he had labored so long and earnestly to collect especially for the saints at Jerusalem. Whether his beloved Philippians had given him personal gifts before his last journey to Jerusalem, or whether his tentmaking had gained him enough for all this, or whether he had come into a family inheritance, or whether any combination of these or other circumstances gave him this command of funds, we are not told. We note only that he was evidently not in financial need and would probably not be for some time to come, with the Roman government bearing the expenses of his food, lodging and transportation.

PAUL BEFORE FESTUS

"Now when Festus was come into the province, after three days he ascended from Caesarea to Jerusalem.

"Then the high priest and the chief of the Jews informed him against Paul, and besought him,

"And desired favor against him, that he would send for him to Jerusalem, laying wait in the way to kill him.

"But Festus answered, that Paul should be kept at Caesarea, and that he himself would depart shortly thither.

"Let them therefore, said he, which among you are able, go down with me, and accuse this man, if there be any wickedness in him.

"And when he had tarried among them more than ten days, he went down unto Caesarea; and the next day sitting on the judgment seat commanded Paul to be brought.

"And when he was come, the Jews which came down from Jerusalem stood round about, and laid many and grievous complaints against Paul, which they could not prove.

"While he answered for himself, neither against the law of the Jews, neither against the temple, nor yet against Caesar, have I offended anything at all.

"But Festus, willing to do the Jews a pleasure, answered Paul, and said, Wilt thou go up to Jerusalem, and there be judged of these things before me?

"Then said Paul, I stand at Caesar's judgment seat, where I ought to be judged: to the Jews have I done no wrong, as thou very well knowest.

"For if I be an offender, or have committed anything worthy of death, I refuse not to die: but if there be none of these things whereof these accuse me, no man may deliver me unto them. I appeal unto Caesar.

"Then Festus, when he had conferred with the council, answered, Hast thou appealed unto Caesar? unto Caesar shalt thou go."

—Acts 25:1-12

Sacred and secular histories both show Festus in a much more favorable light than Felix. Both show him to have been basically reasonable and just, as well as active and energetic in the discharge of his duties as governor of Judaea, which position he held for only two years before his death.

Having arrived at Caesarea, he lost no time in becoming acquainted with those over whom he was to reign. After only three days he went up to Jerusalem, evidently to meet the rulers of Israel.

No sooner had he arrived upon the scene, however, than he found himself involved in a characteristic web of intrigue. Immediately the Jewish leaders began "informing" and "beseeching" him with regard to Paul and, if his own account of it may be trusted, "all the multitude of the Jews" set up a clamor "crying that he ought not to live any longer" (Ver. 24).

Indeed, the rulers brought this pressure to bear upon Festus to back up their request that, as a *favor*, he would send for Paul to be tried at Jerusalem. Actually, however, they had no intention of letting Paul reach Jerusalem alive, for their plan was to have him ambushed and killed *en route*.

How corrupt and wicked mere religion can be! Two years had passed since these spiritual leaders had first invented their false charges against Paul, clamoring for his execution and even plotting to murder him. Now, after all this time, their hate is as bitter and relentless as ever and they are still as determined to destroy him, if not by false accusation and trial, then by the assassin's dagger.

The governor's response to their petition, however, was dignified and just. Paul would be kept at Caesarea, he said and, since he himself was soon to go there, those in power, or more powerful,[1] among them, could go down with him and make their complaints there at the Roman seat of authority. If in this case too, Festus' later account is to be trusted, he also pointed out that it was not the "manner of the Romans" to deliver an uncondemned man up to his accusers as a mere favor (See Ver. 16).

In fulfillment of his promise Festus went back to Caesarea "not more than eight or ten days" later (See Ver. 6, R.V.) and, on the very next day, commanded Paul to be brought before him.

This was no private interview but a public trial, for the governor occupied "the judgment seat" and the Jews, who had already appeared on the scene, "stood round about" charging Paul with many grave crimes centered, however, in the three major charges of the previous trial, as his defense indicates (Ver. 8).

Once more they were unable to produce evidence, however, that he was actually guilty of either heresy,

---

1. Gr. *dunatoi*.

sacrilege or sedition. He, therefore, merely stood firm in his denial that he had committed any offence, either against the law of Israel, or against the temple, or against Caesar.

If the number and the gravity of their charges against Paul had made Festus suspicious, their failure to produce legitimate evidence had fully convinced him of the bankruptcy of their case against Paul. Festus himself acknowledged this later (Ver. 25).

Yet there was much to be considered at this, his first court session in Judaea. If history is correct, the Jews had been responsible for Felix' removal by Nero. If Festus acquitted Paul and released him now, he would bitterly antagonize the Jewish rulers at the very outset of his reign, when he most needed their friendship and support.

He therefore made a proposition which, though designed to appease the Jews, still showed that he did not mean to be wholly unjust: Would Paul agree to go up to Jerusalem and there be tried in Festus' presence, or at least under his supervision?[2] He understood perfectly that Paul need not agree to this, so left the decision with him.

But that would still be a trial by the Jewish Sanhedrin and Paul knew, as Festus may not have known, how utterly hopeless it would be to look for justice there. Thus he responded to the governor's suggestion by standing firmly on his rights as a Roman citizen: *"I stand at Caesar's judgment seat, where I ought to be judged,"* he said, explaining that if he had committed any crime worthy of death, he would have accepted the

---

2. The trial itself, however, would then be by the Sanhedrin, as Verses 11 and 20 indicate.

sentence manfully, but since, as Festus very well knew, the charges against him were false, no one had the right to deliver him up to his accusers.

And then the apostle pronounced those words which surprised and upset Festus as they placed him in an even more embarrassing position:

"I appeal unto Caesar."

There is historical testimony to the fact that certain, if not all, Roman citizens at that time had the right to suspend trials in which they were involved in the lower courts by appealing directly to the Emperor. Thus the apostle now, doubtless judging this was his only escape from sure death on the one hand, or another long imprisonment on the other, availed himself of this right. Perhaps he also remembered the promise of the Lord that he should testify at Rome (Acts 23:11) and felt this was the course *He* would have him take.

But this left Festus in an embarrassing predicament, for it would hardly help him, in the eyes of Imperial Rome, to have his first official act as governor thus challenged. He therefore conferred with his assessors,[3] evidently to make sure that Paul's Roman citizenship could not be questioned and to see if there were any other possible escape from his dilemma.

But the governor *dare not* deny the apostle's appeal, and we detect a tone of resentment as well as derision in his reply, as he says: *"Hast thou appealed unto Caesar? unto Caesar shalt thou go."* "Little do you know," he intimated, "what an appeal to Caesar means."

---

3. The "council" of Verse 12 is not, of course, the Sanhedrin, for they were not even present. Moreover a different word, *sumboulion*, is used.

Now the case was out of Festus' hands. There remained only the official report to the supreme tribunal, with all the records and documents involved, and a review of his own judgment in the case. He was responsible, too, to see that the defendant was taken safely to Rome.

Thus Israel is left farther and farther behind in the apostle's ministry and experience, and he emerges more and more distinctively as *"the apostle of the Gentiles."*

HEROD AGRIPPA VISITS FESTUS

AGRIPPA'S INTEREST IN PAUL'S CASE

"And after certain days King Agrippa and Bernice came unto Caesarea to salute Festus.

"And when they bad been there many days, Festus declared Paul's cause unto the king, saying, There is a certain man left in bonds by Felix:

"About whom, when I was at Jerusalem, the chief priests and the elders of the Jews informed me, desiring to have judgment against him.

"To whom I answered, It is not the manner of the Romans to deliver any man to die, before that he which is accused have the accusers face to face, and have licence to answer for himself concerning the crime laid against him.

"Therefore, when they were come hither, without any delay on the morrow I sat on the judgment seat, and commanded the man to be brought forth.

"Against whom when the accusers stood up, they brought none accusation of such things as I supposed:

"But had certain questions against him of their own superstition, and of one Jesus, which was dead, whom Paul affirmed to be alive.

335

"And because I doubted of such manner of questions, I asked him whether he would go to Jerusalem, and there be judged of these matters.

"But when Paul had appealed to be reserved unto the hearing of Augustus, I commanded him to be kept till I might send him to Caesar.

"Then Agrippa said unto Festus, I would also hear the man myself. Tomorrow, said he, thou shalt hear him."

—Acts 25:13-22

Festus was now faced with an embarrassing problem. The formal charges brought against Paul had not been sustained by one iota of firsthand testimony. They should therefore have been thrown out as invalid, the case should have been dismissed and Paul should have been liberated. Yet, how could Festus anger the Jews now? And—was there something more behind all this clamor for Paul's life? Was there some *other* charge which might be validly made against him?

The "many and grievous complaints" made against Paul—all unproved (Ver. 7) had left Festus in a quandary as to what it was they really had against him and, to make matters worse, Paul had taken the case out of his hands by appealing to Caesar. What kind of a report could Festus now send to the Emperor without making himself appear a most incompetent judge (Vers. 26,27)? This would be bad so soon after assuming office in Judaea.

It came to pass at this time, however, that Herod Agrippa II and Bernice appeared upon the scene, having come, evidently, to give formal recognition to the new procurator.

Agrippa II, the last of the Herods, was not even, like his predecessors, "King of the Jews." Luke calls him simply "the king" (Ver. 14, Ctr. Luke 1:5). The domain which Caesar had first granted Herod the Great, had been cut in two, so that Archelaius was "ethnarch" over *half* the province. This half had again been cut in two, so that Herod Antipas was a "tetrarch," or governor over *one quarter* of a province. And the present Herod had been given even less territory, including part of Galilee, but not Judaea, so that he was not even "King of the Jews." The title "king" was conferred upon him only as a courtesy. History does record, however, that he was the appointed guardian of the temple with the right to nominate the high priest.

In this all we have further evidence of the steady decline of the nation Israel. For years the kings of Israel, who should have come from the royal line of David, and the high priests, who should have come from the priestly line of Aaron, had been *appointed* by heathen emperors; the Emperor directly appointing the king, giving the king, in turn, the power to name the high priest. But these Herods not only lacked the royal blood of David's line; they were Idumaeans, aliens by birth, though they did go through the motions of embracing the Jewish religion.

Since Agrippa represented at least some of the people of Israel, it was advisable for him to maintain the best possible relations with the Roman procurator at Caesarea. Hence this visit. Furthermore, Festus needed him too—especially now—for his knowledge of the Jewish religion and Jewish laws and customs.

Again we have a wicked couple before us. Herod, of course, came from wicked parents and had a dark, infamous past. Bernice, who is mentioned three times as with him (Vers. 13,23; 26:30) was none other than the sister of Drusilla, Felix' depraved paramour, and thus

Herod's own sister, with whom he lived in incestuous relationship.

It was "many days" (Ver. 14) before Festus got round to mentioning Paul's case to Agrippa; days spent, doubtless, in processions and festivities in honor of "the king." But finally the time came when Festus related his problem concerning Paul to the man he hoped could help him.

His account of the case, while basically factual, betrays more than his ignorance of Jewish religion and law; it betrays his utter spiritual blindness.

He stated that the charges brought against Paul were not such as he had expected. Yet Paul had been charged with profaning the temple (which was under Roman protection) and even with *sedition*. Were these not such charges as he should have been able to deal with? The answer is evidently that the accusers had so completely failed to produce evidence of the truth of these charges that Festus had considered them invalid.

The Jews, said Festus, really had "certain questions" against Paul "of their own superstition,[4] and of one Jesus, which was dead, whom Paul affirmed to be alive" (Ver. 19).

Festus' reference to "one Jesus" shows that he knew little or nothing about Christ, though he *had* observed that Jewish feeling at Paul's trial had most deeply concerned this One, who, in his opinion, was evidently dead, but "whom Paul affirmed to be alive." However Paul's accusers might try to misrepresent the real issue—*this was it*.

---

4. *Deisidaimonia, fear of the demons*, was *their* word for *religion*. Festus would not offend his royal visitor, himself a Jew, by calling the Jewish religion *superstition*. See our notes on Acts 17:22 and the R.V. on both passages.

But why Paul should insist that this Jesus was alive, or why the Jews should so bitterly object to this, or how a court decision about it would solve anything, was more than Festus could see.

Poor blind pagan! He did not see that it was not a question of "their religion" or "our religion," but of *the truth*. He did not see that these "questions" affected *him*. He did not see that man's redemption—*his* redemption—depended on whether or not Christ really was alive.

How many "respectable" people today are as blind, spiritually, as Festus! Let others hold to "their religion" if they will; let them consider these "questions"; let them deny or believe that Christ rose bodily from the dead, but "how does this concern me?" Thus millions pass lightly over the most vital truths—truths essential even to their own salvation.

Festus did not tell the truth, at least not the *whole* truth, as to his reason for suggesting a Jewish trial to Paul, for Luke's inspired record does not indicate that Festus had felt that a trial at Jerusalem would be more *just*, but rather that he sought "to do the Jews a pleasure" by giving Paul into their hands (Ver. 9).

Agrippa, unlike Festus, had heard a great deal about Jesus, and doubtless also about Paul. This latter is indicated by his remark: *"I also was wishing to hear the man myself"*[5] to which Festus responded: *"Tomorrow...thou shalt hear him"* (Ver. 22).

---

5.   See R.V. Margin.

Chapter XLVI — Acts 25:23-26:32

PAUL BEFORE HEROD AGRIPPA

"And on the morrow, when Agrippa was come, and Bernice, with great pomp, and was entered into the place of hearing, with the chief captains, and principal men of the city, at Festus' commandment Paul was brought forth.

"And Festus said, King Agrippa, and all men which are here present with us, ye see this man, about whom all the multitude of the Jews have dealt with me, both at Jerusalem, and also here, crying that he ought not to live any longer.

"But when I found that he had committed nothing worthy of death, and that he himself hath appealed to Augustus, I have determined to send him.

"Of whom I have no certain thing to write unto my lord. Wherefore I have brought him forth before you, and specially before thee, O King Agrippa, that, after examination had, I might have somewhat to write.

"For it seemeth to me unreasonable to send a prisoner, and not withal to signify the crimes laid against him."

—Acts 25:23-27

Since Festus had invited Agrippa to hear Paul on the morrow, he evidently decided to use the occasion to show himself friendly to the military and civil leaders of Caesarea at the same time. They would be interested in Paul's case.

Thus, at the appointed time, we find Agrippa and Bernice arriving at the Audience Hall "with great pomp," along with the military chiefs and leading citizens of the community.

After Paul had been brought into the chamber Festus addressed the entire audience, frankly explaining the awkward position in which he had been placed, having to send a prisoner to Caesar without being able to supply any definite information as to his case.[1]

Festus' opening words: *"Ye see this man,"* lends pathos to the scene. There stands the great apostle, who should have been lavished with high honors rather than accused of crimes—there he stands before all these dignitaries, a prisoner in chains.

Did they pity him? Perhaps, but he surely pitied them, as we shall presently see. And what of Herod Agrippa, in his purple robes, with Bernice, bedecked with jewels beside him? They had entered upon the scene in splendor and pageantry. But now as Agrippa beheld Paul, did he recall his great grandfather, Herod, and the slaughter of the innocents? (Matt. 2:16). Did he recall his great uncle, Herod Antipas, and the murder of John the Baptist? (Matt. 14:1-11). Did he recall his father, Herod Agrippa I and the murder of James? (Acts 12:1,2). Did it occur to him that all these ancestors of his had died or been disgraced soon after their commission of these crimes? Did the "great pomp" of his own parade to the Audience Hall remind him of the time, sixteen years ago, when the people had shouted that his much-more-powerful father was a god, and how he had been instantly stricken with death and

---

1. Note that Festus not only calls Nero *Augustus (the august one)* but *kurios, "my lord"* (Vers. 21,26). This is another instance of Luke's accuracy, for while the earlier Augustus and Tiberius had refused this title, Nero had accepted and used it.

eaten by worms "because he gave not God the glory"? (Acts 12:21-23). When we consider the extreme vanity and self-importance of this phantom king, it is doubtful that *any* of these things even entered his mind.

Here was Paul before a different audience from any he had ever been called upon to address. Festus, the Roman Procurator, King Herod Agrippa II, high ranking military officers and eminent civic leaders were all in his audience that day. The Lord was fulfilling His promise: *"He is a chosen vessel unto Me, to bear My name before...kings..."* (Acts 9:15).

PAUL'S DEFENSE BEFORE AGRIPPA

We come now to the third account of Paul's conversion in the Book of Acts. The first is Luke's inspired record of it in Chapter 9, the second is Paul's account before the multitude at Jerusalem in Chapter 22 and the third is Paul's account before Herod Agrippa, here in Chapter 26.

Paul's hearing before Agrippa was not in any sense a legal trial. His accusers were not there to prefer any charges, nor did either Festus or Agrippa have any right to pass sentence upon him since he had appealed to Caesar. This was rather a special hearing before one who was better qualified than Festus to judge the merits of Paul's case, and Festus had called for it so that he might be better able to send a report to Caesar.

Paul, however, would not be benefited by helping Festus explain the charges laid against him! Thus, as in his private hearings before Felix, he scarcely refers to these charges, but takes advantage of the opportunity to seek to win his hearers to Christ.

THE QUESTION AT ISSUE

"Then Agrippa said unto Paul, Thou art permitted to speak for thyself. Then Paul stretched forth the band, and answered for himself:

"I think myself happy, King Agrippa, because I shall answer for myself this day before thee touching all the things whereof I am accused of the Jews:

"Especially because I know thee to be expert in all customs and questions which are among the Jews: wherefore I beseech thee to hear me patiently.

"My manner of life from my youth, which was at the first among mine own nation at Jerusalem, know all the Jews;

"Which knew me from the beginning, if they would testify, that after the most straitest sect of our religion I lived a Pharisee.

"And now I stand and am judged for the hope of the promise made of God unto our fathers:

"Unto which promise our twelve tribes, instantly serving God day and night, hope to come. For which hope's sake, King Agrippa, I am accused of the Jews.

"Why should it be thought a thing incredible with you, that God should raise the dead?"

—Acts 26:1-8

As honorary chairman of the session, Agrippa now invited Paul to tell his side of the story, and Paul, with that characteristic gesture of his, "stretched forth the hand"[2] beckoning all those present to hear him.

---

2. This very hand, as well as the other, may have been chained to a Roman soldier. We gather this from the use of the plural in Verse 29: *"these bonds"* (cf. Acts 12:6 *"two soldiers...two chains"*).

In this situation, as well as in others which we have already considered, we find the apostle completely objective in his outlook. The pomp and pageantry connected with the occasion, the vanity of the "royal" couple, the presence of military and civil dignitaries, the fact that *he* stood before them in chains: all this does not appear to have distracted him for one moment. At perfect ease throughout the hearing, the apostle used the opportunity to offer his defense, of course, but, as we have seen, even more to win his hearers to Christ.

In his introductory remarks we find again that combination of candor and courtesy which so become the man of God. He does not flatter the wicked Agrippa, nor commend him for either character or accomplishments, but he does sincerely express his gratification at being granted a hearing before one so intimately acquainted with Jewish affairs. And this acknowledgment of Agrippa's qualifications in the case opens the way naturally for the apostle to request the king to hear him "patiently."

Again the apostle pleads that his *"manner of life"* was well known to all the Jews (Ver. 4.) He had been brought up among them at Jerusalem as one of that promising and privileged group of young men who studied under Gamaliel, the renowned doctor of Moses' law (22:3). He had "profited in the Jew's religion above many of [his] equals...*being more exceedingly zealous of the traditions of [his] fathers*" (Gal. 1:14). His accusers well knew, though they would not testify, that from the beginning he had lived a Pharisee, following the teachings and customs of the very strictest sect in Israel (Acts 26:5).

And now he stands trial—*for what?* For repudiating his faith in God's promise to the fathers? No! but *for proclaiming the very hope upon which that promise rested* (Ver. 6).

344

A DISPENSATIONAL BLUNDER

We pause here to take note of a blunder into which extreme dispensationalists sometimes fall in studying this passage.

If the failure to observe dispensational *distinctions* in the Scriptures has brought harm and loss to the Church, the failure to recognize the *unity* of God's plan for the ages, and to observe dispensational *connections* is fraught with peril fully as great.

Those who jump to hasty and extreme conclusions, dispensationally, generally see some "distinctions" which do not exist. The result, interestingly enough, is that in seeking to establish non-existent "distinctions" they generally blunder back into the camp of those who fail to note some of the *most basic distinctions*.

An example of this is seen in the erroneous contention that Paul here asserts before Agrippa that it is for proclaiming the kingdom of Messiah that he has been accused of the Jews. During Paul's early ministry, it is argued, he preached practically the same message as the twelve, and his special ministry *for us* did not begin until after Acts 28:28. Strangely, the question why the remaining members of the twelve were not then suffering along with Paul, does not seem to occur to these brethren. But we pose it here. If the Jews were so angry at Paul for proclaiming the kingdom, how is it that the multitudes of those who believed and proclaimed this very message in Jerusalem and Judaea went on unmolested at this time?

The fact is that from the beginning Paul's apostleship and commission had been separate and distinct from that of the twelve or any other—and he *says* this in

345

Acts and in his early epistles (See Acts 20:24; Eph. 3:1-3; Gal. 1:11,12; 2:2,7,9; etc.). Now, considering the passage before us, it must be carefully observed that the apostle does *not* say that he was being judged for proclaiming *"the promise"* made to the fathers. To the fulfillment of this promise (the millennial kingdom) the "twelve tribes" themselves "hoped to come." Why, then, should they find fault with him for believing and proclaiming it?

It was for proclaiming "the *hope* of the promise" that he was hated and persecuted. And what was "the *hope* of the promise?" It was *the resurrection* in general, and *the resurrection of Christ* in particular. The Sadducees—poor apostates!—who had so bitterly opposed him, did not see that the resurrection, and particularly the resurrection of Christ, was the only basis for any expectation of the promised kingdom. Christ alone was—and is—the rightful King, and the thousands of believers gone before could not see that kingdom unless they were raised from the dead.

The Pharisees, of course, joined the Sadducees in their persecution of Paul because he had further pointed out how the resurrection of Christ was a proof of a *finished* redemption and of justification by grace without religion or works.

But his purpose here was to point out that he had been opposed by the Jews for proclaiming a doctrine which was the very—the *only*—hope of the fulfillment of a promise to which the twelve tribes[3] themselves hoped to come (Vers. 6,7). They "served" God intensely, day and night, offering prayers and sacrifices and

---

3. This passage shows the fallacy of the theory of "Anglo-Israelism," that the ten northern tribes of Israel never rejoined Judah and Benjamin after their exile, but wandered to more distant parts and turned up as the Anglo-Saxon races.

346

oblations, longing for the establishment of the kingdom long promised. But the resurrection, especially the resurrection of Christ, was the hope of that promise and, mark well, the apostle repeats that *this* is what the Jews opposed:

"For now I stand and am judged for the HOPE of the promise....For which HOPE'S sake, King Agrippa, I am accused of the Jews" (Vers. 6,7; See also 23:6; 24:15; 25:18,19; 26:22,23).

And "why," he asks, "should it be thought a thing incredible with you [Jews] that God should raise the dead?" (Ver. 8). In posing this question the apostle directly confronts Agrippa with many obvious arguments for the resurrection. Did not the Scriptures teach it? Did they not record instances of it? Did not all nature bear witness to it, and—strongest argument of all—does not the very name *God* comprise a myriad of miracles? Would He be *God* if He could not raise the dead? *"Why should it be thought a thing incredible with you, that GOD should raise the dead?"*

Doubtless Paul thus faced Agrippa directly with the question of the resurrection because he felt Agrippa might have a closer relationship with the Sadducees, some of whose high priests he had nominated.

PAUL'S FORMER ENMITY AGAINST CHRIST

"I verily thought with myself, that I ought to do many things contrary to the name of Jesus of Nazareth.

"Which thing I also did in Jerusalem: and many of the saints did I shut up in prison, having received authority from the chief priests; and when they were put to death, I gave my voice against them.

347

"And I punished them oft in every synagogue, and compelled them to blaspheme; and being exceedingly mad against them, I persecuted them even unto strange cities."

—Acts 26:9-11

In Paul's testimony before Agrippa he shows how perverted the human conscience can become. He verily thought *"with himself"* that he *"ought"* to do *"many things"* against Christ—that is, that he ought to oppose Him in *every way possible.*

Our Lord Himself had forewarned His disciples: *"...the time cometh, that whosoever killeth you will think that he doeth God service"* (John 16:2). Did this, then, justify Saul in his actions? By no means. He could and *should* have known that Jesus was the Christ, for the Scriptures were clear enough as to this, but as the Pharisee of Luke 18:11 had "prayed with himself," so the Pharisee of Acts 8 and 9 had "thought with himself," and his conclusions, though *sincerely* arrived at, made him an enemy of God and a murderer of His people.

No, Paul's sincerity did not excuse him, though it did afford God grounds for showing him *mercy* (I Tim. 1:13).

Paul doubtless had a threefold purpose in referring to his former bitter enmity against Christ. First, it would indicate that he had not *lightly* changed his attitude toward Christ. Second, it would indicate that if one so utterly sincere could be so wrong, the position of his hearers, in God's sight, might be far worse. Third, his *"I verily...myself"* expresses the apostle's sympathy with his hearers and his hope that God might save them too.

And with this the apostle proceeds to recall some of the details of his persecution of the followers of Christ

348

at Jerusalem. He not only "thought," he "also *did*" many things contrary to the name of Jesus.

"Many" of Christ's followers he had "shut up"[4] in prison, by *"authority from the chief priests"* (who now opposed him) and when these disciples were condemned to death he cast his vote[5] against them.

Paul's testimony that *"many"* of the saints were thus imprisoned and put to death, indicates that Stephen was not the only martyr during this period. Doubtless Stephen's martyrdom is the only one mentioned by Luke because it was crucial and representative in Israel's history, but Luke does inform us that Stephen's murder touched off a *"great persecution"* in which Saul *"made havock of the church"* (Acts 8:1,3) and went forth "breathing out *threatenings and slaughter* against the disciples of the Lord" (9:1). Moreover, at his conversion, the Jews at Damascus exclaimed: "Is not this he that *destroyed* them which called on this name in Jerusalem?" (9:21). Finally, Paul himself later wrote to the Galatians: *"Beyond measure I persecuted the church of God and wasted it* [Lit. *laid it waste*]" (Gal. 1:13). Thus there is no reason to doubt Paul's testimony before Agrippa, or to conclude that it is contradicted by the fact that Luke records Stephen's martyrdom alone.

But it was not enough that those apprehended for their faith in Christ were imprisoned, tried and executed, for Saul had first tortured many of them to force them to recant. "I punished them *oft*," he says, "in

---

4. This intense term, *katakleio*, is used only here and in Luke 3:20, and shows how vexed he was with the believers.
5. "Voice," Gr. *psephos*, a stone used for voting. See R.V. The fact that Paul could cast such votes would seem to indicate further that he was a member either of the Sanhedrin or of the larger body, "the estate of the elders" (cf. Gal. 1:14).

every synagogue [in Jerusalem, Ver. 10 and 22:18,19] and *compelled*[6] them to blaspheme" (Ver. 11).

And the flaming leader of the rebellion against Christ was not satisfied even with this. Jews in *other* cities must learn to dread the worship of Christ as a plague. Maddened with raging fury against the believers, he "persecuted them *even unto strange cities*"[7] (Ver. 11) seeking to stamp out the worship and memory of Jesus of Nazareth.

This is Paul's considered analysis of his former state as he recalls it before Agrippa and the others present. He states it thus that he might be seen as one who has come to know *the truth*—to know *Christ*—and has thus come to his senses.

The apostle's bid for the souls of his hearers is further seen in the fact that he now calls those whom he had so fiercely persecuted *"saints"* (holy or consecrated ones) and states that he punished them to make them *"blaspheme"*—blaspheme *Christ*, of course. Could he imply any more clearly that he *now* looked upon Christ *as God?*

HIS CONVERSION TO CHRIST

"Whereupon as I went to Damascus with authority and commission from the chief priests,

"At midday, O king, I saw in the way a light from heaven, above the brightness of the sun, shining round about me and them which journeyed with me.

6. This refers to the *object*, rather than the result of the punishment, for the imperfect tense is used. Those tortured did not necessarily yield, otherwise "many" would not have been "put to death."

7. This proves that his journey to Damascus was not the first and only such venture, but the last of many like it.

"And when we were all fallen to the earth, I heard a voice speaking unto me, and saying in the Hebrew tongue, Saul, Saul, why persecutest thou me? it is hard for thee to kick against the pricks.

"And I said, Who art thou, Lord? And He said, I am Jesus whom thou persecutest.

"But rise, and stand upon thy feet: for I have appeared unto thee for this purpose, to make thee a minister and a witness both of these things which thou has seen, and of those things in the which I will appear unto thee;

"Delivering thee from the people, and from the Gentiles, unto whom now I send thee,

"To open their eyes, and to turn them from darkness to light, and from the power of Satan unto God, that they may receive forgiveness of sins, and inheritance among them which are sanctified by faith that is in Me."

—Acts 26:12-18

It was without question Saul himself who had kindled the persecution that raged against Messiah's followers. According to the record it was he who had "made havock" of the church (8:3) who had "destroyed" the believers at Jerusalem (9:21) who had "persecuted the Church of God" and had "laid it waste" (Gal. 1:13). It was *he* who had gone to the high priest *asking* for letters of authority to bind any of Christ's followers in Damascus and bring them to Jerusalem for punishment.

But it must not be assumed from this that the chief priests were not more than glad to have this young zealot stir up hatred against Christ and His followers, and Paul is careful to stress this fact. In his account of his conversion given before the multitude at Jerusalem he had referred to "the high priest...and all the estate of the elders" as witnesses of his persecutions, and had added: *"from whom also I received letters...to Damascus, to bring them which were there bound unto Jerusalem for to be punished"* (Acts 22:5). And now in his second account, before Agrippa he likewise declares that he had persecuted the saints *"having received authority from the chief priests"* (26:10) and that it was *"with authority and commission from the chief priests"* that he had gone to Damascus to bind the believers there (Ver. 12). Thus he had gone forth as the appointed representative of Israel and her rulers, and his bitter enmity against Christ and His followers was but the expression of theirs.

It is in this account of Paul's conversion that he says that the light which shone from heaven was brighter than that of the noonday sun. Only those who know the blinding glare of the Syrian sun at high noon can begin to appreciate this. This was no subjective vision, experienced by the apostle alone. The light from heaven shone round about Paul *and his companions* that day (Ver. 13) as actually as the glory of the Lord had shone round about the shepherds at Christ's birth (Luke 2:9). And like the shepherds, they were all "sore afraid"[8] and *all* fell to the earth (Ver. 14).

This fact alone indicates how important an event in history was the conversion and commission of Paul.[9] Indeed, a comparison of the narrative in Luke 2 with that which we have here will emphasize this still further.

---

8. "The glory of the Lord" *would* make men afraid, since *"all have sinned and come short of the glory of God"* (Rom. 3:23).

9. For a fuller discussion of this subject see Chapter XIV in Volume 1.

The glory of the Lord which shone about the shepherds appeared "by night" (Luke 2:8,9) but the glory that blinded Saul—and opened his eyes—eclipsed the noonday sun. It was the glory from the face of Him who had been exalted *"far above all heavens"* (Eph. 4:10 cf. Eph. 1:20,21; Phil. 2:9; Heb. 7:26) whom Paul had been blindly persecuting, but who now appeared to him in love and grace.

It is in this account, too, that we learn that the Lord addressed Paul in the sacred tongue of his fathers, *"the Hebrew tongue,"* tenderly asking him: *"Saul, Saul, why do you persecute Me?"* (Ver. 14).

Again it is in this account that we learn of the Lord's gentle remonstration: *"It is hard for thee to kick against the pricks [goads]"*[10] (Ver. 14). And this reveals to us a fact hitherto not made known: that the persecutor of Christ had not been quite sure of himself, at least at the time just preceding his conversion.

His inability to *answer* Stephen (Acts 6:10) Stephen's transformed countenance before the Sanhedrin (6:15) his testimony about seeing "the Son of man" (7:56) his prayer for his murderers (7:60) and a hundred other such incidents in connection with those he had persecuted and helped to put to death, may well have brought about an uncertain inward condition which his stubborn determination had failed to overcome.

Finally, in this account of Paul's conversion we have the fullest report of what the Lord said to him from heaven.

---

10. Expressing *futile resistance*, as when oxen kick against the goads of their drivers. This phrase is not found at 9:5 in most texts.

First, it should be observed that Saul was not, like those saved under the ministries of John the Baptist and the twelve, a repentant Jew. He had not sought Christ or wished to know Him. His salvation was clearly by *sovereign grace*. The Lord had appeared to Paul in his obstinacy, not to punish him but to *save* him and commission him as His apostle.

Secondly, we learn that the truths he was to proclaim were to be further made known to him in a series of revelations in which the Lord Himself would appear to him:

"...I have appeared unto thee for this purpose, to make thee a minister and a witness both of these things which thou hast seen, and of those things in the which I will appear unto thee" (Ver. 16 cf. II Cor. 12:1-4).

This refutes the teaching that Paul's "revelation ministry" did not begin until after Acts 28:28. The apostle, in his first revelation of Christ, had already seen the Lord in a glory far excelling that in which the twelve had ever seen Him. *They* had known only the Christ on earth; Paul, from the beginning had known only the Christ "exalted far above all" and had *seen* Him in His heavenly glory. *They* had been sent to proclaim His kingdom rights, even after His ascension (See Acts 1:6-8; 3:19-21; etc.). *He* had been sent "to testify *the gospel of the grace of God*" (Acts 20:24). Hence the apostle never speaks of "*my gospels*" (in the plural) but always of "*my gospel*" (Rom. 2:16; 16:25; II Tim. 2:8); nor does he ever say or imply that the revelations of Christ to him concerned *different* messages, but rather that *one* message was gradually committed to him in a series of revelations (Acts 20:24; 26:16; I Cor. 9:17; II Cor. 12:1-4; Gal. 1:11,12,15,16; Eph. 3:1-4; Col. 1:24-26; etc.).

354

Third, we learn from this passage that from the day of Paul's conversion he was chosen from Israel and from the Gentiles as Christ's apostle to both.

The word "delivering" (Verse 17, A.V.) is almost certainly an incorrect rendering of the Greek here, for Paul was *not* "delivered" from the Gentiles in the sense that would be intended here; in fact he was finally beheaded by Nero. The Greek *exaireo* means simply *to take out*. Thus it *can* refer to deliverance, as in Acts 23:27, where it is correctly rendered *"rescued."* But surely it could *not* be rendered "rescue" or "deliver" in Matthew 5:29. In *this* passage it is correctly rendered: "And if thy right eye offend thee, *pluck it out*, and cast it from thee." Neither, we believe, is "delivering" the correct rendering here. Dean Howson translates it: "thee have I chosen," in *Life and Epistles of St. Paul* (pg. 673). And J. N. Darby, in his *New Translation*, renders it: *"taking thee out."*

This is a more consistent rendering, for Paul was indeed *chosen* and *taken out* from both his own people[11] and the Gentiles, and sent back to both[12] with the message of grace. This distinguishes him, too, from the twelve. *They* represented the *twelve tribes of Israel* (Matt. 19:28). *He*, as *one* apostle, represents the *one Body* (Col. 1:24; Eph. 4:4).

And how complete a representative! He was a *Hebrew*, a *born* Hebrew and *intensely* Hebrew (Phil. 3:5).

---

11. The term "the people," in Scripture, refers to Israel (See Psa. 2:1 and cf. Acts 4:25,27).

12. Some hold that the "unto whom" refers only to the Gentiles, not *both*. It is true that Paul was sent especially to the Gentiles, as over against the *nation* Israel, but his ministry to the end, included both Jews and Gentiles (See Ver. 20; I Cor. 12:13; Eph. 2:14-18; etc.).

He was also, as we have seen, a Roman (Acts 22:25) a *born* Roman (22:28) and *intensely* Roman (21:39; 25:9-11). Here, then, we have a Hebrew and a Roman in one person! Moreover, he was a former *enemy*, reconciled to God by *grace—"exceeding abundant" grace!* What an ideal representative of the believing Jews and Gentiles in this dispensation, who have been "reconciled to God in one body," who have "the forgiveness of sins *according to the riches of His grace!"*

The Book of Acts, of course, is primarily the account of the fall of the nation Israel, *not* "the history of the founding of the Church," but the record of Acts *does* confirm the testimony of Paul's early epistles that the reconciling of believing Jews and Gentiles to God in one body began with *Paul*, during his *early* ministry. Further, the Lord's words: "unto whom *now I send* [Gr. *apostello*] thee" (Ver. 17) indicate that Paul was commissioned as an apostle on the very day of his conversion.

But, despite the pageantry of the scene, the apostle is speaking here to a depraved half-Jewish king with a poor fallen woman at his side, along with a heathen governor and many other lost souls. Thus he does not discuss God's plan to form the Body of Christ but deals rather with basic moral and spiritual matters.

"The glorified Christ said to me on that day," he recalls:

"Thee have I chosen from the house of Israel and from the Gentiles; unto whom now I send thee:

"To open their eyes

"and to turn them from darkness to light,

"and from the power of Satan unto God,

"that they may receive forgiveness of sins.

356

"and inheritance among them which are sanctified by faith that is in Me" (Vers. 17,18 cf. *Life and Epistles of St. Paul*, pg. 673).

How Agrippa, Bernice, Festus and all the rest should have been touched by this progressive unfolding of what the rejected, but glorified, Christ was willing to do for them! Blindness dispelled, light beheld, sins forgiven, riches of grace bestowed. All this and more could now be theirs for the asking.[13]

HIS MINISTRY SINCE HIS CONVERSION

"Whereupon, O king Agrippa, I was not disobedient unto the heavenly vision:

"But showed first unto them of Damascus, and at Jerusalem, and throughout all the coasts of Judaea, and then to the Gentiles, that they should repent and turn to God, and do works meet for repentance.

"For these causes the Jews caught me in the temple, and went about to kill me.

"Having therefore obtained help of God, I continue unto this day, witnessing both to small and great, saying none other things than those which the prophets and Moses did say should come:

"That Christ should suffer, and that He should be the first that should rise from the dead, and should show light unto the people, and to the Gentiles."

—Acts 26:19-23

The apostle does not recall, merely, that he was *obedient* to the heavenly vision. He says: "I was *not*

---

13. The phrase "by faith *that is in Me*," however, does not refer to *their* faith but to *His faith*, or *fidelity*. The word *faith* here is used *subjectively* rather than objectively (cf. Rom. 3:3; Gal. 2:20; etc.).

*dis*obedient," indicating that the only alternative to the course he had taken would have been to *disobey* orders direct from heaven, received under such arresting circumstances. This would have been unthinkable, yet it was because he had not disobeyed the divine commission that the Jews had gone about to slay him. This, of course, was calculated to have its effect upon those present too, including especially Agrippa himself, as indicated by the earnest manner in which Paul addressed him personally.

In the apostle's brief account of the carrying out of his commission it should be noted that the word "then" in Verse 20 is supplied by the translators in the Authorized Version; it is not contained in the original. Albert Barnes comments on this:

"It would seem from that word [*then*] that he had *not* preached 'to the Gentiles' until *after* he had preached 'at Jerusalem and throughout all the coasts of Judaea,' whereas, in fact, he had, as we have reason to believe...before then 'preached' to the Gentiles in Arabia" (*Barnes* at Acts 26:20).

While Barnes does not prove even in his notes on Acts 9, that Paul *preached* in Arabia, his general argument is correct. For one thing, after his return to Jerusalem from Damascus (Gal. 1:17,18) he *"came into the regions of Syria and Cilicia"* (Gal. 1:21) apparently in connection with his journey to Tarsus (cf. Acts 9:29,30). Evidently this was the occasion of the founding of Gentile churches there, for later we find letters being sent along with Paul and others, to the Gentile believers there, to confirm them in grace (Acts 15:23-27).[14] Now all this time, Paul himself tells us,

---

14. See our notes on Galatians 1:21, in Volume 1, pgs. 322-324.

he *"was still unknown by face unto the churches of Judaea which were in Christ"* (Gal. 1:22, R.V.). He could not, therefore, have preached "throughout all the coasts of Judaea" before going to the Gentiles. His ministry in Judaea more probably took place at the time when the Gentiles at Antioch sent financial "relief unto the brethren which dwelt in Judaea" (Acts 11:29,30) or else on one of his subsequent visits to that region.

The order of the reading in the Greek, at Verse 20, would indicate that the word "first" refers to *Damascus*, where he began to witness for Christ. It *is true* that wherever he went, until the end of Acts, he consistently ministered to the Jews first, but he surely did not go "first" to the Jews in Palestine and "then" to the Gentile regions.[15] The meaning of Verse 20 is simply that he ministered to *both* Jews and Gentiles.

But Verse 20 presents still another problem.

Paul's declaration that he had taught Jews and Gentiles alike "that they should repent and turn to God, and do works meet for repentance," has led some to the unwarranted assumption that the apostle, during this period, had preached "the gospel of the kingdom," even as John the Baptist, our Lord and the twelve had done.

Such a conclusion would be contrary to the whole record, however. A moment's reflection will show that the true soul winner, still today, will seek to persuade men to "repent," lit. "change their minds" and "turn to God" and then "do works" consistent with that change. This is still so, even though the *theme* of our message is the finished work of Christ and the riches of His grace.

---

15. See our notes on this in Volume 1, pgs. 321-322.

In the presentation of Messiah to Israel, however, the *emphasis* was placed upon repentance. Most of the Jews rested in the fact that they, as Abraham's descendants, were God's people regardless of their conduct. Hence their need to change their minds and do works consistent with this change. It is doubtless because Paul was particularly addressing one with a Jewish background that he put the matter in this way.

It was because of Paul's obedience to the divine commission that the Jews had sought to kill him (Ver. 21)—this latter now attested in the legal records which Festus had in his possession. Paul no doubt brought up this fact to emphasize to the judges the poverty of the Jews' case against him. It was evident, as John Calvin points out, that "their cause and conscience were both evil" (See *Acts*, Vol. II, pg. 348) otherwise they would have granted him a fair trial.

But Paul had obtained the help that was from God,[16] and had continued to that very day his course unchanged.

ANOTHER DISPENSATIONAL BLUNDER

Extreme dispensationalists, seeking to prove that Paul *did* preach a kingdom message during his early ministry, have often cited Acts 26:22 to prove their point.

"Having therefore obtained help of God, I continue unto this day, witnessing both to small and great, *saying none other things than those which the prophets and Moses did say should come.*"

---

16. This is the sense of the original, the definite article appearing before "help."

Does not this prove, they argue, that Paul *could not* have proclaimed the mystery before Acts 28? Does he not *say* he had proclaimed *nothing* which the prophets and Moses had not already foretold? Here these brethren show again their inability to think a subject through or to follow it through in Scripture.

Paul had, up to this time, proclaimed numerous truths which cannot be found in the writings of either the prophets or Moses. Neither the prophets nor Moses had foretold the salvation of the Gentiles through the *fall* of Israel, nor the "gospel of the grace of God," in which neither circumcision nor the law was to have any part. Nor had they even hinted that Jews and Gentiles would be baptized into one body by the Spirit. Nor had they said—or known—anything about believers being "caught up" to heaven by "the Lord Himself." Yet all this had been proclaimed by Paul prior to this time (Rom. 11:11,12; Acts 20:24; I Cor. 12:13; I Thes. 4:16,17).

And had not Paul written of *"the mystery"* and its associated *"mysteries"* in his *early* epistles? (Rom. 11:25; 16:25; I Cor. 2:6,7; 4:1; 15:51). Is the *mystery* to be found in *prophecy*—that which was "hidden" and "kept secret," in that which had been "made known"?

Indeed, even if we were to admit that Paul proclaimed the kingdom during his entire Acts ministry, he would then still have taught more than "the prophets and Moses did say should come," for even in "the gospel of the kingdom," our Lord uttered things which had been *"kept secret from the foundation of the world"* (Matt. 13:35); truths which neither the prophets[17] nor Moses had even known about.

---

17. It is true that our Lord Himself was a prophet, but Paul clearly refers to the prophets whom Agrippa believed (Ver. 27).

Do the facts, then, contradict Paul's statement before Agrippa? In no wise. The trouble is that our extremist friends have quoted only half his statement. The first part of his statement, in Verse 22, is clearly qualified by the remainder, in Verse 23:

"That Christ should suffer, and that He should be the first[18] *that should rise from the dead, and should show light unto the people, and to the Gentiles."*

In other words, the facts that Christ should suffer, rise from the dead and show light to Israel and the Gentiles, were nothing but what the prophets and Moses had already predicted. Why then should the Jews so bitterly oppose Paul's ministry to the Gentiles? This alone was Paul's argument.

It is always difficult for us to understand how any sound teacher of the Word can quote Acts 26:22 alone, making it an unqualified statement by Paul that until that time he had preached *nothing* but what the prophets and Moses had predicted. Both the rest of Paul's statement here and the rest of his early teachings and writings, would seem to pronounce them guilty, not merely of misinterpreting but of *misrepresenting* his plain words. This is especially so since most of them have been faced again and again with these facts.

PAUL'S DEFENSE INTERRUPTED

"And as he thus spake for himself, Festus said with a loud voice, Paul, thou art beside thyself; much learning doth make thee mad.

"But he said, I am not mad, most noble Festus; but speak forth the words of truth and soberness.

18. Not in time, but in rank. See I Corinthians 15:20,23 and Colossians 1:18.

"For the king knoweth of these things, before whom also I speak freely: for I am persuaded that none of these things are hidden from him; for this thing was not done in a corner.

"King Agrippa, believest thou the prophets? I know that thou believest.

"Then Agrippa said unto Paul, Almost thou persuadest me to be a Christian.

"And Paul said, I would to God, that not only thou, but also all that hear me this day, were both almost, and altogether such as I am, except these bonds.

"And when he had thus spoken, the king rose up, and the governor, and Bernice, and they that sat with them:

"And when they were gone aside, they talked between themselves, saying, This man doeth nothing worthy of death or of bonds.

"Then said Agrippa unto Festus, This man might have been set at liberty, if he had not appealed unto Caesar."

—Acts 26:24-32

This passage in Acts has caused some to look upon Festus as a coarse, rude individual. What we have seen of him thus far, however, indicates that he was anything but rude. The fact that he interrupted Paul *"as he thus spake,"* and did so *"with a loud voice"* evidently indicates that he was deeply agitated.

It is true that "the natural man receiveth not the things of the Spirit of God" (I Cor. 2:14) and that the proclamation of "Christ crucified" is "unto the Greeks foolishness" (I Cor. 1:23). It is true that, *apart from the working of the Holy Spirit*, all this about One who had died, rising again to "show light" to the nations, along

363

with the story of Paul's miraculous conversion, would have seemed to Festus as the sheerest superstition. But Imperial Rome sanctioned the fanatical superstitions of many religions. Why then, should Paul's words have caused such an outburst by Festus before Agrippa and all the other dignitaries present?

Whether Festus was himself moved by Paul's stirring testimony, and sought to cover up his feelings by this outburst, or whether he was concerned about the effect it was having upon the others present, we cannot, perhaps, tell, but surely the incident indicates the spiritual power of Paul's address as he spoke of darkness and light, the power of Satan and of God, the forgiveness of sins and Christ, the only Savior.

The translation: *"much learning doth make thee mad,"* is doubtless further responsible for misconceptions about Festus' character. The Greek word *"gramma"* simply means *"writings"* and is twice used of the Holy Scriptures (John 5:47; II Tim. 3:15). Surely a man of Festus' character and position would not object to *learning*. It was evidently to the *"writings"* which Paul held so dear, that Festus referred. These Paul quoted fluently; these he cited as final authority on many a question, and these he had doubtless been studying diligently during his two years' confinement at Caesarea, especially in connection with the further revelations he had received from the glorified Lord.

Thus what Festus really said was: *"Your many writings are turning you mad."*

Paul, understanding Festus' agitation, replied with calm and simple dignity: *"I am not mad, most noble Festus; but speak forth the words of truth and soberness"* (Ver. 25) then immediately referring himself back

364

to the king. This combination of firm protest with courtesy is characteristic of Paul. He treats Festus with deference, yet firmness, as a strong man might treat a weak opponent, and proceeds to demonstrate to him that his deep earnestness comes, not from madness, but from *"truth and soberness."*[19]

In an adroit use of adverse circumstances, the apostle explains to Festus that King Agrippa knows about these things; that he can speak freely before him, and that he is convinced that the details of his account have not been "hidden" from him, since they were not done "in a corner."

Unquestionably Paul was correct in this, for Agrippa had not only been brought up in the Jewish religion, but had long been intimately associated with Israel politically. Surely, then, the conversion of Saul, the persecutor, to Christ and the apostle's widespread ministry and the phenomenal spread of the gospel could not have been unknown to him.

And now he does something more likely to convince Festus than any argument in his own defense. Addressing Agrippa personally, he asks:

"King Agrippa, believest thou the prophets?" and then immediately adds: *"I know that thou believest"* (Ver. 27).

To have waited for an answer would, under such circumstances, have been improper as well as foolish. *He*, not Agrippa; had been called for a hearing, and to put the king in an embarrassing position would only have angered him. Thus, tactfully, the apostle immediately

---

19. The Greek *sophroneo* indicates *soundness of mind* (see Mark 5:15; Luke 8:35; II Cor. 5:13).

answers his own question. He *knows* King Agrippa believes the Old Testament writings—and surely Festus would not call *Agrippa* mad! Nor could Agrippa, in his position, deny this and accept Festus' opinion of the sacred Scriptures. Thus with superb tact the apostle appeals to Agrippa himself and uses *him* as his witness, at the same time driving home the *truth* of his argument.

WAS AGRIPPA "ALMOST PERSUADED"?

There has been a great deal of controversy about the significance of Agrippa's response to Paul's appeal: *"Almost thou persuadest me to be a Christian."* The various views on the subject are substantially as follows:

1. That the Greek *"en oligo,"* or *"in a little,"* gives the sentence the meaning: *"in brief, you would persuade me to become a Christian."*

2. That the words *"en oligo"* refer to Paul's *argument*, making the sentence to read: *"With a little [a brief argument] you would persuade me to become a Christian."*

3. That he said in *sarcasm*: "In a little while you will persuade me to become a Christian."

4. That the words *"en oligo,"* here, *do* have the sense of *"almost,"* and that he meant, either in sarcasm, or in greater or less sincerity: *"Almost you persuade me to become a Christian."*

5. A few translators and commentators hold that the word "persuadest" refers to *Paul*, and that Agrippa actually said: *"In a little you will persuade yourself to make me a Christian."*

It is held by some that the phrase "thou persuadest me," would be more correctly rendered: "thou *wouldest* persuade me," but other commentators reject this view and a considerable majority of our Bible translations fail to bear it out.

In view of this fact, and considering the emotional effect which Paul's address had upon Festus, we reject interpretations 1, 2 and 3. We also reject interpretation 5 as lacking support.

As to interpretation 4, the idea of "almost" fits more naturally with Paul's reply in Verse 29. Also, while in his reply Paul may simply have ignored any sarcasm on the part of Agrippa, the circumstances again: Paul's moving address, his appeal to the Scriptures, the stirring account of his conversion, the evident power and effect of his ministry, Festus' emotional outburst—all this, leads us to believe that Agrippa was experiencing the convicting power of the Holy Spirit, even though he may have meant to brush this off by a remark *apparently* sarcastic. Thus he becomes the symbol of all those who are never *quite* persuaded to trust in Christ as their Savior.

Whatever the degree of Agrippa's sincerity in the matter, Paul was quick to take advantage of the situation. Revealing his burden of heart, not only for Agrippa, but for Festus, Bernice and *all* those present, he replied with great feeling:

"I would to God, that not only thou, but also all that hear me this day, were both almost and altogether such as I am, except these bonds" (Ver. 29).

What a truly great servant of God the apostle was! How deeply in earnest: *"I would to God."* How large-hearted: *"not only thou, but also all that hear me this day."* How self-effacing: *He* is in chains, but longs for *their* salvation. How triumphant: "I wish *you* could be as *I* am." How powerful his plea: "Almost" is not enough. It must be *"altogether."*

And the most exquisite touch of Christian courtesy and grace is found in his words: *"except these bonds."* He had suffered much for Christ, but he wished none of *that* for them. He wished them to know only the peace and assurance and joy in his heart. He may have added this phrase with a twinkle in his eyes, too, for it indicated he *was* sane; he did *not* enjoy his chains.

Conviction was doubtless taking hold—perhaps of many there present. The unbelieving heart says it must not go too far. Agrippa, as chairman of the session rises and, with the others, leaves the chamber. How many since have followed his example!

Discussing the matter between themselves they all agreed that Paul was worthy neither of death nor bonds, and Agrippa remarked that he might have been set free had he not appealed to Caesar. Festus had not told him how this had come about, indeed, had actually misrepresented the case (Acts 25:25).

This was not the first time Paul's innocence had been confirmed (Acts 23:9; 23:29; 25:25) yet he had not been released. And now he *could* not be released. There was no retreat for either him or Festus. To Caesar he must go and Festus is responsible to see to it that he arrives safely at Rome.

368

THE VOYAGE TO ROME

ANCIENT SHIPPING AND NAVIGATION

We come now to one of the most exciting episodes in the history of Paul's ministry: the voyage to distant Rome, with its long weeks of hardship and peril on a storm-tossed sea.[1] Before discussing this section in detail, however, we would do well to acquaint ourselves somewhat with the shipping and navigation of those days.[2]

It is evident from II Corinthians 11:25 and other Scripture passages, that the sailing vessels of ancient times foundered in far greater proportion than those of more modem times.

This was largely due to their construction. Besides having a less streamlined hull, the ancient vessels used little or no more than one large mast with its mainsail and, perhaps one or two smaller sails, located near the center of the ship. Rather than distributing the strain on the ship in strong winds, this naturally centered all the strain amidships, tending to spring the planks below and cause leakage.

---

1. The reader is urged to consult the map on Page 402 in the study of this section of Acts.

2. One of the most complete studies of this subject is to be found in *The Voyage and Shipwreck of St. Paul*, by James Smith of Jordanhill, England, one of the first to consider this passage from the viewpoint of a seaman. Smith's book appeared in 1848, when England's interest in sailing vessels was at its height. It is to this book and its author that we are chiefly indebted for the nautical information we give in connection with Paul's voyage to Rome.

This explains why "they used helps,[3] undergirding the ship," in the storm we are soon to consider (Ver. 17). It also explains why, in the storm in which Jonah figured, the mariners *"cast forth the wares that were in the ship...to lighten it of them"* (Jonah 1:5) and why in *this* storm they cast overboard much of the cargo, and even *"the tackling of the ship"* (Acts 27:18,19) when one would suppose that ballast would have been the more necessary in a storm.

It is a mistake, however, to suppose that these primitive vessels were necessarily small in size. The ship in which the apostle sailed from Myra to Melita accommodated 276 passengers and crew *besides her cargo*, and the *next* ship sailing from Melita to Italy, accommodated all these 276, *besides her cargo and her own passengers and crew*. Indeed, Josephus refers to a ship on which he sailed with 600 passengers aboard. Many ancient merchant vessels, then, were large sea-going craft, capable of carrying heavy cargoes and hundreds of passengers.

It would be a mistake, too, to assume that the simple rigging on these ancient ships would prevent their working to windward. On the contrary, the passage we are to consider may well confirm the contention of some naval authorities that they could sail against the wind to within perhaps 8 points of a 32-point compass,[4]

---

3. These consisted of cables, chains, or even heavy ropes, passed around the hull to prevent it from going to pieces. This procedure has been called "frapping" by earlier seamen of the British and American Navies. With the appearance of more modern sailing vessels and then steamers, however, these measures became unnecessary.

4. Though Roman and Greek navigators did not use compasses but went mostly by the stars when out of sight of land.

for they did make a considerable part of this journey *against* the wind, obviously by "tacking."

It is true, however, that the very nature of the rigging, while advantageous to a quick run before the wind, would prove a disadvantage when sailing *against* the wind.

In this connection it is well to observe again that the prevailing wind in the Levant blows from the northwest most of the year, becoming stronger in the autumn months and blowing up fierce storms in the winter. Thus winter voyages, from November to March were avoided in those days, all navigators seeking harbors in which to "winter" (cf. Ver. 12).

DISPENSATIONAL SIGNIFICANCE
OF THE VOYAGE

We have long ago learned in these studies that Acts is more than a spiritual story book. Like any other book of the New Testament it has a distinct line of teaching. Furthermore, presenting as it does, the transition from the kingdom program to that of the present day, it has a peculiar and important *dispensational significance.*

Luke was not inspired to go into such detail and make so much of this voyage to Rome merely to provide us with a thrilling and dramatic narrative.

Paul was a seasoned traveler and had already faced many grave dangers; among them, "perils in the sea" (II Cor. 11:26). Indeed, some years previous to this voyage he had already been able to write: *"...thrice I suffered shipwreck; a day and a night I have been in the deep"* (II Cor. 11:25). But this voyage to Rome had a peculiar dispensational significance, hence more is made of it.

371

Paul had gone to Jerusalem, among other reasons, "to testify the gospel of the grace of God," but had found the nation hardened in its rejection of Christ, and the believers there farther then ever from a true understanding of grace (21:20). And now, for the last time, he leaves his countrymen behind to go to Rome, as "the prisoner of Jesus Christ for [the] Gentiles."

But his departure as a prisoner by no means signifies that he has walked off the stage of history into oblivion. On the contrary, he is more than ever to occupy the center of the stage. God's plan revolves around him while, for the present, Israel and Judaism are left behind and the *world* looms into view.

Already his great message has been proclaimed far and wide. Already he has written letters to establish the saints in grace. And now, from Rome, he will send more letters, containing truths which have been rightly called "the capstone of divine revelation," and which are to lead the Church into the blessings of full-orbed grace.

Thus Paul's departure from Jerusalem to Rome is significant of the transfer of God's blessing from Israel to the Gentiles. Soon the apostle's ministry will no longer be to "the Jew first." When he arrives at Rome he will tell the Jewish leaders there that *"the salvation of God has been[5] sent unto the Gentiles"* (28:28). The *Gentile* is now to occupy the prominent place in the purpose of God as more Gentiles than Jews worship Israel's God and His Christ.

Those who find difficulty in reconciling this with the doctrine of the one joint body should observe that while abundant grace is *offered equally* to Jew and Gentile and

---

5. This is the correct sense.

the merits of Christ crucified *apply equally* to both (Rom. 10:12) and while believing Jews and Gentiles are indeed reconciled to God in one body by the cross (Eph. 2:16) yet *practically* speaking, this is a Gentile dispensation, for the simple reason that Israel, as a nation, has rejected Christ and believing Jews in the Body form so small a minority. This is why God's work today is called: *"this mystery among the Gentiles"*[6] (Col. 1:27).

Further, since Acts is the story of the fall of *Israel* it is not strange to find this voyage teaching a *figurative* dispensational lesson too, for signs, parables and figures have always been significant in Israel's history.

Thus the passage depicts the voyage of the Church[7] through the present dispensation, as it leaves Judaism behind. The sea symbolizes the unsaved masses (Isa. 57:20); the contrary wind, the antagonism of Satan[8] (Eph. 2:2). The *ship* is finally wrecked, but all who sail with Paul are brought safe to shore (Ver. 44).

Paul is the outstanding figure aboard ship. *He* gives advice as to the journey (Vers. 9,10) and when this is rejected and trouble results, he rebukes them saying: *"Sirs, ye should have hearkened unto me"* (Ver. 21). It is *he* who cheers his fellow-passengers as, by divine revelation, he declares that all those sailing *with him* will survive the storm (Vers. 24,25) and it is *he* who persuades them finally to partake of food and presides in the giving of thanks (Vers. 34-36).

6. The fulfillment of *prophecy* among the Gentiles awaits Israel's conversion (See Zech. 8:13; Rom. 15:8-10; etc.).

7. The *professing* Church, *within which*, in *this present* dispensation, are the members of the Body of Christ.

8. Thus our Lord *"rebuked"* the wind (Mark 4:39). In the passage before us the wind is always *against* them, except once, when it deceives them (Vers. 13,14).

These dispensational lessons must be borne in mind as we proceed to study the account of the apostle's voyage to Rome.

THE LAST FAMILIAR SCENES

"And when it was determined that we should sail into Italy, they delivered Paul and certain other prisoners unto one named Julius, a centurion of Augustus' band.

"And entering into a ship of Adramyttium, we launched, meaning to sail by the coasts of Asia; one Aristarchus, a Macedonian of Thessalonica, being with us.

"And the next day we touched at Sidon. And Julius courteously entreated Paul, and gave him liberty to go unto his friends to refresh himself.

"And when we had launched from thence, we sailed under Cyprus, because the winds were contrary.

"And when we had sailed over the sea of Cilicia and Pamphylia, we came to Myra, a city of Lycia.

"And there the centurion found a ship of Alexandria sailing into Italy; and he put us therein."

—Acts 27:1-6

The time had at length arrived to leave the military barracks at Caesarea and begin the journey to Rome, for "a ship of Adramyttium" lay in the harbor, ready to sail to the coasts of provincial Asia, of which Adramyttium lay at the far north. There connections might be made for the rest of the journey to Italy. From Verse 9 we conclude that this voyage, which was to have so great an effect upon the history of mankind commenced sometime near the end of August.

The prisoners being sent to Rome were in the custody of one Julius, "a centurion of Augustus' band,"[9] but *Paul,* as we have said, is the central figure of the narrative. It is written about *him.* In Julius' custody are *Paul* and *"certain other prisoners"*[10] (Ver. 1). Indeed, besides Paul and Julius, only two others are identified: Luke (See the "we" and "us" of Verses 1,2) and Aristarchus, *Paul's attendants.*[11] *He* gives advice, rebukes, cheers, commands, promises safety and presides over the famous "meal in the storm." Moreover Julius shows him respect and even some affection, permitting him to go ashore at Sidon to visit his friends and later risking his life to save him.

Thus the Lord provided for His apostle by giving him a position of unique influence aboard ship, along with a sympathetic centurion, two devoted believers as his companions in travel—*and* Christ's own promise of safe passage (Acts 23:11) to further sustain him.

---

9. Perhaps a centurion of some local cohort named after Augustus, but more probably one of the *Praetorian Guard,* who may have been in the vicinity in connection with Festus' installation into office.

10. It would appear that these, unlike Paul, were already condemned to death and now probably sent to Rome to fight with wild beasts for the amusement of Nero and the Roman populace.

11. For other references to these two, see Acts 19:29; 20:4; Colossians 4:10; Philemon 24; II Timothy 4:11. There is no indication that these were *prisoners.* Pliny writes how a man "of consular rank" was permitted attendants in such cases (Epist. III. 16). Since Paul was not being *sent* to Rome as a criminal, but had himself demanded trial by Caesar, Luke was evidently permitted to attend him as his physician, and Aristarchus as his servant. This is another indication that the apostle was probably not in the poorest circumstances, financially, at this time. Unlike the other prisoners, he was doubtless responsible for his own fare to Rome. Luke, on the other hand, *may* have secured free passage as a physician, but Aristarchus could hardly have gone along free of charge.

The first part of the journey would still bring the apostle into contact with familiar scenes and faces. As we have seen, the ship was scheduled[12] to sail to the coasts of provincial Asia, but there was first one stop to be made at Sidon, about seventy miles to the north.

That Julius held Paul in high esteem, and was even affectionately disposed toward him, already becomes evident in Verse 3 of this passage. There we read that he treated Paul with kindly affection,[13] giving him liberty to go ashore to his friends and "refresh himself" (Lit. "be cared for").

After two years in prison the apostle would hardly possess the necessities for a long sea voyage. Also, he may have suffered physically from his long confinement, for he was far from robust. This special consideration, then, with the material help and Christian fellowship it afforded, must have heartened him greatly. It was one happy day with friends ashore to prepare him for many fearsome weeks on a storm-tossed sea.

The centurion's kindly feeling toward Paul was not unique in the apostle's experience. Other Roman officers, both civil and military, had shown him similar kindnesses, as Julius also would again (See 18:14,16; 19:31,37; 24:23; 28:16,31; etc.). This speaks well of Paul's character as a Christian.

But many discouragements lay ahead. From here on the voyage was one long series of delays, perils and accidents which ended, after two months, in fearful shipwreck on the rocky shores of Malta.

---

12. The word here rendered "meaning" refers to the vessel, not to the company boarding it.
13. More than "courtesy." The Greek word *philanthropos*, from *philos*, "loving," *anthropos*, "man."

Luke explains that they sailed "under" (Lit. "in the lee of") Cyprus, "because the winds were contrary" (Ver. 4). Ramsay states that Luke's explanation "stamps him as a stranger to these seas" (*St. Paul the Traveler*, pg. 317) since, according to Ramsay it was *normal* at this time of the year to avoid navigation in the open sea. But Ramsay is surely wrong here. Not only is this an *inspired* record, but Luke's amazing accuracy of detail and his familiar use of nautical language indicates that he was no stranger to sea travel and was, indeed, familiar with this part of the Mediterranean.

Evidently the original plan had been to sail south of Cyprus by the open sea straight to the southern coast of "Asia," but because the strong westerly winds had begun to blow unseasonably early, it had been decided to sail to the north and east of Cyprus so as to get more protection from the wind. That they did *not* sail south of Cyprus, as some conclude from the word "under," in Verse 4, is evident from the fact that they reached Myra by way of the sea of Cilicia and Pamphylia (Ver. 5, and see map, pg. 402).

While the wind in these waters was already "contrary," the *current* is said to flow always westward. This would afford some help, so that we read of no *extraordinary* difficulty encountered sailing north of Cyprus to Myra.

The first lap of the journey had, however, taken longer than expected. The same winds which had previously sped Paul so prosperously from Patara to Tyre (See notes, pg. 237, and map, pg. 134) were now "contrary," keeping him for a considerable length of time in familiar territory. To the north lay his native Cilicia and to the east, Antioch, from whence he had departed on his first apostolic journey, while to the south lay

Cyprus, the island on which he had first labored after leaving Antioch. Many memories must have crowded the apostle's mind as the navigators sought, with difficulty, to make headway against the wind.

Finally they arrived at Myra, where the centurion was fortunate—or, as it turned out, *un*fortunate— enough to find "a ship of Alexandria," bound for Italy. Its presence in the harbor of Myra may be accounted for by the same early winds which had baffled the mariners of the coastal vessel from which the centurion and his prisoners had just disembarked.

It is also possible, however, that Myra was one of its ports of call, for this ship bore grain.[14] Egypt was then the granary of the world, and a local inscription has described Myra as *"harrea,"* a "storehouse of corn."

Probably this Alexandrian ship was a seagoing vessel, considerably larger than the previous coastal vessel, for the Egyptian sea freighters are reputed to have been the largest on the Great Mediterranean.

It was in this great vessel that the direst perils were soon to be encountered.

TROUBLE AHEAD

"And when we had sailed slowly many days, and scarce were come over against Cnidus, the wind not suffering us, we sailed under Crete, over against Salmone;

"And, hardly passing it, came unto a place which is called The Fair Havens; nigh whereunto was the city of Lasea.

---

14. It may have been either corn or wheat, for the Greek *sitos*, used in Verse 38, may apply to either.

"Now when much time was spent, and when sailing was now dangerous, because the fast was now already past, Paul admonished them,

"And said unto them, Sirs, I perceive that this voyage will be with hurt and much damage, not only of the lading and ship, but also of our lives.

"Nevertheless the centurion believed the master and the owner of the ship, more than those things which were spoken by Paul.

"And because the haven was not commodious to winter in, the more part advised to depart thence also, if by any means they might attain to Phenice, and there to winter; which is an haven of Crete, and lieth toward the south west and north west."

—Acts 27:7-12

The wind still "contrary," it took the vessel "many days" to cover the short distance from Myra to Cnidus, on the southwest coast of "Asia." And having managed "with difficulty"[15] to bring the ship "over against" Cnidus, they were evidently unable to enter its harbor, *"the wind not suffering"* them (Ver. 7).

Some have supposed that this last phrase refers to their inability to continue their course to the north of Crete, but we conclude that it refers to their inability to enter the harbor at Cnidus, for the following reasons:

1. The term *"over against Cnidus,"* coupled as it is with: *"the wind not suffering us,"* seems to imply that they could get no *closer* to it than they did.

2. They brought the ship "over against" Cnidus only "with difficulty." Why should they try so hard to

---

15. Not "scarce." The same word is rendered "hardly" in Verse 8, but both should be *"with difficulty."*

get that close to Cnidus if they did not mean to enter its harbor?

3. After struggling with contrary winds for "many days" it would be natural to seek a harbor on the mainland.

4. Cnidus was evidently a prosperous city with a large harbor and it would have been folly, under the circumstances, to pass it by with only the *hope* of making some smaller harbor on the island of Crete.

Beaufort says of Cnidus: "Few places bear more incontestable proofs of former magnificence....The whole area of the city is one promiscuous mass of ruins; among which may be traced streets and gateways, porticoes and theatres" (*Karamania*, pg. 81). And to this Howson adds: "But the remains which are the most worthy to arrest our attention are those of the harbors...because these remains have been less obliterated by violence or decay" (*Life and Epistles of St. Paul*, pg. 694).

Evidently, then, the navigators would have entered the harbor at Cnidus, had the wind permitted it, but they were compelled by the force of the gale, to turn southward, hoping to round Cape Salmone, on Crete's eastern extremity, and so gain the protection of the island's lee shore (For A.V. "under," see above).

This they managed to do, but again "with difficulty," arriving at length at "The Fair Havens," evidently a roadstead more than a harbor, where they might at least lie at anchor. A bit to the west of The Fair Havens lay Cape Matala. Had they rounded this they would again have been exposed to the full force of the gale. It was necessary therefore, to wait at The Fair Havens for the wind to change.

"Much time was spent," however, waiting in vain for a favorable wind—so much time that "sailing was now dangerous, because the fast[16] was now already past" (Ver. 9). The sailing had already been difficult because of the unseasonably early northwest gales, but even if the winds changed, it would now be dangerous to venture forth because the Autumnal Equinox had ushered in the season when no favorable breeze could be depended upon and sailing was invariably hazardous.

As they still waited for the wind to change, therefore, Paul "admonished" the seamen not to venture further. The apostle was by now a veteran traveler and seaman. Thrice he had been shipwrecked and on one occasion he had spent "a night and a day" in the deep, doubtless clinging to some floating object, so he was well acquainted with "perils in the sea" (II Cor. 11:25,26).

He declared, therefore, that he "perceived" that this voyage, if pursued further, would bring "hurt" (Lit. *violent injury*) and "much damage" (or *loss*) not only to the cargo and the ship, but to their lives as well.

That Paul's advice was even considered[17] by the centurion and those in charge of the vessel, indicates that they held him in high regard. Perhaps they also knew by now that he was a traveler of considerable experience.

While there was a small town some seven miles from their present "haven," there lay beyond Cape Matala the city of Phenice,[18] with a well-equipped harbor. This

---

16. Doubtless that of the Day of Atonement (Lev. 16:29) which fell about October 1st.

17. We fail to see, as some suppose they do, any evidence of a formal ship's council in which Paul was invited to take part. It was obviously Paul who took the initiative in the matter (See Ver. 9).

18. Identified as the modern *Lutro*.

was only about forty miles distant and it was hoped that, should the wind turn favorable, they might make this harbor and winter there.

To both the "master" (the navigator in charge) and the "owner" of the ship, it seemed worth the risk. Furthermore, Paul had claimed no supernatural guidance in this matter. He had simply said that he *"perceived"* danger ahead. His declaration was a *warning*, not a prediction.

The centurion,[19] therefore, can hardly be blamed because he was "convinced" ("believed," in A.V., is incorrect) by the professional seamen aboard, even though Paul eventually proved to have been right in the matter. Also, because "the haven was not commodious to winter in," the majority of the crew, or passengers, or both (doubtless excluding the prisoners) urged that they "depart thence also," and attempt to reach Phenice. They had already survived many dangers; they would survive this one too, they hoped, and thus spend the winter in more acceptable surroundings—but they were wrong, with the result that the pilot and owner lost their vessel and cargo and all aboard would probably have lost their lives had not the Lord promised Paul their safety.

There is one technical problem in Verse 12 which should be explained before we proceed further with our study of the voyage. The harbor of Phenice, we are told, *"lieth toward the south west and north west."* First, how could it lie in *two* directions? The answer is simply that an island lay at its mouth, so that it might be entered from *two* angles. But, it may further be asked, would it not be folly for the mariners, already fighting strong

---

19. It appears that he had final authority in the matter. This would lend support to the view that he was one of the Praetorian Guard.

winds from the west, to seek haven in a harbor open to those very winds? The explanation to this problem is found when we adopt the *sailor's* viewpoint. The passage does not state that the *mouth* of the harbor faced southwest and northwest; it simply states that the harbor lay in that direction. Now, the harbor *did* lie to the southwest and northwest *as the seamen approached it.* A ship would have to turn its bow either to the southwest or to the northwest *to enter the harbor*, depending upon the direction it had come from. Thus the *mouth* of the harbor actually faced toward the south*east* and north*east*, sheltered from the winds that had given them so much trouble.[20] This is another reason why the attainment of this harbor was so much to be desired.

THE GREAT TYPHOON

"And when the south wind blew softly, supposing that they had obtained their purpose, loosing thence, they sailed close by Crete.

"But not long after there arose against it a tempestuous wind, called Euroclydon.

"And when the ship was caught, and could not bear up into the wind, we let her drive.

"And running under a certain island which is called Clauda, we had much work to come by the boat:

"Which when they had taken up, they used helps, undergirding the ship; and, fearing lest they should fall into the quicksands, strake sail, and so were driven.

---

20. R.V. renders this passage: "looking north-east and south-east," and gives as an alternate rendering: "down the south-west *wind* and down the north-west *wind*." While both these renderings are doubtless correct *interpretations* from the *landsman's* point of view, they are still *interpretations* and not, as far as we can ascertain, *faithful renderings of the text.* Leaving the text *as it is*, the passage is simply explained as above.

"And we being exceedingly tossed with a tempest, the next day they lightened the ship;

"And the third day we cast out with our own hands the tackling of the ship.

"And when neither sun nor stars in many days appeared, and no small tempest lay on us, all hope that we should be saved was then taken away."

—Acts 27:13-20

DECEIVED BY THE WEATHER

Ah, this soft south wind! Just what they had been waiting for!

It was only thirty-odd miles to the port of Phenice, and, while the south wind would make it somewhat more difficult to round Cape Matala, it would prove a great advantage all the rest of the way.

And so it was that "loosing thence" (Lit. *weighing anchor*) they "sailed close by Crete" (only to round the cape, of course). At last they were on their way, presumptuously anticipating a carefree voyage across the bay to Phenice, perhaps indulging in a good-natured laugh at Paul for the advice which might have caused them to throw away such a golden opportunity. So confident were they in this warm, soft breeze, that they even left their skiff, or row boat,[21] towing behind.

A SUDDEN STORM

Little did they realize, as the great ship sailed smoothly along in the balmy breeze, that all of a sudden they would find themselves in a fearful crisis.

---

21. That mentioned in Verses 16 and 30. Doubtless of considerable size.

384

The words "arose against it," in Verse 14, give the impression that a wind had come up against the ship. This is incorrect. The words are *ebalen kar autes*: *"came down it."* The idea is that a storm swept down Crete, whose mountains at this point tower to more than 7000 feet. The fierce storms in this part of the Mediterranean often begin in the same way today, with strong down drafts from the mountains.

This was no ordinary storm, for the word here rendered "tempestuous," is the adjective *tuphonikos*. It was a wind of typhonic force—a *typhoon*, locally named *Euroclydon*, or *The Northeaster*.[22] Today it is called *The Levanter*, because it blows from the Levant.

So suddenly had this fierce storm swept down upon them that there was no time to furl the great mainsail or to do anything to control the ship. They had been "caught" in a tempest so fierce that it was impossible to "bear up into the wind" (Ver. 15) or heave to, as we would call it. There was nothing to do but let her drive madly before the gale.

It was fortunate for them that the storm had not begun any later than it did, or they would have been driven into the island of Clauda, some 20 miles to the southwest. As it was they cleared the island, running "under," it, or in the lee of its southern shore. The narrow escape must have been a frightening experience.

In the lee of Clauda, the mariners exhibited excellent seamanship, using the temporary and comparative calm to attend to three matters of pressing importance.

---

22. Actually it often blew from the East North East, but on this occasion it must have blown more from the North East, as is evident from the course along which they had already drifted, and from their fear of being driven upon Syrtus Major (Ver. 17).

First the skiff must be hauled aboard—and as quickly as possible. Whether this was already water-logged or not, the record does not reveal, but we do know that in this stormy sea, the task of hoisting it aboard was not easily performed (See Ver. 16). From the "we," in Verse 16, we conclude that Paul and his two associates, or at least Luke, helped in this.

Second, the ship must be "frapped" or undergirded with cables or ropes,[23] to keep her from going to pieces. This, of course, was no work for a landlubber. "They" executed it without help from the passengers.

Third, there was great danger that the northeast wind might drive them upon "the quicksands[24] off the coast of what is now known as Tripoli, and definite precautions must be taken against this. They therefore "strake sail" or, literally, "lowered the gear" (Ver. 17). It is evident from the context that this does not mean that they took down all the sails. To do this would have been a sure way to run into Syrtis for the wind was already driving them in that direction. Furthermore, to allow the ship to drift along the breakers would be to invite it to capsize into a trough of the sea. She *must* be hove to, or brought to face the wind as directly as possible.

They must therefore have taken down the great mainsail and any higher sails and gear, leaving only a

---

23. The procedure explained on Page 154. It is interesting to observe that the noun here rendered "helps" is found in only one other place in the New Testament: Hebrews 4:16, where it should also appear as a noun: *"that we may find grace for timely help."* Thus we go to the throne of grace, often in times of desperate need, to obtain the grace that will undergird us and keep us from going to pieces.

24. Gr. *The Syrtis*, designated on most maps as *Syrtis Major*, an extensive area of shoals and reefs in which many sea-going vessels were caught.

small storm sail, or sails, to help steady the ship. Indeed, navigators of more modern sailing vessels insist that the very term: "lower the gear," under such circumstances, would imply the setting of a storm sail, or sails.

Their object was not so much to make progress but to weather the storm and avoid Syrtis. From the course which the ship now followed, it is evident that she was facing as near as possible into the wind, with her right, or starboard, side to the wind, and the storm sail so set that she kept drifting astern but always forging northward,[25] and so was "driven," as the map shows, about 8 degrees north of west, at an average rate of perhaps one and a half miles per hour,[26] bringing her to the island of Malta in about thirteen days, or fourteen from Fair Haven (Ver. 27).

NO SMALL TEMPEST

As the fierce storm continued unabated through the first night and the passengers and crew were "exceedingly tossed," it became necessary to "lighten" the ship. Actually, the original word is in the imperfect tense, and indicates that they *kept* lightening it (by casting overboard whatever could be missed) a probable indication that leakage had already begun.

But matters were to become still worse. The picture is one of growing panic. "The third day," says Luke, "we cast out with our own hands the tackling[27] of the ship" (Ver. 19). Every man was pressed into service. All that

25. In such a case "the direction in which the ship drifts is not that in which she appears to sail, or toward which her bow is turned" (*Conybeare and Howson*).

26. Smith and Penrose agree that this would be normal.

27. The Greek word for "tackling" here is evidently used in a broader sense than to include only the rigging.

was not necessary to survival must be cast overboard; beds, luggage, chests, cables and sails doubtless included, and perhaps even some of the cargo. Evidently the ship was taking more water. Furthermore, they had no compasses in those days, and without sun or stars to take reckonings by they were at still another grave disadvantage. And this continued day after day, night after night.

The ship now reduced to a leaky, battered, dismantled hulk, imagination fails us as we try to picture the physical and mental state of the hopeless, godless souls aboard. There was no relief from the fierce gale, the pounding sea, the drenching rain and spray. No fire could be lighted, no cooking done, no one could relax, until the weary, famished wretches began to give up hope. Luke closes this portion of his inspired record with the words:

"And when neither sun nor stars in many days appeared, and no small tempest lay on us, all hope that we should be saved was then taken away" (Ver. 20).

A MESSAGE OF HOPE

"But after long abstinence Paul stood forth in the midst of them, and said, Sirs, ye should have hearkened unto me, and not have loosed from Crete, and to have gained this harm and loss.

"And now I exhort you to be of good cheer: for there shall be no loss of any man's life among you, but of the ship.

"For there stood by me this night the angel of God, whose I am, and whom I serve,

"Saying, Fear not, Paul; thou must be brought before Caesar: and, lo, God hath given thee all them that sail with thee.

"Wherefore, sirs, be of good cheer; for I believe God, that it shall be even as it was told me.

"Howbeit we must be cast upon a certain island."

—Acts 27:21-26

It was in this situation of grim despair that Paul was used of God to offer hope and assurance, by a declaration, which at the same time teaches a valuable spiritual and dispensational lesson to the Church.

"After long abstinence" on the part of all, the apostle "stood forth in the midst" to address all those aboard. While they, doubtless (except Paul's companions) had been crying to their heathen gods (as in Jonah 1:5) Paul had been in communion with *God* and had received further assurance of safe arrival at Rome—and that for those who traveled with him as well.

"Sirs," he cried above the noise of the storm, "Ye should have hearkened unto me, and not have loosed from Crete, and to have gained this harm and loss" (Ver. 21).

It was not like Paul to thus embarrass the captain and his crew, the owner of the ship and Julius, the centurion, before all, but the present circumstances called for such measures so that they all might *now* heed his words.

How similar is the situation in the Church today! It is because believers, and especially their leaders, have ignored Paul's God-given instructions that the Church is "tossed to and fro" and has suffered so much harm and loss. And once more, as the dispensation of grace appears to be drawing to a close, it is Paul who cries: *"Ye should have hearkened unto me."* [28]

---

28. Note the analogy with Eutychus, who fell asleep under Paul's teaching, plunged from his position in "the third loft" and was then restored through Paul's instrumentality (Acts 20:6-12; see pgs. 198-207).

And now the apostle exhorts his hearers to be of good cheer, assuring them that there will be no loss of life among them, but only of the ship. This can as surely be said of the Church which is Christ's Body. Not one of its members shall be lost, though the organization will go down a dismal failure.

But how had Paul received this assurance? Hear him tell it as he stands there in the raging storm:

"For there stood by me this night the angel of God [Lit. "an angel of the God"] whose I am, and whom I serve,[29]

"Saying, Fear not, Paul; thou must be brought before Caesar: and, lo, *God hath given thee all them that sail with thee*" (Vers. 23,24).

Again there is a striking spiritual and dispensational analogy. In the present dispensation, all those who sail with Paul, and *only* those, are saved and safe. Ill-taught preachers may mix law and grace, prophecy and the mystery, the kingdom and the Body, but their hearers are saved only as they hear and receive the Pauline revelation regarding the finished work of Christ and salvation by grace through faith alone. Indeed the *hearers*, by erroneous association, may read these truths into passages which do not actually teach them, but the fact remains that they are saved through *these truths* of the glorious revelation committed to Paul. Certain it is that they are *not* saved by bringing sacrifices, as was Abel (Gen. 4:4,5) nor by efforts to keep the law, (according to Ex. 19:5 and Lev. 18:5) nor by repentance and water baptism (according to Mark 1:4 and Acts 2:38) but only by "the preaching of the cross" and "the gospel of the grace of God."

---

29. Cf. I Kings 17:1: *"As the Lord God of Israel liveth, before whom I stand."*

This scene in Acts closes with a most remarkable demonstration of faith: a man standing on a storm-battered deck, crying above the roar of a raging sea to more than two hundred seventy famished, fainting men:

"...sirs, be of good cheer; for I believe God, that it shall be even as it was told me" (Ver. 25).

Doubtless, the prediction that they should be "cast upon a certain island" was made so that they might be assured that their deliverance had not been by chance.

THE LAST DREADFUL NIGHT

"But when the fourteenth night was come, as we were driven up and down in Adria,[30] about midnight the shipmen deemed that they drew near to some country;

"And sounded, and found it twenty fathoms: and when they had gone a little further, they sounded again, and found it fifteen fathoms.

"Then fearing lest we should have fallen upon rocks, they cast four anchors out of the stern, and wished for the day.

"And as the shipmen were about to flee out of the ship, when they had let down the boat into the sea, under color as though they would have cast anchors out of the foreship,

"Paul said to the centurion and to the soldiers, Except these abide in the ship, ye cannot be saved.

"Then the soldiers cut off the ropes of the boat, and let her fall off."

—Acts 27:27-32

---

30. This designation then included not only the Adriatic Sea, but also that part of the Mediterranean which lies to the south of it.

But there was still more anxiety to endure, as the battered ship was "driven up and down in Adria." This clause, in Verse 27, is not meant to indicate that their course was not fairly steady, however. We have seen that the vessel was headed as directly as possible into the northeast wind, with her starboard side toward the wind and her storm sail, or sails, set so that she kept drifting astern, yet always forging northward. According as the velocity of the gale rose and fell, therefore, she would be "driven up and down," though in a general direction of about 8 degrees north of west.

And now, on the fourteenth night of this raging tempest, the practiced senses of the seamen, discerned that "some country was approaching,"[31] either by the sound of breakers on the shore, or a glimpse, now and then, of their phosphorescent whiteness.

In the daytime such a discovery might have been welcome indeed, but on a pitch black night in a howling storm, the sudden realization that land was near would be anything but comforting.

Quickly they let down the lead and found the depth to be twenty fathoms and, a little farther on, fifteen fathoms. This meant that immediate action must be taken to prevent their being driven upon the rocks. Four anchors must be dropped from the stern at once (Ver. 29).

But why from the *stern* rather than from the bow, the more usual place? The reason for this has by no means been agreed upon.

The majority of commentators, it seems, hold that the vessel was probably anchored from the stern lest

---

31. This is the literal rendering and again expresses the viewpoint of the mariner, to whom the ship is the center of everything. The land approaches *it!*

she swing round and strike rough or rocky places, and also that in the morning she might be in a position for the sailors to weigh anchor and beach her more easily should this be possible.

It appears to us, however, that most commentators have "followed the leader" here, failing to take several important factors into consideration.

First, it is quite generally agreed that the land which the vessel now approached was the island of Malta (cf. 28:1) and that she now lay opposite what has since come to be called St. Paul's Bay. But this bay is located on the northeast side of the island and the reader will recall that the ship had also been facing in this general direction, into the northeast wind and hence *away* from the shore.

We conclude, therefore, that the mariners cast anchor from the stern so that the ship *would* swing round to face the shore. In such a gale the first anchor would, of course, have affected this result and then three more would have been dropped to insure her against slippage. Fifteen, or even ten fathoms[32] of water would doubtless have offered plenty of depth to effect this maneuver.

But, even having done this, their position was still perilous. The anchors might give way, for who knew what they were holding to? And even if they held, billows from astern might engulf the sinking ship or, weakened as she was, the very fact that anchors were holding her against the gale might cause her to fall to pieces. Little wonder that, having done all they could, they "wished for the day" (Ver. 29).

---

32. One fathom, approximately six feet.

It is evident that the mariners did not expect the vessel to survive, for in the darkness of that stormy night they formed a desperate plot which was utterly unworthy of their traditions and responsibilities.

They let down the skiff, ostensibly to carry[33] anchors out from the bow and drop them there to steady the ship. Actually, however, they planned to use the skiff (evidently large enough to hold them all) to desert the ship and its passengers.

But Paul, suspecting their purpose, took immediate action to intercept it. How could the difficult maneuver of beaching the ship be affected *without the crew*?

With the alertness and presence of mind so characteristic of him,[34] the apostle simply spoke a few quick words to the right people and the cowardly plan was thwarted.

Had he remonstrated with the sailors themselves, they might well have escaped in spite of his words. He therefore spoke "to the centurion and to the soldiers." And he showed God-given wisdom in his approach to *them*. Taking into consideration the human instinct for self-preservation, he said: "Except these abide in the ship, *ye* cannot be saved" (Ver. 31).

The result was instantaneous. Without further discussion, the soldiers cut the ropes, let the boat fall into the water, and another crisis was passed.

Paul's moral ascendancy on this voyage is worth observing. To begin with he was permitted the company

33. The term rendered "cast" in Verse 30 is not the same as that used in Verse 29. It means, literally, "to stretch out."

34. Paul is probably the foremost Scriptural example (excepting Christ Himself) of that which he urges upon his son Timothy: "Be *instant*, in season, out of season" (II Tim. 4:2).

394

of two attendants, and the centurion treated him with kindly affection. Then at Fair Havens, while the centurion (who had final authority aboard) did not ultimately accept his advice, it is significant that this advice should even have been heard and weighed against that of both the "master" and the "owner" of the ship. But as, through fearful experience, they all learned the truth and wisdom of his warning, his influence among them grew steadily greater, until he, the passenger and prisoner, could stand and address all aboard and rally them to new hope and courage, and could issue a warning to the centurion and his soldiers which had the practical effect of an order.

Many words have been wasted in connection with the so-called contradiction between Verses 22 and 31. The simple fact, however, is that the response to the warning of Verse 31 *did not* render the prediction of Verse 22 untrue, for the sailors stayed with the ship and all *were* saved. Indeed, God's promise in Verse 22 was realized as the *sailors* "ran the ship aground." Thus their action was *included* in his prediction. This bears out a principle which we observe both in Scripture and in human experience: that human agency is deeply involved in the fulfillment of God's sovereign purposes.

ENCOURAGEMENT FOR THE FINAL ORDEAL

"And while the day was coming on, Paul besought them all to take meat, saying, This day is the fourteenth day that ye have tarried and continued fasting, having taken nothing.

"Wherefore I pray you to take some meat: for this is for your health: for there shall not an hair fall from the head of any of you.

395

"And when he had thus spoken, he took bread, and gave thanks to God in presence of them all: and when he had broken it, he began to eat.

"Then were they all of good cheer, and they also took some meat.

"And we were in all in the ship two hundred three-score and sixteen souls."

—Acts 27:33-37

In the fearful night spent off the coast of Melita, Paul had been used of God to foil the attempted escape of the sailors and to keep them with the ship. This victory, however, carried with it another danger, for men whose plans have been thwarted are apt to be sullen and uncooperative.

In this new and critical situation we again see the apostle's practical insight and presence of mind as well as his human sympathy. Grasping the situation clearly and realizing that now, if ever, the soldiers, sailors and all needed to be drawn together and encouraged, he took prompt action.

As the early dawn began to reveal the haggard faces of the exhausted wretches who had now spent thirteen days in this awful storm, Paul did the one thing most apt to help them both physically and emotionally: He proposed, yes urged, that they take the time to partake of food.

We do not suppose that Verse 33 indicates that they had eaten *nothing whatever* these thirteen days, but rather that they had prepared no regular meals. With the ship rolling and pitching in the storm, with the almost constant need for action and with life itself in the balance every fearful moment, it is to be doubted whether anyone had much time or even appetite for food. Doubtless they had snatched, now and then, only what they felt was absolutely necessary to their physical survival and often had gone without even that.

Imagine, then, the reaction as Paul began to urge them to pause to eat, reasoning: "This is for your deliverance,"[35] and assuring them confidently: *"There shall not an hair fall from the head of any of you"* (Ver. 34). And imagine the effect as he then proceeded to show his confidence in the truth of his declaration by taking bread, giving thanks to God for it in the presence of all and then beginning to eat it.

Ah, such courage, or "pluck," as Plumptre calls it, is fully as contagious as fear! "Then were they all of good cheer," says the record, and joining him, also partook of food (Ver. 36).

It is here that Luke records the number of those aboard. Perhaps this is because it was most natural to count them under such circumstances, but the Holy Spirit doubtless led him to do this at this point so as to impress upon us the wonder of the scene: two hundred seventy-five men, having come to the end of their own resources, now cheerful and ready to face grave dangers calmly, under the divinely-appointed leadership of one faithful and fearless man of God.

Oh, that the Church would come to the end of herself; to the end of her efforts to save the organization, now being tossed to and fro and foundering in a stormy sea! Oh, that she would heed the instructions of Paul, her God-appointed leader! (Rom. 11:13; I Cor. 3:10). How united and ready she would be to face the opposition of the adversary! (See Phil. 1:27,28).

---

35. This is the correct rendering of Verse 34.

SAFE TO LAND

"And when they had eaten enough, they lightened the ship, and cast out the wheat into the sea.

"And when it was day, they knew not the land: but they discovered a certain creek with a shore, into the which they were minded, if it were possible, to thrust in the ship.

"And when they had taken up the anchors, they committed themselves unto the sea, and loosed the rudder bands, and hoisted up the mainsail to the wind, and made toward shore.

"And falling into a place where two seas met, they ran the ship aground; and the forepart stuck fast, and remained unmovable, but the hinder part was broken with the violence of the waves.

"And the soldiers' counsel was to kill the prisoners, lest any of them should swim out, and escape.

"But the centurion, willing to save Paul, kept them from their purpose; and commanded that they which could swim should cast themselves first into the sea, and get to land:

"And the rest, some on boards, and some on broken pieces of the ship. And so it came to pass, that they escaped all safe to land."

—Acts 27:38-44

Thanks, under God, to the apostle's confidence and leadership, the darkness of this last early morning, the most critical of all, finds the efforts of those aboard best coordinated.

The few hours before they could see land were to be used to the best possible advantage in preparing the ship for a possible run ashore.

When they had "eaten enough,"[36] and were strength-ened, they began to lighten the ship by unloading their cargo of grain, or whatever was left of it, into the sea. They must get the ship floating as high as possible, for the less her draft the farther she could be run ashore should it be possible to beach her.

Nothing is said of the food brought along for *provisions* and, not yet having been able to determine whether or not they were near *inhabited* land, it is doubtful that they would have disposed of this. Perhaps the ship could be beached and these provisions salvaged for their sustenance.

The light of dawn finally revealed the land, but no one aboard recognized it. They did, however, see, through the rain (cf. 28:2) "a certain bay,"[37] with a beach" (Ver. 39). Here, it was hoped, the ship might be run aground, and plans were made accordingly.

Here the *Authorized Version* again fails to give the true picture. First, the original does not say that the anchors were "taken up," but "cut," or "cleared" away. What would have been gained by retrieving four heavy anchors when the ship was to be run aground and they had just lightened her for this purpose? Second, the word "themselves" (in Verse 40) is supplied by the translators and erroneously so. Third, the Greek indicates that they did three things *simultaneously*.

A better rendering of Verse 40, therefore, would be: *"And having cut away the anchors they left them in the sea. At the same time, having loosened the rudder bands,*

---

36. The Greek term describes a full and hearty (if simple) meal.
37. "Creek" is wrong. The word *kolpos* is rendered "bosom" in Luke 6:38, but was also the nautical word for *bay*.

and having hoisted the mainsail to the wind, they made for the shore."

Indeed, to avoid disaster in a situation of this kind, they *must* have done these three almost simultaneously.

Most commentators seem to feel that it was a "foresail," rather than the "mainsail" that was hoisted to the wind at this time. We question this, however, for the following reasons: First, there is little or no *proof* that the word *artemon* must or may signify a *foresail*. Second, there is no indication, and little probability, that the ship *had* a foremast (See notes on pg. 369). Third, we know that the mainsail had been lowered (Ver. 17) and that this was then used as a storm sail, or that a small storm sail was set. Finally, it was naturally their purpose to run the ship as far ashore as possible. It would appear, therefore, that a larger sail would afford the *force* needed to accomplish this.

Even so, they failed to achieve their purpose, for, heading toward shore they ran aground on a shoal formed by two opposing currents (Ver. 41, "where two seas met").

Here, for the first time, the usual word for ship (*ploin*) gives way to another (*naus*). The vessel was no longer a ship, but a mere floating hulk. Thus, with its bow stuck fast in the mud, the stern of what had been a great sea-going vessel immediately began breaking to pieces under the violent pounding of the waves.

Now quick decisions must be made, especially with regard to the prisoners. The severity of Roman military discipline caused the soldiers to urge their immediate execution, for should any of them escape, it would then cost the soldiers *their* lives. These soldiers were as ready to sacrifice the lives of others to save their own as the sailors had been on the previous night! (Ver. 30).

One of these prisoners, however, had already been signally used to save all their lives and Julius, the centurion, was too just, or thought too much of Paul, to permit his execution. The word "willing," in Verse 43, indicates far more than acquiescence. He *willed* to save Paul, and thus kept the soldiers from carrying out their plan. And so again Paul becomes, indirectly, the deliverer of others so that *all* may be brought safe to land.

But in all this there was no panic. The centurion issued orders for all who could swim to dive overboard first (Ver. 43). These would then be in a position to help the rest to shore. This may well have been Paul's suggestion, for he had already experienced three shipwrecks (II Cor. 11:25). Those who could not swim were then instructed to get to shore as best they could on planks and "pieces" (not necessarily *broken* pieces) of the ship.

"And so it came to pass that they escaped all safe to land" (Ver. 44).

> "The calm, the breeze, the gale, the storm,
>   The ocean and the land,
> All, all are Thine, and held within
>   The hollow of Thy hand."

> —Edward A. Dayman

The measures taken under lee of Clauda, the thwarting of the sailors' plot, the help and inspiration of "the meal in the storm," the final measures taken to beach the ship, the centurion's determination to save Paul—all these had but formed parts of God's gracious purpose, which had now been completely and wonderfully fulfilled.

401

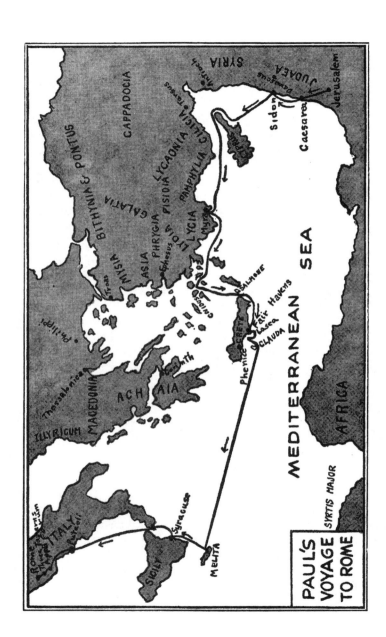

PAUL'S VOYAGE TO ROME

MEDITERRANEAN SEA

MELITA AND THE APPROACH TO ROME

THE LANDING ON MELITA

"And when they were escaped, then they knew that the island was called Melita.

"And the barbarous people showed us no little kindness: for they kindled a fire and received us every one, because of the present rain, and because of the cold.

"And when Paul had gathered a bundle of sticks, and laid them on the fire, there came a viper out of the heat, and fastened on his hand.

"And when the barbarians saw the venomous beast hang on his hand, they said among themselves, No doubt this man is a murderer, whom, though he hath escaped the sea, yet vengeance suffereth not to live.

"And he shook off the beast into the fire, and felt no harm.

"Howbeit they looked when he should have swollen, or fallen down dead suddenly; but after they had looked a great while, and saw no harm come to him, they changed their minds, and said that he was a god."

—Acts 28:1-6

MELITA THE MODERN MALTA

It is now all but certain that the 276 survivors made the shore of what is now known as the Island of Malta, that rocky citadel that successfully withstood such continuous bombing during World War II.[1]

---

1. In April of 1942 alone the enemy flew 5715 sorties, dropping 6728 tons of bombs on this small island without cracking its defenses.

There is another Melita in the Adriatic Sea, off the coast of Illyricum, high up in the Gulf of Venice, but the arguments identifying this island with Paul's shipwreck are so trivial as to be hardly worth considering, while the arguments *against* it are irrefutable.

With a gale blowing from the northeast, so fierce that it was only barely possible to keep the ship under control, how could they possibly have arrived at a point so far to the north, and that with a comparatively narrow channel to navigate between Italy's heel and Macedonia and many islands in their path to make their passage still more precarious? Also, if they landed at the northern Mileta, how could they then have traveled *north* to Rome, as they clearly did, by way of Syracuse, Rhegium and Puteoli (Vers. 11-13).

On the other hand there is remarkably conclusive evidence that they landed at Malta, and even at the site traditionally known as St. Paul's Bay. This evidence is, in part, as follows:[2]

1. The direction and rate of drift, as we have described it, would have brought the vessel to the vicinity of Malta, and approximately in this length of time.

2. In the direction of their drift they could very well have arrived off the coast of Koura Pt., the eastern boundary of St. Paul's Bay, without having previously neared any other part of Malta's coast.

3. Breakers from the northeast would strike this point violently, yet a ship could come within one quarter of a mile of it without striking sunken rocks. This is evidently why the sailors "deemed" that they were

---

2. Much of this evidence is gleaned from Smith's *Voyage and Shipwreck of St. Paul.*

approaching land, yet the ship did not immediately run aground.

4. The depth off Koura Pt., within hearing distance of the breakers, is about 20 fathoms, and a little farther on—in the direction of their drift—it is about 15.

5. The old *English Sailing Directions*, used before the turn of the century, say of this area: "While the cables hold, there is no danger, as the anchors will never start," so firm is the bottom there.

6. On the farther side of the bay, the rocky coast descends to a sandy, or pebbly beach, such as that toward which the sailors finally headed the stricken craft.

7. This bay on the northeast coast of Malta has traditionally been called *"St. Paul's Bay,"* while there is no such tradition in favor of the northern Melita.

8. The presence of another ship of Alexandria, which had wintered there on its way to Italy (28:11) is strong evidence that the island was Malta. Malta lay in the usual path of navigation from Alexandria to Italy, while the other "Melita" was altogether out of the way.

THE RECEPTION AT MELITA

Paul had already suffered three shipwrecks (II Cor. 11:25); now, by the grace of God, he had survived a fourth.

It is in connection with this landing at Melita that we first read of the "rain" and the "cold." It must therefore have been heartening to the 276 survivors, chilled and drenched as they were, to find that the island was inhabited with people, of a foreign tongue,[3] indeed, but eager to show them "no little [Lit. *unusual*] kindness."

Luke records, gratefully, that they "received us *every one*." It made no difference to these generous-hearted people whether the survivors were soldiers, sailors, passengers, or even prisoners; they were men in distress and needed help. Immediately therefore, they started a blazing fire (perhaps in one of the island's many caves) so that all might gather round to warm and dry themselves. This was the first comfort they had enjoyed for fourteen long days and nights and we doubt not that with many, or most, of them, long pent-up anxiety now gave way to tears of grateful relief.

But there was still one strong, firm soul among these wretched survivors, extending his hand to steady the rest; helping while others were being helped and doing what he could to alleviate the sufferings of his fellows, apparently unmindful of his own. His was a courage that the centurions and soldiers of the Roman army could admire. Little wonder he had so many friends among them!

But the sticks the apostle had gathered for the fire concealed a poisonous serpent, a viper, and as he lay the wood on the fire the beast leaped out from the heat and fastened itself upon his hand.

Ordinarily this would have resulted in widespread inflamation and sudden death, and as the Melitans saw the viper hanging on his hand they concluded among

---

3. The term "barbarous people" is not used in a derogatory manner. The Greek *barbaroi* means simply, *people of another tongue*, and referred to all who were not Greek in language or culture. The *Scythians* were the uncivilized savages who lived beyond the boundaries of the Roman Empire (See Rom. 1:14; I Cor. 14:11; Col. 3:11).

themselves that he was doubtless a murderer who, though having escaped the sea, was about to be executed by *Vengeance*, or *Justice*, the goddess who supposedly sat beside *Jupiter* and disposed of such cases.

But the apostle shook the viper back into the fire and felt no harm,[4] so that the Miletans, looking in vain for him to die, now concluded he must be a god! Their feelings had changed as suddenly and completely as those of the Lystrians in the opposite direction, where first it was sacrifices, then stoning (Acts 14:11-19).

This incident in the last chapter of Acts is followed by others, which prove that the era of miraculous demonstrations had not even yet passed. Also, it is another of those narratives in the Acts record which have a striking symbolic significance.

A VIPER'S BITE AND THE GRACE OF GOD

It is highly significant that a *viper* should leap out of the fire to attack Paul just as Israel was about to be set aside in the purposes of God.

That Israel's rulers, and especially the Pharisees, at this time, were considered as vipers in the sight of God is evident from the inspired record. Three times in the Gospel according to Matthew we find them called vipers.

In the first instance John the Baptist, detecting their hypocrisy in coming to his baptism, rebukes them with the words:

"O generation [or brood] of vipers, who hath warned you to flee from the wrath to come?

---

4.   This was not a fulfillment of Mark 16:18. The *taking up* of serpents should rather be associated with Exodus 4:2-5.

"Bring forth therefore fruits meet for repentance" **(Matt. 3:7,8).**

In the second, our Lord Himself, after they had blasphemed Him, showed why they *could* not bring forth good fruit, saying to them:

"O generation of vipers, how can ye, being evil, speak good things? For out of the abundance of the heart the mouth speaketh" **(Matt. 12:34).**

In the third, after pronouncing woe after woe upon them, He says:

"...ye are the children of them which killed the prophets.

"Fill ye up then the measure of your fathers.

"Ye serpents, ye generation of vipers, how can ye escape the damnation of hell?" **(Matt. 23:31-33).**

Even after the resurrection and ascension of our Lord, the rulers of Israel continued their relentless opposition against Him. They threatened His apostles, scourged them and cast them into prison. And when Stephen dared to say: "Ye do always resist the Holy Ghost," they dragged him out, stoned him to death, and waged "a great persecution" against the saints at Jerusalem (Acts 7:51,58,59; 8:1).

All this does not indicate, however, that their bitter campaign against Messiah was succeeding. On the contrary they lost round after round of the contest, and never even got to settle on a consistent plan of attack. While the apostles pursued a course which was straight as an arrow, the rulers tried first this and then that, only to be defeated and embarrassed again and again.

Peter answers the members of the Sanhedrin with such spiritual power that his accusers are turned into defendants and before he and John leave the chamber of Israel's Supreme Court, they serve them notice that they intend to *continue* preaching Christ (Acts 4:5-21). When the apostles are imprisoned again (more of them this time) an angel delivers them, and when the Sanhedrin convenes and commands that they be brought from prison for trial, it is discovered that they are *in the temple preaching*, the manner of their escape from prison remaining a mystery. And again the apostles declare that they will go right on preaching Christ (Acts 5:17-32). Then Gamaliel advises the rulers to "leave them alone" (5:38) but this proves even less effective, for now we read that "...*daily in the temple, and in every house, they ceased not to teach and preach Jesus Christ*" (5:42).

And as for the stoning of Stephen and the persecution which followed, God countered that with the greatest blow of all: the conversion of Saul,[5] which robbed them of their most outstanding and aggressive leader. At this stinging defeat, we find the rulers creeping in their holes again—and for a considerable time. The churches have rest "throughout all Judaea, and Galilee, and Samaria," and multiply steadily (Acts 9:31).

Ere long the apostles and elders at Jerusalem are freely holding their own council in defiance of the Sanhedrin, with a great multitude from far and near attending (Acts 15). And soon there are "many tens of thousands[6] of Jews" at Jerusalem "which believe" (Acts 21:20) and the rulers can do nothing about it. Like Simon, the apostate Jew of Samaria, they are "in the gall of bitterness."

---

5. Though he was both too young and too sincere to be included in the category of the vipers to which the rulers belonged.

6. This is the correct rendering.

But meantime Paul had been sent "far hence unto the Gentiles," to offer them salvation and blessing apart from Israel, by the grace of God alone and on the basis of the death of Christ. Through his ministry thousands of Gentiles had come to rejoice in Israel's God and in the Messiah Israel had rejected.

This was too much for the rulers to bear and, when Paul visited Jerusalem again, they leaped out of the flame, as it were, to strike at him and destroy him.

"Away with such a fellow from the earth!" they cried, "for it is not fit that he should live." And in their rage "they cried out, and cast off their clothes, and threw dust into the air" (Acts 22:22,23).

It was because of their enmity that Paul was now in chains, that he had suffered this fearful shipwreck and would soon be called upon to stand before Nero. But in this brief symbolic incident the Holy Spirit shows us how futile is the rulers' rage, and how inevitable their doom, for the apostle merely shook off the beast so that it fell *back into the fire*, while he went on unharmed.

Our Lord had warned these rulers that if they blasphemed against the Holy Spirit they could *never* find forgiveness, neither in that age, nor in the age to come (See Matt. 12:31,32). They now *had* persistently blasphemed the Holy Spirit as Christ was preached by the apostles "with the Holy Ghost sent down from heaven." Hence they were to be given up to the fire of God's judgment, while Paul went on to dispense to the Church and the world still greater riches of grace.

PAUL'S MINISTRY AT MELITA

"In the same quarters were possessions of the chief man of the island, whose name was Publius; who received us, and lodged us three days courteously.

410

"And it came to pass, that the father of Publius lay sick of a fever and of a bloody flux: to whom Paul entered in, and prayed, and laid his hands on him, and healed him.

"So when this was done, others also, which had diseases in the island, came, and were healed:

"Who also honored us with many honors; and when we departed, they laded us with such things as were necessary."

—Acts 28:7-10

So completely had God overruled in the storm which had overtaken the great Alexandrian grain ship that it had even been wrecked at the right spot!

It was more than a mere coincidence that Publius, the "chief man," or governor, of the island owned "possessions" in the very area of the shipwreck. Of this man Luke writes: "He received us, and lodged us three days courteously."[7]

We have already learned that the Melitans had *"received...every one"* of the 276 survivors (Ver. 2) but the Greek word rendered "received" in Verse 7 has a different meaning. The former word means to *welcome* or *take to one's self*, but the latter means to *entertain* or *assume responsibility for*. This is why we find it used along with the word "lodged," and in connection with Publius' *"possessions."*

It is perhaps impossible to determine precisely how many are included in the "us" of Verse 7. It is doubtful that it includes all 276 survivors, for if it did, the phrase "every one" would be more appropriate here than at Verse 2. Since Luke is the writer, it doubtless includes

---

7. The original expresses kindness of *feeling* rather than mere kindness of manner.

Paul, Luke and Aristarchus, and probably also Julius, for surely the chief official of a Roman possession would give special recognition to a Roman military officer of considerable importance. Indeed, it may well be that Publius offered *Julius* this generous hospitality, which Paul and his companions were then allowed to share.

At any rate, God was overruling, for by this hospitality on the part of Publius and the subsequent healing of his father, Paul's acceptance and prestige on the island was immediately assured and he found three months of usefulness and blessing among its inhabitants. And this in turn further enhanced his position with Julius, the centurion.

Publius' father had been ill with recurrent fevers[8] and an aggravated form of dysentery. Paul's visit at this time, therefore, was opportune, and his procedure in healing the sick man throws light upon a question which has baffled many commentators.

Strangely, nothing is said in the record about any preaching by Paul at Melita, nor about anyone being converted. We can understand that circumstances doubtless forbade his preaching aboard ship, but now, with three months to spend on the island, surely there was ample opportunity to proclaim Christ and His finished work.

In cases of this kind we must not forget the selective principle in divine inspiration, which is so prominent in the Book of Acts. God's great purpose in Acts is *not* to record "the birth and growth of the Church," as some have supposed, but to record *the fall of Israel* and to vindicate His action in setting them aside while

---

8. The word is plural in the original.

He demonstrates the righteousness and grace of the Messiah they have rejected.[9]

In this closing section of Acts it is not God's main purpose to show Paul's ministry among the Gentiles, but rather to show the apostle as rejected by Israel and sent in chains to Rome *because* of his ministry among the Gentiles (See 22:21-23).

Who can doubt that Paul did preach the gospel to the inhabitants of Melita? True, we read only of his miracles, but had he not written in his letter to the Romans that Christ had used his "mighty signs and wonders" *"to make the Gentiles obedient by word and deed"* as he *"preached the gospel of Christ"?* (Rom. 15:18,19).

Further, it will be observed, that in his initial miracle of healing on the island, he *"prayed"* as he laid his hands on Publius' father and healed him. This, to begin with, would show those present that he was *not* the author of the miracle but only the instrument; *not* a god, as they had supposed, but a *messenger* from God. We may be sure, too, that this prayer, and such words as the apostle would say in addition, would include a testimony to the saving grace of Christ.

While mere tradition cannot be *trusted*, in many cases it is accurate, and in this case it is interesting to note that tradition places an ancient church at Melita, with Publius as its first bishop or overseer.

The healing of Publius' father naturally caused others, who were ill, to come to Paul for healing. It was a great opportunity for Paul to repay the islanders for

---

9. This is why we find no mention of the "one Body," discussed so fully in his epistles written during this time (See Rom. 12:4,5; I Cor. 12:12-27; Gal. 3:26-28).

their generous hospitality, as well as to make Christ known to them. The Melitans had sought no gain in befriending the wretched survivors of the wreck. How richly they had now been rewarded! Malta was now an island of healthy people!

And now *they* showed their gratitude to *him*, whose unexpected visit had brought them so much good. Not only did they honor Paul and his companions with "many honors,"[10] but when the time came to leave, they "loaded" them with provisions. They would never forget the apostle and the blessing he had brought them. Little wonder that this part of Malta is to this day known as St. Paul's Bay!

APPROACHING ROME

"And after three months we departed in a ship of Alexandria, which had wintered in the isle, whose sign was Castor and Pollux.

"And landing at Syracuse, we tarried there three days.

"And from thence we fetched a compass, and came to Rhegium: and after one day the south wind blew, and we came the next day to Puteoli:

"Where we found brethren, and were desired to tarry with them seven days: and so we went toward Rome.

"And from thence, when the brethren heard of us, they came to meet us as far as Appii Forum, and the

---

10. Compare here the treatment which our Lord received at the hands of the Jews. Those who should in gratitude have raised statues and held banquets in His honor in every city, asked Him instead: *"By what authority doest Thou these things? and who gave Thee this authority...?"* (Mark 11:28). They asked the Great Physician to show His credentials!

Three Taverns: whom when Paul saw, he thanked God, and took courage.

"And when we came to Rome, the centurion delivered the prisoners to the captain of the guard: but Paul was suffered to dwell by himself with a soldier that kept him."

—Acts 28:11-16

At length the time arrived to leave Melita, since another "ship of Alexandria," which had wintered there, was about to set sail for Italy.

The "sign" under which this ship sailed was "Dioscuri," signifying Castor and Pollux, the twin sons of Jupiter and Leda. These legendary twins were identified as the two bright stars in the constellation Gemini, and worshipped as the patron deities and guiding stars of sailors. The Apostle Paul aboard this ship, "protected" by heathen gods, is an example of the believer in the world.

Syracuse, the first port at which they landed, was an important city of Sicily, still bearing the same name. Perhaps they "tarried" there for three days to wait for a change of wind, for it was then necessary to reach Rhegium (at Italy's toe) by an indirect course.[11] But after one day at Rhegium a favorable south wind arose, taking them north to Puteoli by the next day.

Puteoli was the most sheltered port on the Bay of Naples, situated at its northern extremity. It was then the chief port of Rome; a harbor for the great Alexandrian grain ships. This was the end of Paul's *voyage* to Rome. The rest must be done on foot.

---

11. The phrase *"fetched a compass,"* in A.V., is most misleading. They had no compasses in those days (cf. 27:20). The word rendered compass means simply *"to go around,"* as in our word *en*compass. The word "fetched" is not found in the original.

415

At Puteoli the apostle, doubtless with the help of Luke and Aristarchus, succeeded in finding a number of Christian brethren. The record states that these brethren urged Paul and his friends to remain with them for seven days,[12] and the implication is that Paul and his associates did this. This is another remarkable indication of Julius' growing interest in Paul, for it meant that the centurion and all his soldiers and prisoners must wait for one week while Paul ministered to these "brethren." Doubtless Paul's miracles and ministry at Melita had further deepened Julius' already profound respect for Paul.

The fact that believers in Christ could be found at Puteoli reminds us of Paul's words in Hebrews 13:24: *"They of Italy* [not merely *of Rome*] salute you," and indicates how widely the gospel of the grace of God had been proclaimed and received.[13]

But a few miles past Puteoli the travelers would now find themselves on the great *Appian Way*, perhaps the most famous highway of antiquity. Slatius called it *"the queen of long-distance roads."* The part from Capua to Rome (132 miles) was built about 312 B.C., but it was lengthened to reach Brundisium by about 244 B.C. Milestones and inscriptions as to its repair are still in existence and, though constructed more

---

12. As at Troas (20:6) and Tyre (21:4).

13. We do not believe the tradition which credits the conversion of these Gentile believers to the ministry of the twelve and their associates (See Gal. 2:2,7,9). It was Paul's gospel that reached to "all nations," "all the world" and "every creature [all creation]" (See Rom. 16:25,26; Col. 1:6; Col. 1:23). Had the twelve, under *their* "great commission," reached all nations, all the world and all creation, with *their* "gospel of the kingdom," the "end of the age" would have come (See Matt. 24:14) but that program was interrupted by *"the dispensation of the grace of God"* through Paul (Eph. 3:1-4).

than two millenniums ago, parts of this great highway still remain intact.

As the apostle and the others made their way toward Rome along this ancient road, two other companies were coming *from* Rome along the same road to meet him. How did they know of his arrival? Evidently the believers at Puteoli had sent word of this to Rome as Paul ministered to them. One of these groups met him at Appii Forum, and the other fifteen miles further on, at The Three Taverns.

The record says, simply, that when Paul saw these brethren, "he thanked God, and took courage." But this brief record still speaks volumes. It indicates that anxiety and fear had attended the apostle's way. Would he have to enter Rome as a criminal, with none but Luke and Aristarchus to stand by? Would the Roman believers remain aloof?

In the last chapter of his Roman Epistle he had sent *personal* greetings to no less than *twenty-seven* members of the church there, and had mentioned others. A considerable number of these he knew intimately. Many of these, no doubt, were included in the two happy welcoming committees: his beloved Aquila and Priscilla, Phebe and Mary, who had helped him much in the work, Andronicus and Junia, his relatives and "fellow-prisoners." Were these among them? What a time of prayer and thanksgiving they must have had; what recollections of their experiences in the proclamation of the gospel; what serious discussions and plans with regard to Paul's stay at Rome and the approaching hearing before Nero! The apostle's affectionate nature was reflected in the love of these believers, who had come all this way to meet and reassure him. Often they must have read his words: "I long to see you," and now they had demonstrated their longing to see him too.

"He thanked God and took courage." His entry into Rome was now to take on a new aspect, with these dear ones nearby to comfort and cheer.[14]

At Rome Julius probably had his last opportunity to show kindness to Paul.

Doubtless the letter sent with Paul (25:26,27) indicated that he was innocent and that *he* had appealed to Caesar. Doubtless, too, Paul's own bearing and the presence of his friends distinguished him as an outstanding personality, but the special consideration given him by the captain of the guard may well have been due in largest part to the intercession and influence of Julius, the centurion, who had by now come to esteem Paul so highly.

Thus, when the prisoners were delivered to the captain of the guard, Paul alone was permitted to live at the home of a friend[15]—perhaps that of his old friend Aquila who, with Priscilla, had entertained him on previous occasions. He was constantly guarded by a soldier, however, to whom he was probably chained. That he was bound by a chain is clear from Verse 20 (cf. Eph. 6:20; Phil. 1:7,13,14,16; Col. 4:18; Phile. 10,13).

---

14. He had entered Jerusalem, too, with many friends, but still with dire forebodings because of the Spirit's warnings (Acts 21).

15. The Greek word *Xenia*, in Verse 23, indicates a place where one is *entertained*, not a cell, nor the "hired house" of Verse 30.

Chapter XLIX — Acts 28:17-31

PAUL AT ROME

THE PRELIMINARY MEETING WITH
THE JEWISH LEADERS

"And it came to pass, that after three days Paul called the chief of the Jews together: and when they were come together, he said unto them, Men and brethren, though I have committed nothing against the people, or customs of our fathers, yet was I delivered prisoner from Jerusalem into the hands of the Romans.

"Who, when they had examined me, would have let me go, because there was no cause of death in me.

"But when the Jews spake against it, I was constrained to appeal unto Caesar; not that I had ought to accuse my nation of.

"For this cause therefore have I called for you, to see you, and to speak with you; because that for the hope of Israel I am bound with this chain.

"And they said unto him, We neither received letters out of Judaea concerning thee, neither any of the brethren that came showed or spake any harm of thee.

"But we desire to hear of thee what thou thinkest: for as concerning this sect, we know that every where it is spoken against."

—Acts 28:17-22

Wherever Paul had gone in his ministry thus far, his policy had been: "The Jew first." One would suppose that this would be changed now. His last earnest appeal to his countrymen at Jerusalem had only served to arouse antagonism so bitter that his present bondage

419

in Rome was his only protection from their rage! He had been forced to appeal to Caesar to escape assassination. Besides, who could expect him to go to the Jew first under *these* circumstances? He was bound with a chain and *could* not attend a synagogue or go where Jews were wont to meet.

Yet, even here in Rome his first care was for his kinsmen. Perhaps some of them might yet be saved. At any rate, the chosen people, from Jerusalem to Rome, would then be without excuse.

Thus it was that after but "three days," doubtless spent in getting settled and meeting with Christian friends old and new, he "called the chief of the Jews together" for a preliminary meeting, at which a date might be set and plans made for a full discussion of the matters which so deeply concerned them all.

With typical tactfulness the apostle addressed them in terminology they would appreciate: "Men and brethren," "the people," "our fathers." Yet he was careful not to give false impressions.

It is only the extreme dispensationalist, trying to prove a point, who interprets the apostle's words in Verse 17 to mean that until this time he had strictly observed the laws and customs of Judaism.

Actually he said nothing of the kind, nor *could* he honestly have done so, for even extreme dispensationalists, who interpret his words in I Corinthians 9:20,21 to mean that his policy was to go back and forth, *under* the law and *from under* it again, would have to admit that he had *not* observed Jewish laws and customs when among the Gentiles.

Thus this passage by no means proves that Paul had until then lived under the law, proclaiming a kingdom message. He did not commit himself to a positive here. He did not say: "I have faithfully observed the customs of our fathers." He merely said: "I have committed nothing *against* the people, or customs of our fathers." The idea is plainly that he was not guilty of *desecrating* their sacred customs. He had not treated either the people or their traditional customs with disrespect.[1] Those who so lightly ridicule beliefs and customs which are sacred to others, would do well to observe Paul's conduct on this occasion.

Next it should be observed that the apostle takes the *defensive* position, as he relates how, though innocent of offense against Judaism, he was delivered a prisoner into the hands of the Romans. This would further tend to win their sympathies, for one of the cruelest things a Jew could do to his brother was to deliver him to the uncircumcised Roman oppressors.

He further points out, however, that his Roman judges had found him innocent of the crimes laid against him, indeed that *they* would have let him go, had not the Jews protested against it.

In this Paul's experience was not unlike that of His Lord. Each succeeding Roman magistrate had found him innocent and each individually should, in justice, have acquitted him but, as with our Lord, the wishes of the Jews played an important part in their decisions.

Thus, the apostle points out, he is here in Rome as a *defendant*, not a plaintiff. He had been *forced*[2] to appeal to Caesar to avoid being handed over to a prejudiced tribunal (25:9,10) and most probably being

---

1. As the Jews at Jerusalem had suspected (Acts 21:27-29).
2. The word "constrained" in Verse 19 is rendered "compelled" in 26:11.

421

assassinated before even coming to trial (25:2,3). Yet he is not here to make any charge against his persecutors. He does not tell how they dragged him out of the temple, beating him and going about to kill him upon the mere *conjecture* that he had brought a Gentile into the sanctuary, nor how the aroused multitude had screamed for his death, casting off their clothes and throwing dust into the air, nor how the high priest had commanded that he be smitten on the mouth at his hearing before the Sanhedrin, nor how more than forty Jews[3] had made a pact neither to eat nor drink till they had killed him—and all these outrages, and more, he could have proved.

He had made not a single counter-charge against his accusers before any Roman judge, nor will he now do so before Caesar, nor, indeed does he even tell *this* audience about all these outrages. His lips are sealed as to all this. He has gone far indeed to conciliate the favored nation and here again he will do so, adding to his explanation of his presence here, the words: *"not that I had ought to accuse my nation of."*[4]

While there was much Paul could have accused his nation of, remember too that there was much they could have accused *him* of. He had at first led them in rebellion against Christ. A message of grace from his pen was therefore most appropriate. It had been fully demonstrated that the children of Abraham were sinners along with all the other children of fallen Adam.

But his main purpose in calling them together was to show them how the truth which his accusers had

---

3. The term "Jews" in this passage is evidently used in its proper, rather than general, sense, of the *Judaeans*.

4. This is consistent with his "dispensation of the grace of God." Compare Peter's accusations in Acts 2:23; 3:14,15; 4:10,11; 5:30.

so bitterly opposed, and which had now cost him his liberty, was the very "hope of Israel."

This truth was not merely that which the prophets had predicted concerning Messiah's reign, for the believers at Jerusalem had been preaching this for some time without serious opposition. It was rather the truth of the resurrection in general and the resurrection of Christ in particular. This truth, which Paul proclaimed with greater light and greater power than any of the twelve could have done, and which so aroused the enmity of the Jews, was actually Israel's only hope. Certainly if it were *not* true that the crucified Messiah had been raised again there could be no hope of a kingdom to come, for there is no *other* Messiah. And, what is more important, there could then be no hope of the forgiveness of Israel's sins, for a *dead* Messiah could not save.

In the passage before us the apostle says: *"For the hope of Israel I am bound with this chain"* (Ver. 20). Now, by examining the Scriptures concerned, any sincere student will learn that Paul was "bound with this chain," *not* for proclaiming that which Israel hoped for, the kingdom, but for proclaiming that which was the *basis* of her hopes, the resurrection.[5] Let us then examine the record:

Before the Sanhedrin the apostle stated clearly why he had been "called in question" by the Jews:

"Men and brethren...*of the hope and resurrection of the dead I am called in question"* (23:6).

Before Felix again, the apostle declared:

"But this I confess unto thee, that after the way which they call heresy, so worship I the God of my

---

5. As *he* preached it, of course.

fathers...*and have hope toward God...that there shall be a resurrection of the dead...*" (24:14,15).

Again, when Festus "declared Paul's cause" to Agrippa, he said:

"...the accusers...brought none accusation of such things as I supposed: But had certain questions...of *one Jesus, which was dead, whom Paul affirmed to be alive*" (25:18,19).

At his hearing before Agrippa, the apostle said:

"And now I stand and am judged for the hope of the promise made of God unto our fathers...For which hope's sake, king Agrippa, I am accused of the Jews" **(26:6,7).**

The *promise*, of course, was the restoration of the kingdom to Israel in glory, but "the *hope* of the promise" was *the resurrection* for the apostle goes on to say:

"Why should it be thought a thing incredible with you that God should raise the dead?" **(Ver. 8).**

All this evidence permits but one interpretation of the last of these passages:

"For the hope of Israel I am bound with this chain" **(28:20).**

Let the sincere and diligent student note carefully that four out of these five passages *state* that Paul was accused, or in bondage, for a *specific reason*; that four out of the five *state* this reason to be his preaching of the *resurrection*; and finally, that in four out of the five this truth is called a *"hope."* In this connection it should be remembered that Peter, at Pentecost, had *warned* Israel that Christ was alive (Acts 2:36; 3:14,15; 4:10) while Paul had later proclaimed that resurrection as the proof that the sin question had been fully dealt

424

with (Rom. 4:25; etc.). It was the resurrection, then, and particularly the resurrection of the crucified Christ, that was *"the hope of Israel."*

Bound, as he was, with "this chain,"[6] the apostle doubtless also hoped that by showing them all this he might gain their sympathy and support in his appeal before Caesar. This seems to be implied in the conclusion, *"For this cause therefore have I called for you, to see you, and to speak with you..."* (Ver. 20).

Their response seems more diplomatic than forthright. They say they have received neither letters nor personal complaints against him. Yet they tell him that they know of "this sect[7]...that everywhere it is spoken against" (Vers. 21,22). Diplomatically they tell him that they would like to hear *his* opinion about it, and with that a date is set for a conference.

THE MAIN CONFERENCE

"And when they had appointed him a day, there came many to him into his lodging; to whom he expounded and testified the kingdom of God, persuading them concerning Jesus, both out of the law of Moses, and out of the prophets, from morning till evening.

"And some believed the things which were spoken, and some believed not.

"And when they agreed not among themselves, they departed, after that Paul had spoken one word, Well spake the Holy Ghost by Esaias the prophet unto our fathers,

---

6. The singular agrees with Verse 16. He was evidently now chained to a single soldier.

7. How did they know he belonged to "this sect" if they had heard no evil reports about him?

"Saying, Go unto this people, and say, Hearing ye shall hear, and shall not understand: and seeing ye shall see, and not perceive:

"For the heart of this people is waxed gross, and their ears are dull of hearing, and their eyes have they closed; lest they should see with their eyes, and hear with their ears, and understand with their heart, and should be converted, and I should heal them.

"Be it known therefore unto you, that the salvation of God is sent unto the Gentiles, and that they will hear it.

"And when he had said these words, the Jews departed, and had great reasoning among themselves.

"And Paul dwelt two whole years in his own hired house, and received all that came in unto him,

"Preaching the kingdom of God, and teaching those things which concern the Lord Jesus Christ, with all confidence, no man forbidding him."

—Acts 28:23-31

The day agreed upon having arrived, "many"[8] of the Jews came to Paul's "lodging."

Here again we should carefully observe just how Paul dealt with them and what this implies.

We read that he "testified" to them of the kingdom of God and sought to "persuade" them concerning Jesus,

---

8. Most translations use the rendering "many" here, though, in fact, the Greek *pleion* is the comparative of *polus*, and means either "more," or "the more part." Thus (as far as we can now ascertain) this second gathering may have been attended by either *more* or *less* Jews than the first. If "more" is meant, than the company was greater; if "the more part," then it was smaller! It is inconceivable that Luke's readers could not have understood *exactly* what he meant, but we are still learning the Greek of that day.

"both out of the law of Moses, and out of the prophets" (Ver. 23).

Does this imply, as some conclude, that until this time Paul had preached only what was contained in the law and the prophets? Those who insist that this is so generally use Acts 26:22 to prove their contention, but we have yet to see one of them add the qualifying clause of Verse 23.

The plain fact is that we find Paul, in his earlier epistles, and even in the Acts record, preaching much that was not contained in the law and the prophets. Indeed, as early as Acts 13:38,39 we find him preaching in a synagogue, proclaiming justification by faith in Christ *without the law*.

But in dealing with Jews under the law, he *must* prove to them *from their Scriptures* that Jesus is the Christ. It is only a pity that in so many cases they refused to be persuaded, so that he could not go on to preach to them the glorious truths he had been specially commissioned to proclaim.

If it be remembered that the *theme* of Acts is *the fall of Israel* and God's vindication of Himself for going to the Gentiles, it will not seem strange that again and again we find the apostle proving to the Jews that Jesus is the Christ, but getting no farther, since they will not accept the proof.

In this particular case he continued "testifying" and "persuading" from morning until evening with results that were indecisive to say the least. Some were persuaded, but others "disbelieved," refusing to be convinced, and, disagreeing among themselves, they "began to depart."[9] Before they left, however, the apostle

---

9. The imperfect tense is used.

pronounced upon them that stern indictment which implies, not merely a patience almost exhausted by the long contest with prejudice and unbelief, but the end of God's present dealings with Israel as a nation.

It is to be noted that in each of the crises at which Paul turned from the Jew to the Gentile it was made clear that the Jew himself was to blame, since he had refused to accept Messiah and the fulfillment of the promises.

At Jerusalem the Lord Himself had appeared to Paul, saying: *"Get thee quickly out of Jerusalem, for THEY WILL NOT RECEIVE THY TESTIMONY CONCERNING ME"* (Acts 22:18).

At Pisidian Antioch the apostle had said to the Jews, with regard to God's Word to them: *"YE PUT IT FROM YOU, AND JUDGE YOURSELVES UNWORTHY OF EVERLASTING LIFE"* (Acts 13:46).

At Corinth, after they had set themselves in opposition and had blasphemed: *"YOUR BLOOD BE UPON YOUR OWN HEADS; I AM CLEAN"* (Acts 18:6).

And now *at Rome*: *"Well spake the Holy Ghost by Esaias the prophet unto your*[10] *fathers....THE HEART OF THIS PEOPLE IS WAXED GROSS [DULL], AND THEIR EARS ARE DULL OF HEARING, AND THEIR EYES HAVE THEY CLOSED; LEST THEY SHOULD SEE...AND HEAR...AND UNDERSTAND..."* (Vers. 25-27).

Seven times the Spirit refers to this judgment upon Israel and shows the peril of hardening the heart against God and His truth.

---

10. The A.V. is evidently wrong here.

428

This indictment of the Jews at Rome by Paul should be compared with that of the leaders at Jerusalem by Stephen. He likewise referred to the unbelieving Jews of former times as *"your fathers,"* calling his hearers *"uncircumcised in heart and ears"* and charging them with *"always resisting the Holy Ghost"* (Acts 7:51).

The Jews (except a remnant) from Jerusalem to Rome had now rejected their Messiah. Stephen's initial pronouncement had now been brought to a conclusion, as Paul said:

"Be it known therefore unto you, that the salvation of God has been[11] **sent unto the Gentiles, and that they will hear it"** **(Ver. 28).**

What folly to assume that this marks the historical beginning of the Body of Christ! Clearly, this is not the *beginning* of something, but the *end* of something—the withdrawal of God's favor from Israel for some time to come.

A great change in God's dealings with men had now been consummated. When on earth our Lord had said to a Samaritan woman: *"Salvation is of the Jews"* (John 4:22). But now the apostle of the *glorified* Lord declares: *"The salvation of God has been sent to the Gentiles"* (Acts 28:28).

God's present work is not, of course, the fulfillment of *prophecy* among the Gentiles. This awaits a future day, when Israel is saved and the Gentiles find salvation *through her* (Zech. 8:13,22,23; etc.). His *present* work is called "this *mystery* among the Gentiles" and we are told that He would have us know what is "the riches of the glory" of it (Col. 1:27).

---

11. See *New Tr.*, et al.

Our hearts should indeed overflow with wonder and gratitude that in this dispensation of grace we Gentiles, to whom God had promised nothing (Eph. 2:11,12) can be saved and assemble to worship Israel's God and Israel's Messiah while she staggers in the blindness of unbelief; indeed, that we may belong to that blessed Body of which He is the living Head, seated with Him in the heavenlies and there blessed with "all spiritual blessings" (Eph. 1:3; 2:4-10,13).

It had been predicted that Jehovah would divorce Israel (Isa. 50:1); that they would be *Lo-Ammi: not* His people (Hos. 1:9) but never had He made known the purpose in His heart of love to bring salvation to the Gentiles through Israel's "fall" and "casting away" (Rom. 11:11-15).

It is true that under this dispensation of grace there is, before God, *"no difference between the Jew and the Greek"* and that *"the same Lord over all is rich unto ALL that call upon Him"* (Rom. 10:12). It is true that *"God hath concluded them all in unbelief that He might have mercy upon ALL"* (Rom. 11:32) and that believing *Jews and Gentiles* are now *"reconciled...unto God in one body by the cross"* (Eph. 2:16). Thus the offer of salvation by grace is extended to all men everywhere, whether Jews or Gentiles.

But all this does not alter the fact that *practically* speaking this is a Gentile age, simply because so few Jews will accept Christ as their Savior. So small is the proportion of Jews in the Body of Christ that nearly all Christian congregations are made up exclusively or overwhelmingly of Gentiles in the flesh.

Thus the pronouncement was true: *"The salvation of God has been sent unto the Gentiles, and...they will hear it."* And thus the Jews departed from Paul's lodging "and had great reasoning among themselves," as they have had ever since.

After some days of entertainment in the home of friends Paul evidently moved to "his own hired house" where he remained for two whole years, receiving all who wished to visit him (Ver. 30). He evidently engaged in a very fruitful ministry here, being used of God, among other things, to establish a church in the very palace of the Emperor (Phil. 1:12,13; 4:22). Nor could his enemies now oppress him, for he was always attended by his Roman guard.

It will be remembered that in the opening verses of Acts, our Lord is said to have taught His apostles for forty days *"the things pertaining to the kingdom of God"* (1:3). This would, of course, involve its establishment on earth, for this was what was to follow His sufferings (Acts 1:6; 2:30; 3:19-21; etc.). Since that time Israel had rejected Messiah and His reign, hence when Paul, in Rome, preached "the kingdom of God and...those things which concern the Lord Jesus Christ," he would naturally explain how Christ had been rejected, so that the *earthly establishment* of the kingdom of God was now held in abeyance, while God sent to a sin-cursed world a wondrous message of grace; an offer of reconciliation through the blood of His Son.

Whether or not the apostle was released after two years and engaged further in a traveling ministry before his trial and execution by Nero, is a question which we will discuss at some length in an appendix.

WHY THE BOOK OF ACTS
CLOSES SO ABRUPTLY

It is evident from the close of Acts, if nowhere else, that the book is not primarily a history of "the birth and

431

growth of the Church," nor even a complete record of "the acts of the apostles." How we should like to know what happened to the Judaean apostles after the raising up of Paul! How we should like to know how Paul fared during these two years in his own hired house *and after!* What reading an inspired record of his last days and his trial and execution would have made!

But God did not cause Luke to write the Book of Acts in order to satisfy our curiosity. The book is rather intended to be the story of Israel's fall and of how salvation was sent to the Gentiles. This having been accomplished, and Israel having rejected Christ at Rome as she had done at Jerusalem and all the way between, the narrative ends. Now, at least, we are in a position to understand why, in the next book of Scripture we find Paul saying:

"I speak to you Gentiles, inasmuch as I am the apostle of the Gentiles; I magnify mine office" (Rom. 11:13).

PAUL'S TRIAL DELAYED

The fact that Paul, after reaching Rome, "dwelt two whole years in his own hired house," receiving callers and freely discussing those things which concerned the Lord Jesus Christ, indicates that his trial was delayed for a considerable length of time.

In the first place, it appears evident that Paul's accusers had not left for Rome when he did (Acts 28:21) and hence *could not* have left until the next spring. Further delay, however, may have been due to one or a combination of several causes. It may have been caused partly by Caesar's lack of interest in either party. Even apart from this, trials at Rome were often delayed for long periods of time, to allow the parties concerned to produce witnesses coming from great distances. In this case, witnesses whom the Jews would probably ask to testify against Paul would have to come from *many* distant places (See Acts 24:5).

It may be, too, that Paul's accusers were discouraged from appearing against him. *They* had not wished the case to come before Caesar; it was *he* who had appealed to Caesar, and the prospects of their winning the case against him were not bright in the light of the opinions of Julius, Festus and Agrippa (Acts 23:26-29; 25:25,26; 26:31,32) and of the formal report which Festus had by now sent to Caesar.

DURING THE DELAY

We have already seen that during this delay, or at least two years of it, the apostle carried on an active and vigorous ministry, receiving visitors and preaching and teaching without restraint. This ministry was bearing abundant fruit.

Imagine the feelings of the soldiers of the Praetorian Guard[12] as, one after another, they found themselves in the midst of gatherings of believers, with Paul presiding! Conybeare and Howson's *Life and Epistles of Saint Paul* contains the following paragraphs regarding Paul's ministry at this time:

"...But nothing in it [his Epistle to the Philippians] is more suggestive than St. Paul's allusion to the Praetorian guards, and to the converts he had gained in the household of Nero. He tells us (as we have just read) that throughout the Praetorian quarters he was well known as a prisoner for the cause of Christ, and

12. Nero's bodyguard.

he sends special salutations to the Philippian Church from the Christians in the Imperial household. These notices bring before us very vividly the moral contrasts by which the Apostle was surrounded. The soldier to whom he was chained today might have been in Nero's bodyguard yesterday; his comrade who next relieved guard upon the prisoner might have been one of the executioners of Octavia, and might have carried her head to Poppaea a few weeks before. Such were the ordinary imployments of the fierce and blood-stained veterans who were daily present, like wolves in the midst of sheep, at the meetings of the Christian brotherhood. If there were any of these soldiers not utterly hardened by a life of cruelty, their hearts must surely have been touched by the character of their prisoner, brought as they were into so close a contact with him. They must have been at least astonished to see a man, under such circumstances, so utterly careless of selfish interests, and devoting himself with an energy so unaccountable to the teaching of others. Strange indeed to their ears, fresh from the brutality of a Roman barrack, must have been the sound of Christian exhortation, of prayers, and of hymns; stranger still, perhaps, the tender love which bound the converts to their teacher and to one another, and showed itself in every look and tone.

"But if the agents of Nero's tyranny seem out of place in such a scene, still more repugnant to the assembled worshippers must have been the instruments of his pleasures, the ministers of his lust. Yet some even among these, the depraved servants of the palace, were redeemed from their degradation by the Spirit of Christ, which spoke to them in the words of Paul. How deep their degradation was we know from authentic records. We are not left to conjecture the services

434

required from the attendants of Nero. The ancient historians have polluted their pages with details of infamy which no writer in the languages of Christendom may dare to repeat. Thus the very immensity of moral amelioration wrought operates to disguise its own extent, and hides from inexperienced eyes the gulf which separates Heathenism from Christianity. Suffice it to say that the courtiers of Nero were the spectators, and the members of his household the instruments, of vices so monstrous and so unnatural, that they shocked even the men of that generation, steeped as it was in every species of obscenity. But we must remember that many of those who took part in such abominations were involuntary agents, forced by the compulsion of slavery to do their master's bidding. And the very depth of vileness in which they were plunged must have excited in some of them an indignant disgust and revulsion against vice. Under such feelings, if curiosity led them to visit the Apostle's prison, they were well qualified to appreciate the purity of its moral atmosphere. And there it was that some of these unhappy bondsmen first tasted of spiritual freedom, and were prepared to brave with patient heroism the tortures under which they soon were destined to expire in the gardens of the Vatican" (pgs. 795,796).

And so Paul became widely known, among Caesar's guards, his "household" and elsewhere, as a prisoner for the cause of Christ (Phil. 1:13; 4:22).

But in addition to all this active ministry at Rome, the apostle still bore "the care of all the churches" (II Cor. 11:28) keeping contact, through representatives, not only with those churches which he had founded, but also with some that had sprung up indirectly through his ministry—groups of believers whom he had never seen.

It was during this imprisonment that he sent Tychicus and Onesimus from Rome with the letters to Colosse and Philemon, and the Ephesian letter[13] (See Col. 4:7-9; Phile. 10-15). After Tychicus and Onesimus had left, it seems, Paul was cheered by the arrival of Epaphroditus with a contribution from his beloved friends at Philippi. The Epistle to the Philippians was, in part, an acknowledgment of this gift.

---

13. Evidently an encyclical letter.

Appendix

DID PAUL SUFFER ONE ROMAN IMPRISONMENT OR TWO?

That Paul closed his ministry as a prisoner in Rome no one, probably, will deny, but did he suffer one imprisonment or two, with a period of release between?

The great majority of those who have looked into this question agree that there were *two* imprisonments, yet the question is often raised, and since the answer to it does not lie on the surface, we devote this appendix to a discussion of it.

Before discussing the Scriptures involved, we would call the reader's attention to Dean Howson's arguments from the testimony of the ancient fathers. Concerning the view that there were two imprisonments, he says: "...no doubt was entertained about it by the ancient Church....The evidence...is all one way" (*The Life and Epistles of Paul*, by Conybeare and Howson, pg. 800). "Most important," he says, is the information "supplied by Clement, the disciple of St. Paul, mentioned in Phil. 4:3, who was afterwards Bishop of Rome. This author, writing *from Rome* to Corinth, expressly asserts that Paul had preached the Gospel 'IN THE EAST AND IN THE WEST;' that 'he had instructed *the whole world*'... and, 'had gone to THE EXTREMITY OF THE WEST' before his martyrdom" (pg. 801). Howson also cites "Muratoris Canon" (A.D. 170) regarding "THE JOURNEY OF PAUL FROM ROME TO SPAIN" (pg. 801). Such a journey had been his desire, as we learn from Romans 15:28.

While there are apparently no early writings to contradict this there are passages all the way from Jerome to Chrysostum to show that this belief was widespread.

While extra-scriptural testimony can never be conclusive, the written testimonies of those historically nearest to the apostle do, necessarily, bear some weight. But stronger still, of course, is the testimony of the Word of God, and to this we now turn.

EVIDENCES FROM THE PASTORAL EPISTLES

First we must consider the historical facts of the Pastoral Epistles. The great majority of these could not possibly fit into any part of the apostle's life before or during his first imprisonment in Rome.

In Titus 1:5 he explains why he had "left" Titus at Crete. This *could not* have taken place on his first journey to Rome, for then he only *viewed* Crete from the ship at Fair Havens (Acts 27:7-13) and he had with him only Luke and Aristarchus (Acts 27:2). But from Titus 1:5 we assuredly gather that by then Paul had visited Crete *with Titus* and had left him there to complete the organization of the churches established.

We learn further, from Titus 3:12,13, that "Zenas the lawyer and Apollos" were with Titus at this time, evidently in the course of a "journey," and that Paul was to send Artemas or Tychicus to him. This all seems to indicate that a work of considerable extent had been launched at Crete. *Certainly* Zenas, Apollos and Titus had not all been "left" at Crete before Paul's original arrival at Rome.

438

From Titus 3:12 we also learn that at the time of his writing he had "determined" to winter at Nicopolis. This would indicate that he was either free at the time, or reasonably assured of his freedom.

There is evidence too that by the time the apostle had written this letter to Titus he had spent enough time at Crete to learn their traits by personal experience. Citing "a prophet of their own" to the effect that "the Cretians are always liars," he adds: *"This witness is true"* (Titus 1:12,13) and indicates that he had left Titus there to correct such abuses (Titus 1:5,10,11,13). Such personal knowledge of the Cretians could not have been gained while the ship to Rome lay at anchor in Fair Havens.

Next let us turn to the first Epistle to Timothy where, in the first few verses we find that Paul had besought Timothy to remain at Ephesus because of false teaching which was gaining ground there. Now Paul had besought him to remain there *while he himself went to Macedonia* (I Tim. 1:3). When Paul addressed the Ephesian elders on his last journey to Jerusalem, and subsequently Rome, as recorded in Acts, such unsound doctrine was as yet undeveloped among them (Acts 20:27-32). Nor was he then bound for Macedonia. He must, therefore have been released and have visited Ephesus—and Macedonia—again. Indeed, it would appear from both Epistles to Timothy that Timothy had by now been subjected to no little pressure from the heretics at Ephesus and needed considerable exhortation to remain in the battle and stand his ground.

In II Timothy 4:6-9, writing on the very eve of his martyrdom, Paul summons Timothy, then at Ephesus, to hurry to Rome. But near the close of the two years of Acts 28:30 Timothy *was* at Rome and wrote, with Paul, to the Colossians (1:1) the Philippians (1:1) and to Philemon (Ver. 1).

Again in II Timothy 4:13-20 there is evidence of two imprisonments. There the apostle refers to incidents which were clearly *recent*, while, if he was executed after his first imprisonment at Rome he would have been a prisoner for four years: two at Caesarea and two at Rome, and these incidents would have transpired four years previous.

Finally, there are such differences in "style, language and ideas" when we come to the Pastoral Epistles, that some have denied their Pauline authorship. In these pastoral letters, says David Smith, there are some 295 cases of language and terminology peculiar to these epistles (*Life and Letters of Paul*, pg. 582). These, we believe, can be best accounted for by the years of hardship which had intervened and by the altered mood and circumstances. Says Smith:

"Accepting as genuine the Pastoral Epistles, we are led, partly by their style, partly by the difficulty of fitting them into any earlier period of Paul's life, partly by traces of a later stage of development, both of truth and error, to assign them to a date subsequent to the two years' imprisonment of Acts 28:30."

ADDITIONAL EVIDENCE

But we also find indications of two imprisonments in the Acts and Paul's other epistles.

Consider Acts 28:30,31. Luke obviously wrote the Acts *after* the two years' imprisonment. If Paul had been executed at this time would it not have been normal to

440

record it, even considering the dispensational aspect of the book? Instead, there is no further narrative. Does not this reservation suggest that much still remained to be told? The post-Acts epistles confirm this view.

Philippians 1:24-26 and 2:24 show that Paul at that time, was confident he would soon be released. In Philemon 22 he shows this same confidence, even requesting Philemon to prepare lodging for him.

If the Hebrews Epistle was written by Paul, as we assuredly believe it was, there can be no question that he was liberated from his first Roman imprisonment, for there we distinctly find him at liberty (Heb. 13:23,24).

THE PERIOD OF RELEASE

We do not presume to theorize on the reasons for the apostle's release, nor is it possible to outline the course of his travels, or even to tell much about his ministry during the time in which he was at liberty. We only know that he carried on an extensive ministry which included Macedonia, Ephesus, Crete, Miletum and probably Nicopolis and Spain (See I Tim. 1:3; Titus 1:5; II Tim. 4:20; Titus 3:12; Rom. 15:24,28). Also, he appeared at Troas, evidently recently, for he had left his mantle and parchments with Carpus there.

Further, we do not know the length of his period of liberty, nor when or where he was again apprehended. We only know that he *was* again taken into custody and finally slain as a martyr for Christ.

THE SECOND IMPRISONMENT

There can be no doubt that when Paul wrote his second Epistle to Timothy he was again *at Rome*, not now "in his own hired house," under military custody as one who had appealed to Caesar, but suffering bonds "as an evil-doer" (II Tim. 2:9).

His request for his cloak (II Tim. 4:13) might well indicate that he was in a dungeon, a dank excavation in the ground, like that at Philippi (Acts 16:24,29; note the words "inner prison" and "sprang in").

The persecution then evidently raging under Nero, or the general change in circumstances seems to have tried the loyalty and thinned out the ranks of his friends. Aquila and Priscilla, perhaps again forced to leave Rome (See Acts 18:2) were now at Ephesus (II Tim. 4:19) and Paul had sent Tychicus there too, to be with Timothy (II Tim. 4:12) Demas had forsaken him (II Tim. 4:10); Crescens had gone to Galatia, Titus to Dalmatia (II Tim. 4:10). Only Luke, his "beloved physician" was still there to minister to him (II Tim. 4:11).

It must have been a keen disappointment to the apostle, at the first part of his second trial, that not one of the Roman believers had the courage to appear in his behalf (II Tim. 4:16). Doubtless the persecution had driven them all into hiding. Less excusable were men like Demas, who had accompanied him to Rome and had left when needed most.

His defense (unsupported by witnesses) must however have been powerful from the very fact that he was remanded to prison to await further trial (II Tim. 4:16,17).

Evidently he was "oft refreshed" by Onesiphorus of Ephesus, and his family (II Tim. 1:16; 4:19) but this probably after his "first answer."

Was it perhaps *while* writing his second Epistle to Timothy that the apostle's case took an adverse turn and he realized that his doom, physically, was sealed? Is this the reason for his urgent appeals to Timothy to hurry to Rome to be with him at the end? (See II Tim. 1:4 and cf. 4:6-8,9,21).

At any rate he could include in the closing words of his last letter, the following note of victory:

"For I am now ready to be offered, and the time of my departure is at hand.

"I have fought a good fight, I have finished my course; I have kept the faith:

"Henceforth there is laid up for me a crown..." **(II Tim. 4:6-8).**

SCRIPTURE INDEX

Acts (Cont'd)

Acts (Cont'd)

The Berean
Searchlight

The *Berean Searchlight* is the outgrowth of a small church bulletin containing brief weekly Bible lessons by Pastor Cornelius R. Stam in 1940. Its publication has become the largest and most important function of the *Berean Bible Society*, reaching monthly into every state of the Union and more than 60 foreign countries.

The *Searchlight* includes in its mailing list thousands of ministers, missionaries and other Christian workers. Also, it is on display in the libraries of hundreds of Christian Colleges and Bible Institutes. The purpose of the *Berean Searchlight* is to help believers understand and enjoy the Bible.

**Send for our FREE Bible
Study Magazine today!**

BEREAN BIBLE SOCIETY
PO Box 756
Germantown, WI 53022

www.bereanbiblesociety.org

OTHER BOOKS BY THE SAME AUTHOR

Write for a Free Price List of All Our Literature

Berean Bible Society, PO Box 756,
Germantown, WI 53022

www.bereanbiblesociety.org

Things That Differ

By Cornelius R. Stam

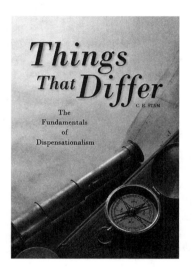

This volume demonstrates how the dispensational method of Bible study is the method God approves, and the only one by which the Bible makes sense. It shows the perfect harmony between the changeless principles of God and His changing dispensations.

HARDCOVER   290 PAGES

Orders:

Berean Bible Society
PO Box 756
Germantown, WI 53022

www.bereanbiblesociety.org

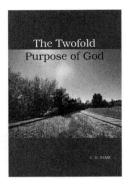
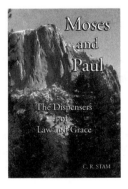

Two Minutes with the Bible

By Cornelius R. Stam

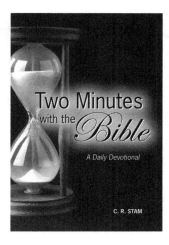

Two Minutes with the Bible is a timeless classic that our beloved Founder, C. R. Stam, compiled from newspaper articles he had written for various publications. We are firm believers at the *Berean Bible Society* in the importance of daily devotions to further spiritual growth.

366 DAILY DEVOTIONALS   PAPERBACK

Orders:

Berean Bible Society, PO Box 756,
Germantown, WI 53022

You can sign up to receive
Two Minutes daily e-mails at

www.bereanbiblesociety.org